LAND, STEWARDSHIP, AND LEGITIMACY

Endangered Species Policy in Canada and the United States

Canada and the United States are similar in terms of the species of wildlife that mingle freely across their shared border. Despite this similarity, however, there are significant differences between approaches to wildlife management in these two nations. In *Land, Stewardship, and Legitimacy*, Andrea Olive examines the divergent evolution of endangered species policy on either side of the 49th parallel.

Examining local circumstances in areas as distant and diverse as southern Utah and the Canadian Arctic, Olive shows how public attitudes have shaped environmental policy in response to endangered species law, specifically the Species at Risk Act in Canada and the Endangered Species Act in the United States. Richly researched and accessibly written, this is the first book to compare endangered species policy on both sides of the Canada–US border. It will appeal to students and scholars of environmental policy, politics, and ethics, and anyone interested in current approaches to wildlife management.

(Studies in Comparative Political Economy and Public Policy)

ANDREA OLIVE is an assistant professor of political science and geography at the University of Toronto Mississauga.

Studies in Comparative Political Economy and Public Policy

Editors: MICHAEL HOWLETT, DAVID LAYCOCK (Simon Fraser University), and STEPHEN McBRIDE (McMaster University)

Studies in Comparative Political Economy and Public Policy is designed to showcase innovative approaches to political economy and public policy from a comparative perspective. While originating in Canada, the series will provide attractive offerings to a wide international audience, featuring studies with local, subnational, cross-national, and international empirical bases and theoretical frameworks.

Editorial Advisory Board

For a list of books published in the series, see page 287.

Land, Stewardship, and Legitimacy

Endangered Species Policy in Canada and the United States

ANDREA OLIVE

UNIVERSITY OF TORONTO PRESS
Toronto Buffalo London

ISBN 978-1-4426-4768-8 (cloth)
ISBN 978-1-4426-1574-8 (paper)

∞

Printed on acid-free, 100% post-consumer recycled paper with vegetable-based inks.

Library and Archives Canada Cataloguing in Publication

Olive, Andrea, 1980–, author
Land, stewardship, and legitimacy : endangered species policy in Canada and
the United States / Andrea Olive.

(Studies in comparative political economy and public policy)
Includes bibliographical references and index.
ISBN 978-1-4426-4768-8 (bound). – ISBN 978-1-4426-1574-8 (pbk.)

1. Endangered species – Government policy – Canada.   2. Endangered species –
Government policy – United States.   3. Endangered species – Law and legislation –
Canada.   4. Endangered species – Law and legislation – United States.   5. Wildlife
conservation – Canada – Citizen participation.   6. Wildlife conservation – United States
– Citizen participation.   I. Title.   II. Series: Studies in comparative political economy
and public policy

QL84.24.O45 2014   333.95'220971   C2013-908070-8

This book has been published with the help of a grant from the Federation for the
Humanities and Social Sciences, through the Awards to Scholarly Publications
Program, using funds provided by the Social Sciences and Humanities Research
Council of Canada.

University of Toronto Press acknowledges the financial assistance to its publishing
program of the Canada Council for the Arts and the Ontario Arts Council.

 Canada Council   Conseil des Arts
for the Arts   du Canada

 ONTARIO ARTS COUNCIL
CONSEIL DES ARTS DE L'ONTARIO
50 YEARS OF ONTARIO GOVERNMENT SUPPORT OF THE ARTS
50 ANS DE SOUTIEN DU GOUVERNEMENT DE L'ONTARIO AUX ARTS

University of Toronto Press acknowledges the financial support of the Government
of Canada through the Canada Book Fund for its publishing activities.

Contents

List of Tables

List of Figures

Acknowledgments

Who really knows when a book begins? I could argue that I started writing this book at the age of twelve, when I was elected environmental president of my elementary school. Or perhaps it was the first time I laid eyes on Banff National Park. Maybe it was at age five, when a bird crashed into our family home and my brother and I insisted on carrying out a proper funeral for the creature. It is near impossible to pinpoint the moments at which thoughts become ideas. I think I formally began writing this book in 2006, however, when I changed my PhD major concentration from political theory to public policy. In this book you will see that I am both an environmental philosopher and a political policy scholar.

Some of this book's arguments and data arise from my dissertation, which I wrote at Purdue University in 2007–9. Thus, first and foremost, I would like to thank my dissertation committee: Leigh Raymond (chair), Laurel S. Weldon, Ann Clark, and Patricia Boling. Although only Chapter Four and part of Chapter Six come from my dissertation, all knowledge is cumulative, so this project would not have been possible without hundreds of conversations and comments on numerous drafts. Thanks also to the Purdue Research Foundation for providing funding to collect some of the data I present here.

I would like to thank my colleagues at the University of Michigan – Dearborn, especially Mitch Sollenberg and Lara Rusch. Their friendship and intellectual camaraderie embraced me when I needed them most. This book also would not have been possible without the assistance of Drew Buchanan and Patricia Turnbull in the UM-Dearborn Research Office. Nor would I have ever completed my data collection without the diligent assistance of Sue Steiner and Christine Kelly-Williams in the political science department. Finally, Martin Hershock and Georgina Hickey, both department chairs *par excellence*, deserve much credit, as they gave me ample time and space to carry this project through to its conclusion.

Dennis Moore at the Canadian Consulate in Detroit has been immensely helpful in my career, and I would like to acknowledge the financial support of the Canadian Embassy in Washington, DC, to conduct research in Nunavut and at Pelee Island, Ontario.

I would like to give a special acknowledgment to Katherine Fierlbeck and Louise Carbert at Dalhousie University and Laurel S. Weldon at Purdue University. These women are my feminist gurus – mothers, wives, friends, and leading scholars in their field. Thank you for always being honest about the sacrifices and the rewards.

During the course of writing this book, I interviewed 101 landowners in the United States and 31 in Canada. This book is about these landowners. I would like to thank them for participating in this study and for sharing their honest and thoughtful opinions. I would especially like to thank Patty on Middle Bass Island for letting me stay at her cottage while I conducted research. In Ohio, I would also like to thank Megan Seymour, USFWS, and Kristen Stanford. On Pelee Island in Ontario, I would like to thank Gina. Your bed and breakfast was the perfect research station!

I would like to thank my colleagues, especially Stephen Brooks, at the University of Windsor, where I taught a graduate seminar in comparative politics in the fall of 2011 that is reflected particularly in Chapter Seven.

The University of Toronto, my new home, has provided an incredibly encouraging atmosphere. I would like to thank all my colleagues in the departments of Geography and Political Science, particularly Graham White.

At the University of Toronto Press, I would like to thank Daniel Quinlan, whose optimism always catches me off guard. I apologize again for the lack of Oxford commas in earlier drafts. I would also like to thank three anonymous reviewers, whose feedback was immensely helpful and encouraging. Similarly, my gratitude extends to Barry Norris, my freelance copy editor, and Wayne Herrington, my managing editor at the University of Toronto Press.

I must thank the government of Canada for continuing to fund social science research and real hand-held books. My husband often reminds me (and his students) that the printing press was one of the most influential inventions to ever come into existence. In a world of e-books and digital technologies, I am grateful that there is still a place, a valued place, for written ideas. This book has been published with the help of a grant from the Federation for the Humanities and Social Sciences, through the Awards to Scholarly Publications Program, using funds provided by the Social Sciences and Humanities Research Council of Canada.

I would like to thank my family. Some of my earliest memories in life revolve around nature and wildlife. Buffalo Pound Provincial Park, Crystal Lake, and Big Sky Montana are forever etched in my heart. My parents, Wilson and Carole Olive, have given me everything I have ever needed to write this book. My grandparents, Harold and Edith Olive (whom we lost in 2005 and 2011), were farmers of British lineage and perhaps the first people to teach me – through their lived experience – about John Locke's private property and Aldo Leopold's stewardship. To farm in Saskatchewan is to mix labour with love. My other grandparents, Gus and Mary MacDonald (lost in 1989 and 2011), were deeply religious and incredibly political. Morality and legitimacy, the other themes of this book, motivated most every action they took.

My husband, Christopher Petrakos, and our cats were absolute necessities in seeing this book through to completion. I married an American who studies British history. He is city-folk, and I have been trying to re-wild him since we first met in 2007. Our lives are filled with books, newspapers, and plane tickets. It has been a real joy to spend my days with someone interested in the world and willing to challenge my ideas and discuss the way things ought to be. He is too much Locke and I am too much Leopold, but living under the same roof we have struck a balance and made a beautiful life.

Finally, I would like to dedicate this book to Leigh Raymond and Stephen Brooks. Leigh, you are undoubtedly the ideal form of mentor. You and the Indiana Brown Bat changed my life. Your teaching, your writing, your Boston Marathon qualifier, and your humanity have been my guideposts all the way. Steve, you reminded me that I am Canadian. You too changed my life. You brought me home. Your composure, your humour, and your patriotism have been a gift.

LAND, STEWARDSHIP, AND LEGITIMACY

Endangered Species Policy in Canada
and the United States

1 Introduction

There is no such thing as *Canadian* wildlife or *American* wildlife. Animals possess no national identity or display any signs of patriotism. Deer roam and birds migrate freely across the forty-ninth parallel without valid documentation. Why, then, when it comes to wildlife management, does an animal's citizenship matter? Why does a polar bear in Alaska fear no rifle while there is almost an open season on hunting polar bear in Nunavut? Why is a water snake on Pelee Island, Ontario, protected by law while a water snake a few miles away on North Bass Island, Ohio, is not? It would seem a matter of scientific determination as to whether or not a species is threatened with extinction, but in Canada and the United States, the management of wildlife – particularly endangered species – falls within the category of domestic boundaries, with little thought given to nature's boundaries. This division of labour is significant because biodiversity loss is the most important shared environmental problem facing Canada and the United States.

This book compares the US approach to the conservation of biodiversity – namely, the Endangered Species Act (ESA) – to the Canadian approach – particularly the Species at Risk Act (SARA). I begin by explaining the two countries' policy approaches and the institutional rationale for their differences. I then examine the attitudes of non-agricultural landowners in the two countries, using interviews and survey data. This is not a book about which country can boast to be a better wildlife manager; rather, it is about what Canada and the United States share and how they can better manage a common resource that is intimately bound to their future prosperity.

My central argument is that affirmative motivations to cooperate with conservation laws exist among residents and landowners in the two countries, and that policy design, with tools such as incentives and regulation, must take advantage of these affirmative motivations to permit society to reconcile the power of private property with the need for conservation. Affirmative motivations, often overlooked in public policy, stem from a sense of legitimacy and personal morality: landowners are willing to engage in conservation efforts and to steward land because they believe that the legislation is legitimate and/or that conservation is the right thing to do from an ethical or moral standpoint. Currently, however, neither country is capitalizing on these affirmative motivations.

As different as the ESA and SARA appear to be, a degree of policy convergence between the two countries suggests that private property and stewardship are more important, and harder to balance, than policy makers have realized. Canada had the advantage of reviewing thirty years of American experience before passing its own law, and SARA was written to avoid some of the problems that plague the US law, particularly as it pertains to private property (Fox and Adamowicz 1997; Illical and Harrison 2007). The ESA, however, has also been slowly transformed over the past three decades, with more incentives created for landowners and greater attempts to implement cooperative management strategies. The ESA is now transitioning from a hard command-and-control policy to a "stewardship-first" policy backed by incentive tools such as tax credits, Habitat Conservation Plans, Safe Harbor Agreements, and other landowner programs. In Canada, SARA is propped up by provincial legislation that leans towards a regulatory approach. The Ontario legislation, in its form as of 2011, looks a bit like the US ESA circa 1970s. Nova Scotia, Quebec, and Manitoba have laws that contain discretionary power to regulate property and protect habitat. In both countries, therefore, there is a greater degree of regulation and stewardship mixing across all land parcels. Once affirmative motivations are realized and policy makers focus on ways to enhance such motivations, conservation policy will be better able to navigate this balance of stewardship and regulation.

The United States and Canada share of lot of natural capital and, as a result, have forged a close relationship.[1] As former British colonies, the two hold many of the same values; it is perhaps not surprising that they also face many of the same environmental problems, often revolving around constrained land use as urbanization and intensive agricultural practices increase across the continent (Beazley 2001; Czech and Krausman 2001; Venter et al. 2006).

What the Two Countries Share

Canada is the largest country to share a border with only one other country, and that border, including the stretch along Alaska, is 8,891 kilometres, or 5,525 miles, long. The US State Department notes that "the relationship between the United States and Canada is among the closest and most extensive in the world. It is reflected in the staggering volume of bilateral trade – the equivalent of $1.6 billion a day in goods – as well as in people-to-people contact. About 300,000 people cross the border every day" (United States 2011). Most Canadians live within two hundred miles of the border, and given its population of expatriates, Los Angeles is jokingly referred to as Canada's fourth-largest city. Although it is not true that more than a million Canadians live in Los Angeles, in the United States as a whole the Canadian-born population numbers 920,000 according to the 2010 US census, along with as many as 65,000 to 75,000 undocumented Canadians (Fix, Passel, and Sucher 2003).

Canadians and Americans also share the closest energy relationship in the world (Doern 2005; Naugle 2011; Sinclair 2010). Energy infrastructure – including oil and gas pipeline networks and electricity grids – is tightly integrated. Canada is the United States' largest and most secure supplier of oil, natural gas, electricity, and uranium (Canada 2011). According to the Canadian federal government, in 2009 Canadian energy exports to the United States – almost 2.5 million barrels per day of crude oil and refined products – were valued at C$76.27 billion, while Canada's energy imports from the US totalled almost C$11.5 billion. The two countries also share an integrated electricity grid and supply almost all of each other's electricity imports. Finally, Canada also supplies approximately one-third of the uranium used in US nuclear power plants (Canada 2011). If the Keystone pipeline is approved, Alberta is prepared to send its oil straight through America's heartland into Texas, where it can be refined and used in the US economy. When it comes to energy, perhaps no two countries are so integrated and so mutually interdependent in a peaceful way.

Beyond energy, the economies of Canada and the United States are thoroughly intertwined (Clarkson and Mildenberger 2011; MacDougall 2006; Morales and Medina 2011). The two countries conduct the world's largest bilateral trade relationship, with total merchandise trade (exports and imports) exceeding C$533.7 billion in 2006 (Ferguson 2008). This relationship revolves around the themes of "integration and asymmetry:

integration from successive trade liberalization from the Auto Pact of 1965 leading to the North American Free Trade Agreement" in 1992 (Ferguson 2008, 1). Autos and auto parts are the top US exports to, and imports from, Canada. But other goods such as computer equipment, electrical equipment, engines, turbo-engines, recorded media, optical equipment, and precision instruments are also major US exports. And Canada exports engines, aircraft equipment, wood, and paper products (Ferguson 2008). The importance of this close trade relationship cannot be understated for the economic prosperity of the continent. As Chapter 7 shows, however, this close relationship has not yet translated into commensurate communication or collaboration in biodiversity conservation.

Other than commercial and energy goods, the countries also share other precious resources in the form of water, air, birds, marine life, and a countless array of land species ranging from small insects to massive prairie bison. Aside from the coastlines more than three hundred rivers and lakes (some of the largest in the world) lie along, or flow across, the border (Canada 2011). The two countries thus have not only hydro-electricity relations, but also a shared fresh water supply (Annin 2006; Fry 2005). In 1972 President Richard Nixon and Prime Minister Pierre Trudeau signed the Great Lakes Water Quality Agreement (GLAWQA), the first step towards restoring and enhancing the water quality and ecosystems of this resource. Today, after ongoing revisions and negotiations, this treaty stands as emblematic of the potential for diplomacy and collaboration that could be of great benefit to conservation.

Beyond the GLAWQA, at least fifty bilateral arrangements concerning the environment exist between the two federal governments and more than one hundred at the state and provincial level (Canada 2011; see Le Prestre and Stoett 2006 for a more comprehensive overview of Canada-US environmental relations). These agreements include the well-known Boundary Waters Treaty, with its International Joint Commission and the Air Quality Agreement. The North American Free Trade Agreement (NAFTA) is probably the best-known agreement between Canada and the United States (as well as Mexico), but less well known is the environmental agreement among the three countries that was created at the same time. The Commission for Environmental Cooperation is a collaborative effort to address regional environmental concerns, help prevent potential trade and environmental conflicts, and promote the effective enforcement of environmental law (see the Commission's Web site at http://www.cec.org).

Canada and the United States also share biodiversity, ecosystems, and cross-border species. The most obvious examples are marine life and fisheries, such as the Gulf of Maine eco-system and the Salish Sea eco-system on the West Coast, where almost a thousand species of land birds travel between Canada, the United States, and Mexico. Canada and the United States also share the Rocky Mountains, the Great Lakes, the Great Plains, and Arctic waters such as the Gulf of Alaska and the Beaufort Sea. The two countries are partners in the Roosevelt Campobello International Park on Campobello Island, New Brunswick. This international park, created by a treaty signed in 1964, contains the summer home of President Franklin D. Roosevelt and is a testament to the close relationship between the two countries (Canada 2011).

Despite this positive relationship, however, few bilateral agreements focus specifically on biodiversity or endangered species. Game and fishing agreements date back to the nineteenth century – as does the protection of national parks. But "endangered" species did not enter the US and Canadian vocabulary until the buffalo began to disappear in 1870 and the passenger pigeon went extinct in the wild in the 1880s. In 1911 Canada and the United States, along with Russia and Japan, signed the Convention for the Preservation and Protection of Fur Seals. And in 1916 came the first US-Canada bilateral endangered wildlife agreement: the Migratory Birds Convention (in fact, Britain signed this treaty on behalf of Canada, which did not then have an independent foreign policy). Through these treaties the continental partners acknowledged the importance of wildlife and agreed to work together to protect a shared natural biological resource and treasure.

Bilateral environmental and wildlife agreements recently have become a bit more numerous. There is the 1986 North American Waterfowl Agreement (which Mexico joined in 1994), the 1987 Agreement on the Conservation of the Porcupine Caribou Herd, and in 1999 came the renewal of the US-Canada Pacific Salmon Treaty. These agreements are all positive indications of a collaborative relationship, but are too few considering that the two countries share so much. Chester (2006, 14) argues that the border is "chalked full of efforts to conserve transborder biodiversity," and points to the prominent example of the World Heritage Area of Alaska-Yukon and British Columbia. He also identifies thirty-seven examples of US-Canada and US-Mexico cross-border conservation, but admits that, by and large, these are not government efforts but informal and led by civil society actors. In reality each country treats endangered species management as a domestic problem, and very little cooperation exists between government agencies, even in the case of cross-border species. And where cooperation does exist, it is directed at species, such as commercial fish, with high economic value (Balis-Larson, Dauphine, and Jewell 1999), rather than at less-valued species such as the Lake Erie water snake, the example I examine in Chapter 7.

What Is in Danger

As of October 2013 SARA listed 513 endangered or threatened species in Canada, while the ESA listed 1,380 endangered or threatened species in the United States. Of these Canada also considers 338 to be endangered or threatened, according to the independent scientific Committee on the Status of Endangered Wildlife in Canada (COSEWIC; see NatureServe Explorer 2012) – although not every species that COSEWIC considers endangered is listed under Canadian federal law, as I explain in Chapter 3. These 338 species, with a few exceptions, are not cooperatively managed. In fact, it is unlikely that the US Fish and Wildlife Service (USFWS) even knows which US species are also endangered in Canada. The two countries do not conduct cooperative scientific status reports or co-manage lists of species. Instead, each independently assesses and lists species within its own territory, with little regard to the species range beyond the border. In 2011, for example, the USFWS delisted the Lake Erie water snake as "recovered," while two miles away in Canada, with the same food sources, the species remains listed as endangered because the population there is lower than across the nearby border. It is as though the border creates endangered species by limiting the species' habitat. On occasion the USFWS will work with Environment Canada or provincial agencies on recovery teams for shared species, but except with respect to endangered migratory birds, examples of government-led efforts are few and far between.

Thus, it is hard to know how many species are endangered north of Mexico. There is a general consensus among the scientific community about what types of species and ecosystems are particularly under pressure: wetlands, grasslands, migratory birds (especially grassland birds), salmon, Pacific Coast sea otters, northern populations of caribou, polar bears, and whales, and Western old-growth forests (Brandt 2009; Canada 2010b; Pew Oceans Commission 2003). In 1995 eighty-two eco-systems in the United States were identified as threatened, endangered, or critically endangered (Noss, LaRoe, and Scott 1995). Both countries are working independently on ways to slow the damage, protect what remains, and enhance the recovery of those being lost most quickly.

Why Species Are Going Extinct

Recent data from the International Union for the Conservation of Nature (IUCN), which analyses and reports on worldwide efforts to reduce biodiversity loss, reveal that of the known species that scientists have examined (just 3 per cent of those thought to exist), 869 are already extinct or extinct in the wild, 290 are critically endangered, and 16,928 are threatened with extinction (IUCN 2012). It is important to remember that the loss is not just a reduction in species, but an actual extinction of life forms. As Soule and Wilcox (1980, 168) point out, "death is one thing, an end to birth is something else."

Reasons for extinction and biodiversity loss include habitat destruction, hunting, pesticide use, and pollution (Vaughn 2011). Leaky and Lewin (1995) explain that human beings endanger the existence of species in three main ways: through exploitation, the introduction into ecosystems of alien species, and the destruction of habitat, the last of which is a major factor in the endangerment and extinction of species in Canada and the United States. Venter et al. (2006) use COESWIC data to show that agricultural activity and urbanization are the most prevalent causes of endangerment in Canada. Of the 341 species included in their study, 46 per cent were threatened by agriculture, 44 per cent by urbanization, 35 per cent by human disturbance, 33 per cent by extraction, and 28 per cent by infrastructure development. In the United States, in contrast, 49 per cent of endangered species are threatened by invasive species (Wilcove et al. 1998), but this is a particular problem in Hawaii, where 99 per cent of birds and plants are so affected. Excluding Hawaii, invasive species are a factor for a similar share of endangered birds and plants in the two countries – 31 per cent in the United States, 27 per cent in Canada (Venter et al. 2006). ˙

The largest contributing factor in the United States, however, is habitat loss (Czech and Krausman 2001), mainly due to urbanization; in Canada, habitat loss is more often the result of agricultural practices (Francis et al. 2012). Nevertheless, both countries have seen significant fragmentation and destruction of habitat. For example, over 99 per cent of the native tall-grass communities and 75 per cent of the mixed grass communities on the Canadian prairies have disappeared, due to farming, the oil and gas and potash industries, and increasing human populations. More than 90 per cent of southern Ontario's Carolinian forests have been converted to farms or human communities. Greater Toronto, reportedly growing at 100,000 people per year (Toronto 2011), is putting enormous pressure on Ontario's biodiversity. In the United States, urbanization in Arizona, southwest Utah, and the East Coast is transforming natural ecosystems into cities and strip malls.

The Arctic landscape is also changing as more people move into northern communities. Although still only a town of about seven thousand people, Iqaluit, in Canada's northern territory of Nunavut, is growing at close to 18 per cent annually, the highest of any urban place in Canada. Nunavut itself has the highest growth rate of any Canadian territory or province, 1.1 per cent, followed by the Yukon. Alaska, already more heavily populated than Canada's North, continues to grow slowly and now has a population of just over 700,000 people, mostly gained between 1950 and 1990 when the state's economy was booming and the annual growth rate fluctuated between 35 and 80 per cent. The result is a rapidly changing Arctic landscape and an increasingly threatened bioregion, which is reflected in declining populations of numerous species. For example, the George River herd of caribou has declined by 60 per cent over the past decade (Canadian Boreal Initiative 2012), while the Bathurst population of caribou on the central Barrens has declined by almost 75 per cent (Russell and Gunn 2011).

Why It Matters

In their 1995 book *The Sixth Extinction*, Leaky and Lewin posit that biological diversity is in the midst of its sixth great extinction but, unlike the first five historical extinction crises, the sixth is being caused almost entirely by human beings. The great American biologist E.O. Wilson (1992) considers this sixth extinction the most important irreversible environmental problem in the world. The loss of biodiversity is hard to quantify, but it will create "consequences for survival that cannot be indefinitely ignored or displaced" (Johnston, Gismondi, and Goodman 2006, 13). Biodiversity loss, moreover, is occurring rapidly, unevenly, and unpredictably (Millennium Ecosystem Assessment 2005; Rockström et al. 2009). The number often quoted is fifty to one hundred life forms lost every day, with the possibility that 25 per cent of species will go extinct in the next few decades (Johnston, Gismondi, and Goodman 2006).

Reasons for worrying about this extinction vary, however, as individuals and governments have different ideas of why biodiversity is significant. For some (see Beazley 2001), the reasons are entirely anthropocentric or instrumental: *nature serves humanity, and if biodiversity is lost, then fewer services will be available*. Such an argument typically focuses on medicine/genetic resources, the food web (including bee pollination), ecotourism, wetlands, and other ways that human beings can use biodiversity. These are all practical and important reasons for valuing biodiversity. The UN Convention on Biological Diversity, for example, considers all these reasons as valid to sustain conservation efforts. Sometimes these services are quantified such that it is possible to put a dollar price on biodiversity (Costanza et al. 1997; Kenny, Elgie, and Sawyer 2011). For example, a major study by the United Nations Environment Programme reports that the loss of ecosystem services will cost between US$2 trillion and US$4.5 trillion annually by 2050 – equal to 7 per cent of global gross domestic product – if current rates of ecosystem degradation continue (TEEB 2010). Thus, in economic terms, the loss would be significant, but the loss would be more than just dollars-and-cents services.

Others (such as Dowie 1996; Eckersley 1992; Hayward 1994) take a more eco-centric view of biodiversity that focuses on the intelligence and splendour of nature, and considers the world to be an interconnected web of relations of value: *nature has an intrinsic worth and should be protected on that basis*. Closely related to such arguments is a subdiscipline of philosophy known as eco-ethics, whose underlying tenet is to "create a conceptual framework for human interaction with the environment, a framework that can assist us in holding our own lives together and enable us to act with discipline, understanding and reverence toward the natural world" (Miller 1991, 12; see also McKenzie 2002). From this principle emerge moral arguments for the conservation and protection of nature and wildlife. Rockefeller (1992), drawing inspiration from Rachel Carson, argues that human beings have a moral obligation to future generations. Aldo Leopold, in his *A Sand Country Almanac* (1949, 30), argues that "all ethics so far evolved rest upon a single premise: that the individual is a member of a community of independent parts. His instincts prompt him to compete for his place in that community, but his ethics prompt him also to cooperate." The existence of an eco-ethic plays a central role in the development of affirmative motivations for stewardship, as I discuss throughout the remainder of this book.

In the United States and Canada, species are valued for all the reasons mentioned above. The ESA concedes, in its first section (ESA 16 U.S.C., 1531), that "species of fish, wildlife, and plants are of aesthetic, ecological, educational, historical, recreational, and scientific value to the Nation and its people." The act lists these reasons alphabetically so as not to give one priority over another. The American people agree that species have anthropocentric worth but also "ecological" worth – although the language of the law does not make it clear if the value is for our sake as humans or for its own sake. Canada takes the division one step further and acknowledges the intrinsic worth of species, as SARA states in its preamble: "Wildlife, in all its forms, has *value in itself* and is valued by Canadians for aesthetic, cultural, spiritual, recreational, educational, historical, medical, ecological and scientific reasons" [emphasis added].

Although one should not read too much into the language of the two acts, word choice suggests that Canadians not only value species for all the same reasons as Americans, but also speak to the "value in itself" that wildlife contains. This is a stronger statement than the ESA, and suggests that all species should be protected not just because they could serve humans, but because they de facto merit saving by the nature of their worth (or their dignity). Newfoundland and Labrador states in its Endangered Species Act (2001) that other species "have a right to exist" (as I discuss in Chapter 3) – perhaps no stronger eco-centric claim exists in North American legislation. But what is written into law and how the law is implemented in practice can be quite different. Thus, part of this book's purpose is to examine empirically the attitudes of Canadians and Americans towards other species.

For anthropocentric and eco-centric reasons, Canada and the United States have been safeguarding biodiversity since the turn of the twentieth century. Their laws are a testament to the values of Canadians and Americans – values that are largely shared and that, in some cases, have been translated directly into affirmative motivations for conservation efforts. Examples range from urban residents of Toronto spending a Saturday planting trees in the Rouge National Park to agricultural landowners in Ohio volunteering for the Partners in Wildlife Program to set aside land for conservation. Canadians and Americans do value other species, and they support the existence of conservation laws.

Saving Endangered Species

Twenty-four major international agreements exist on biological diversity; among the better known are the Convention on International Trade in Endangered Species of Fauna and Flora (CITES) and the United

Nations Convention on Biological Diversity (UNCBD).[2] Both the United States and Canada have ratified the former, but the United States has not ratified the latter.

The development of CITES was in large part a result of US leadership, since the 1969 Endangered Species Conservation Act included a provision to convene an international meeting to develop an agreement on the conservation of endangered species (Vaughn 2011). The United States, in fact, was the first country to ratify the convention, which became effective on 1 July 1975; today there are 175 parties to the convention. CITES does not focus on the protection or recovery of endangered species, but on the international trade of species at risk of extinction in the wild. The African elephant became protected under CITES in 1988, after the United States pushed for its listing, although restrictions were lifted for some African nations that were permitted temporarily to sell stockpiles of ivory. Despite CITES oversight, however, it is estimated that 37,000 African elephants are poached each year (Vaughn 2011). Critics point out that CITES is not well enforced and that there is no real power behind the convention to restrict the actions of individual countries, a common and reoccurring problem for widely based international treaties.

During the Earth Summit in Rio de Janeiro in 1992, the UNCBD was concluded after six years of negotiations. Although the United States was involved in drafting the agreement and although President Bill Clinton signed it in June 1993, the US Senate never ratified the treaty (Vaughn 2011). Today 168 countries, including Canada, are party to the convention, and the United States has been granted an "observer" role, allowing it to attend negotiations and annual meetings of the parties. The rationale behind the UNCBD is largely anthropocentric – the convention acknowledges the goods and services that ecosystems provide, such as food, fuel, shelter-building materials, air and water purification, pollination of plants, moderation of floods, and numerous other benefits that human beings derive.

Under the convention, governments "undertake to conserve and sustainably use biodiversity." All parties are required to develop national biodiversity strategies with action plans that are to become part of environmental planning and development in sectors such as forestry, agriculture, fisheries, energy, transportation, and urban planning (United Nations 2000). Each country must report on its progress and attend yearly meetings to address goals and create action plans moving forward. Since the US has not signed, it is not obligated to develop strategies or action plans at the ecosystem level, nor does it attend meetings for the purposes of joint action or policy making. Were it to sign the convention, as Canada already has, the two countries would make further progress in their collaborative efforts to conserve biodiversity and likely could share resources and streamline data for the purposes of action plans.[3]

For example, in preparation for the 2010 meeting of the UNCBD, the UN created a "Framework for Measuring Progress" with specific goals towards which all signatory parties to the convention were to report their progress, including (i) promoting the conservation of the biological diversity of ecosystems, habitats, and biomes; (ii) promoting the conservation of species diversity and genetic diversity, as well as the sustainable use and consumption of species; (iii) reducing pressures on habitat loss, land use, and degradation and water use; (iv) controlling threats from invasive alien species; (v) addressing challenges to biodiversity from pollution and climate change; and (vi) maintaining the socio-cultural diversity of indigenous and local communities (UNEP 2010). Canada, as a signatory to the convention, collects data and research in each of these domains and prepares annual reports on the status of its biodiversity, which alone has marked a turning point in conservation in Canada. As I discuss in later chapters, Canada is starting to focus more on stewardship initiatives, ecosystems, Aboriginal knowledge, and issues related to joint governance of wildlife management areas. Thus, although Canada once lagged behind the United States on the conservation of biodiversity, it might soon lead the continent in this area.

Beyond large international agreements, Canada, the United States, and Mexico have an agreement to co-manage North American ecosystems: the Trilateral Committee for Wildlife and Ecosystem Conservation and Management, established in 1996, which assists coordination, cooperation, and development of partnerships among wildlife agencies of the three countries and other interested groups. The Trilateral Committee is headed by the directors of the Canadian Wildlife Service, the USFWS, and the Coordinating Unit for International Affairs of the Mexican Ministry of Environment and Natural Resources (SEMARNAT). It develops and oversees programs and projects for conservation and management of biological diversity and ecosystems of mutual interest. The committee also "implements the conservation priorities of each country; develops, implements, reviews, and coordinates specific cooperative actions; and facilitates communication on issues that span international boundaries" (see the Web site of the Trilateral Committee at http://www.trilat.org/about-the-trilateral). Although the three countries have accomplished little for the sake of shared ecosystems, it is important that Canada and the United States continue to invest in research and sustainable development in Mexico. The trilateral agreement has great potential, and will become increasingly important as North America faces an increasingly significant problem of extinction in the twenty-first century.

Although there has been some progress at the international and intraregional levels, most of the heavy lifting takes place within individual states. UN conventions rely on self-reporting and good-faith efforts on the part of signatory countries; the trilateral agreement in North America also does not carry legally enforceable sanctions. So, how should a country conserve its natural biodiversity? For the United States the answer is the Endangered Species Act; for Canada the answer is the Species at Risk Act. Both pieces of legislation are aimed at the protection and recovery of endangered species, but, as I explain, they are quite different. Since the two countries are so similar and suffer biodiversity loss for similar reasons, why did such different policies develop? Chapters 2 and 3 address this question.

The most significant difference is that, in Canada, SARA does not extend mandatory protection of habitat to non-federal lands – in part the outcome of Canada's signature on the UNCBD. But the difference can also be explained by different institutional and ideational factors in the two countries, including federal powers and the precautionary principle. Nonetheless, the two countries' policy approaches are converging, and so I also examine the extent to which this process is occurring. Indeed, Canada's approach leaves the field open for provincial policy to regulate property in the style of the US ESA – Ontario has already adopted a similar law, and other provinces are considering doing so. Thus, both the United States and Canada are relying on voluntary stewardship but backing that approach with the threat of a legal hammer if landowners do not comply.

After analysing the ESA (Chapter 2) and the Canadian national strategy for biodiversity (Chapter 3), in Chapter 4 I explore theories of compliance and cooperation. Specifically, I ask why small private landowners are willing to comply and cooperate with a law, such as the ESA or SARA, that places limitations on their property rights and/or opposes their material interests. The focus is on non-agricultural landowners, who are understudied yet increasingly important for species habitat and protection. Since urbanization is a prominent cause of habitat loss in North America, it is important to include urban landowners in discussions of conservation. To comply means landowners must obey the law as written, whereas to cooperate means landowners take voluntary actions on their property to benefit endangered species conservation. The customary regulatory approach implies that individuals comply with rules because they fear punishment (May 2002, 2004; Winter and May 2001). The traditional policy toolkit for obtaining compliance thus has been through command-and-control legislation such as the ESA, in which the enforcement of actions and the imposition of sanctions are central (May 2002; Sparrow 2000).

Citizens, however, might want to comply with public policy for other reasons, known as "affirmative motivations," that emanate from good intentions and a sense of civic duty (May 2004). In this book I examine two types of affirmative motivations: morality and legitimacy. A motivation through morality arises when an individual wants to cooperate with public policy because he or she believes that the policy is "right" in a moral or ethical sense. For example, a citizen might refrain from drinking and driving, not because of a fear of punishment, but because morally he or she feels compelled to refrain from this action. In Chapter 4 I lay out the possibility that citizens in Canada and the United States might steward endangered species and otherwise cooperate with species-at-risk policy because they feel morally obligated to do so. This is what Leopold meant when he said "ethics prompt him to cooperate" (1949, 30).

A motivation through legitimacy means that one complies with a policy because one feels that the authority enforcing the law has the right to dictate behaviour or that the law was created in a procedurally just manner and is thus worthy of compliance. For example, a citizen might wear a seat belt not because he or she fears punishment or because he or she feels morally compelled, but because seat-belt laws were passed in a fair and democratic society and, therefore, should be obeyed. For motivations through legitimacy to exist, citizens need to believe that laws were created in a democratic process that included public discourse. In fact, the intent behind social regulation in a just society is that individuals will comply voluntarily with the law. In Chapter 4 I also suggest the possibility that citizens might cooperate with endangered species policy because they respect the law and feel government has the right to enforce such policy.

In Chapter 5 I explore the history of private property and of conservation in the United States and Canada. With Chapter 4, this presentation lays the groundwork for a discussion of the tensions that arise when private property and conservation collide. It has been argued elsewhere that society "can sustain ecosystems across boundaries only if we understand how humans behave with respect to the places they claim as territory" (Brunson 1998, 66). The theoretical basis of this book is that small landowners' attitudes towards property regulation and conservation will influence their willingness to cooperate with either the ESA or SARA, despite their material interests. In the case of property, I argue that similar norms exist in Canada and the United States if norms are taken to mean there is an informal rule of behaviour regarding property that is deemed socially acceptable (Axelrod 1986). Specifically, I am interested in attitudes about property that reflect John Locke's influence on landownership in North America, as both Canadian and American politicians historically have looked to Locke's conception of property. This "Lockean norm" is taken to be a concept of ownership that rejects government intervention and gives limited attention to social obligation. The degree to which individual landowners subscribe to this norm and how they balance it against conservation partly determines what kind of policy approach government should take towards the conservation of endangered species on private lands. Ultimately, my goal is partly to show that property norms need not necessarily limit the potential for conservation on private property.

Both the ESA and SARA rely on stewardship by private property owners, but does stewardship exist in the North American psyche? A stewardship norm is said to find its origins in the works of Aldo Leopold, whose *The Sand County Almanac* is "widely held to be the secular equivalent of holy writ within environmental circles" (Minteer 2006, 3). In this work Leopold devised a land ethic based on the principle that an action is right "if it tends to preserve the integrity, stability, and beauty of the biotic community. And an action is wrong if it tends otherwise" (Leopold 1949, 204). But to what extent do Canadian and US landowners think this way about land and biodiversity today? Do they have a motivation to cooperate with respect to the conservation of endangered species for ethical reasons? Do they really feel an obligation to the land and to the non-human members of the biotic community? If so, this suggests that there is an affirmative motivation through morality for conservation.

In Chapters 6 and 7 I present case studies of small non-agricultural landowners and urban residents in Canada and the United States. The main purpose of these empirical chapters is to offer evidence of affirmative motivations. Most landowners in the case studies interpret conservation as consistent with both their own sense of morals and their idea of legitimacy. This suggests that policy makers should be able to maximize conservation by enhancing these types of motivations. This is not to suggest that other tools in the compliance model, such as incentives and regulation, can be ignored; rather, the point is to weave affirmative motivations better into cooperative management strategies.

In Chapter 8 I present a unique case study of non-landowners in the northern Canadian territory of Nunavut. The indigenous people, the Inuit, might also possess affirmative motivations for conservation of wildlife, but since the Inuit have a different relationship to the land and a different source of legal legitimacy, they do not draw upon the intellectual traditions of Locke or Leopold. Aboriginal scholars claim that "the Native mind reveals a profound sense of empathy and kinship with other forms of life, rather than a sense of separateness from them or superiority over them" (quoted in McKenzie 2002, 38; see also Hughes 1996; Knudtson and Suzuki 1992; Preece 1999). Obviously there is great diversity among native cultures in North America, but Knudtson and Suzuki (1992) point out that there is broad consensus on the integrity and intrinsic worth of nature. The Inuit possess an eco-ethic that provides moral foundations for conservation. As Chapter 8 illustrates, however, the legitimacy of conservation laws such as SARA can be questioned since the law's implementation overemphasizes Western science and Western culture while not meaningfully including Inuit knowledge or Inuit people. Environmental justice, a form of procedural justice, demands Inuit participation to create an affirmative motivation via legitimacy for conservation of wildlife in the North.

Finally, in Chapter 9, I summarize the main findings of the book and piece together what this all means for endangered species policy in Canada and the United States. The idea of voluntary willingness to comply is set in the context of landowners who know very little about conservation law or endangered species, yet still harbour deeply entrenched views about government regulation and the importance of other living things on Earth. In this chapter I also explore some of the most important challenges facing endangered species conservation in Canada and the United States, including the oil sands development, Arctic policy, and, in the Canadian context, Conservative Party politics.

Journeys across North America

In this book I present six different, apparently unrelated, but carefully selected cases (see Table 1.1). The first comes from Indiana in 2007 and

involves the brown bat (see Raymond and Olive 2008). My collabora-
tor, Leigh Raymond, and I chose it because it was a "hard case" for the
ESA. As a state, Indiana is fairly conservative – or in the very least it is
not obviously liberal-environmental like California, Washington, and
Maine – and there was no reason to expect that landowners would be
especially empathetic to conservation or to pro-environmental attitudes generally. Moreover, although endangered, the brown bat is not a
charismatic species, so that there was little chance that emotional at-
tachment to the creature would increase positive public perception.

The next two cases – Utah and the desert tortoise, and Ohio and the
Lake Erie water snake – are meant to compare with that of Indiana.
Again, these states are fairly conservative and the two species concerned are also non-charismatic. If landowners in Indiana, Utah, and
Ohio are willing to cooperate with the USFWS to protect a bat, a tortoise, or a snake, then there might be hope for the protection on private
property of really any species in the United States. Although there was
not overwhelming support for the law or for conservation efforts on
behalf of these species in the three states, I did find "pragmatic stewards" (Minteer 2006). Essentially, some of the landowners represent
what Minteer calls the "third way" because they accept "the interpen-
etrating character of intrinsic and instrumental values in experience,
the basic continuity of means and ends in environmental thought and
practice" (2006, 4). Landowners in my case studies shared anthropocentric (instrumental) and eco-centric (intrinsic) reasons for conservation,
and were generally able to relate the preservation of other species to the
preservation of the public good in society. Thus, many landowners were
willing to engage in cooperative management on their own land for the
sake of endangered species – either for instrumental or intrinsic reasons, or even both.

I selected Ontario as the fourth case study because of its similarity to
that of Ohio in every important way save for the key difference of
policy outcome. Ontario and Ohio share an endangered species, the
Lake Erie water snake, which lives on the islands off the coast of Port
Clinton, Ohio, and Leamington, Ontario. The islands are very similar – both Middle Bass and Pelee Island are home to numerous summer cabin owners and a few permanent residents. Ohio and Ontario
have similar endangered species laws – the ESA in Ohio and the
Ontario Endangered Species Act. The USFWS delisted the Lake Erie
water snake in Ohio in 2011, however, while it remains endangered
in Ontario, only a few miles away. Thus, in this chapter I focus on the

Table 1.1. Summary of Six Case Studies

Location	No. of Interviews	Wildlife Law	Government Agency	Species
Indiana	22	ESA	USFWS	brown bat
Utah	35	ESA	USFWS	desert tortoise
Ohio	44	ESA	USFWS, Ohio Department of Natural Resources	Lake Erie water snake
Ontario	18	Ontario ESA, SARA	Ontario Ministry of Natural Resources	Lake Erie water snake
Nunavut	5	Wildlife Act, SARA	Nunavut Wildlife Management Board, Environment Canada	polar bear
Saskatchewan	369 surveys	SARA	Environment Canada	n.a.

existence of affirmative motivations, but I also address cross-border conservation. Given the similarity of Canadian and US laws and the affirmative motivations of landowners on both sides of the border, there should not be such a glaring difference in the status of a shared endangered species.

My fifth case study is that of Nunavut. When I began researching conservation in Canada, I found Nunavut to be a bit of a conundrum. Federally, SARA applies to all Aboriginal reserves, but it does not apply in the same way in the Yukon, the Northwest Territories, and Nunavut. Instead, each territory has its own wildlife act and manages species at risk in collaboration with the federal government and the provinces. The indigenous peoples of North American do not look to Locke or Leopold for inspiration, but instead have their own traditional knowledge and approach to managing biodiversity. Few books or articles have been written about conservation in Nunavut, yet the inclusion of Aboriginal peoples in conservation efforts is important, not only because Canada agreed to do this via the UNCBD, but also because environmental and ecological justice demands inclusion. Like other people in North America, Aboriginal peoples are keenly aware of procedural justice and might be motivated to cooperate with policy because of it. In this chapter I intentionally problematize some of my findings and suggest that affirmative motivations do not come solely from the likes of Locke or Leopold, or even from Anglo-Christian culture.

The last case study is that of Saskatchewan, in the heart of the Canadian prairies. Researching SARA presented me with a surprising fact: Saskatchewan is one of just four Canadian provinces that lack stand-alone species-at-risk legislation. Saskatchewan's Ministry of Environment reports that the province is in the process of writing such legislation, but information is desperately lacking about species status or the attitudes of landowners and residents. In November 2011 I mailed a thousand surveys to registered voters in urban and semi-rural areas of the province to see how much they knew about species at risk in Saskatchewan, and to determine their general attitudes towards private property, conservation, and government regulation.

All my case studies represent "hard cases" for conservation. I specifically selected areas of the United States whose residents have attitudes that are not overly liberal or obviously environmental. Arguing that citizens and landowners in those states care about endangered species and are willing to steward private lands would not be adequate to respond to the "wise use" movement or other public opposition to the ESA or SARA. In Canada, I look to a prairie province without legislation to find a stewardship ethos, instead of selecting a province (such as Nova Scotia) with a long track record of conservation. Moreover, I did not choose charismatic creatures to which individuals would become emotionally attached and favour conserving at high cost. Rather, individual landowners in Ontario and Ohio who are willing to steward their land for snake habitat are an indication of a deeper commitment to biodiversity. Likewise, the landowners and citizens who were asked about bats, tortoises, and snakes were pushed to the limit in terms of what they felt was worth protecting.

There are millions of landowners in Canada and the United States – ranging from small urban landowners to large agricultural landowners to even larger developers and industrial landowners. I have focused only on small non-agricultural landowners and urban residents. The sample is small and not always random, so my results cannot be generalized for either Canada or the United States. Research in environmental law and policy has a solid grasp of the attitudes of farmers and ranchers, especially in the United States (as I discuss in Chapters 2 and 6); there is also a fair amount of research on conservation alliances with larger landowners such as the Nature Conservancy. But the lack of publicly available data or interviews of landowners, especially with respect to Canada-US comparisons, means that my case studies address a gap in the empirical literature by offering a unique in-depth look at conservation from the perspective of small private landowners. Accordingly, future work in this field should address a larger and more representative cross-section of landowners in the two countries. Ideally, this would include a closer examination of the relationship of industries such as forestry and mining with conservation; when it comes to endangered species legislation and policy, we cannot leave agribusiness, mining, oil, gas, and other large land users and developers out of the picture. Indeed, interactions between large extractive industry firms and small property owners are also part of the broader picture here. Thus, although I focus on the small landowner side of the equation, I draw larger implications and conclusions for future work in conservation studies.

My cases are hard, but they present real people going about their everyday lives in places where contact with endangered species and critical habitat is a likely reality. Endangered species no longer live just in "wilderness" areas or provincial/state parks. Urbanization and climate change are altering habitat across North America, pushing species into places inhabited by human beings. Residents of Swift Current, Saskatchewan, are likely to live in close proximity to potential burrowing owl or piping plover habitat, while any landowner in Hurricane, Utah, could come across a desert tortoise in their backyard. The choices that individuals make about how they manage their land and about the kind of legislation they support will affect, deeply and directly, species at risk in their own neighbourhoods.

Conclusion

Species are rapidly becoming endangered all around the world, and climate change will only exacerbate the situation (Hinzman et al. 2005; IPCC 2007; Jia, Epstein, and Walker 2009). As of 2013, 168 countries had ratified the UN Convention on Biological Diversity, and there is growing worldwide recognition that species are valuable and that extinction should be avoided (CESCC 2011; Dobson 2005; Rankin, Austin, and Rice 2010; SCBD 2010). In Canada and the United States, domestic legislation already acknowledges that species have anthropocentric and eco-centric (instrumental and intrinsic) value. The US Endangered Species Act not only started a domestic movement, but also led to an international effort to conserve other species. Although still in force, the ESA officially expired in 1992 and there is political gridlock over its reauthorization, despite the threat of extinction that species face from habitat loss across the country, (Barry 1991; Goble 2009; Mathews 2004; Nash 2011). In Canada, the Species at Risk Act (created in 2002) applies unevenly across the country and is still in its developmental stage. It remains unclear what some provinces will do and whether or not the federal government will get involved in local efforts to conserve at-risk species. It might be too soon to assess the law, but time is quickly running out for some species, and the ramifications of failure need to be taken more seriously.

The Canadian and American publics have supported national, state, provincial, and territorial legislation for the protection and recovery of species in threat of extinction. This is a policy issue of growing importance in both countries as climate change, shale oil and gas development, Arctic exploitation, and the likely flow of oil from northern Alberta to Texas and through the Pacific gateway place increasing pressure on ecosystems. Canada and the United States are similar in so many ways, and they share energy resources, water, and wildlife, which would lead one to suppose they would have similar endangered species laws. Instead, the differences between the two countries are meaningful. As Binnema (2010, 621) points out, comparing the United States and Canada is not like comparing "two Delicious apples." Canada is the second largest landmass in the world and has a population of just 35 million. Its coastline, the longest in the world, touches the Pacific, Arctic, and Atlantic oceans. Canada is also a parliamentary democracy, where federalism is negotiated differently than in the United States – not only between the federal government and the provinces or states, but also between Aboriginal peoples and colonialists. For these reasons, Canada and the United States manage biodiversity differently. Moreover, as Illical and Harrison (2007) note, Canada was able to draw important – negative – lessons from US experience with the ESA. Nonetheless the ESA and SARA are identical in the most important of ways: they require voluntary stewardship from the very people they attempt to regulate. This makes affirmative motivations essential to conservation in North America.

In Canada most land is privately managed and in the United States it is mostly privately owned.[4] This is the consequence of history – of pioneers who were encouraged by government to settle two vast countries. The result today is that most biodiversity relies on private property, and on the people who own and manage it, for survival (Bean and Wilcove 1996; Shogren and Tschirhart 2001). But why would a landowner be willing to steward biodiversity? How can they be motivated to be good stewards? As I explain in Chapter 4, government could force them through stringent regulation, but this likely would be unpopular.

Government could pay them to steward, but this likely would be expensive. Government could also just call on landowners to be good stewards, but that would work only if individuals had an underlying reason to heed the appeal. In this book I search for those underlying motivations, a search that extends across the West, through the Midwest, and to the Canadian North.

My claim is ultimately an optimistic one: many landowners have affirmative motivations for cooperating with endangered species legislation. Most are willing to make some trade-off between their rights and conservation needs without resort to market-based incentives. Thus, it is not necessary to change the idea of private property – the essence of American culture – to solve the biodiversity crisis. The answer, instead, lies in a careful combination of policy tools in the implementation of the law. The path forward will not be easy, but the past gives us some indication that we should be hopeful about the future. At the turn of the twentieth century, the United States and Canada embarked upon what is now referred to as "the dawn of conservation diplomacy" (Dorsey 1998) to conserve forestry resources. This project was immensely successful. Now, more than a decade into the twenty-first century, a new age of conservation diplomacy is required for endangered species. The two countries not only must examine their energy relationship and matters of Arctic sovereignty, but, most important, come to terms with their duty to protect biodiversity for the peoples of North America and for future generations on Earth.

2 The United States' Endangered Species Act

In the United States the federal government has taken responsibility for the protection of endangered species, even though the states technically have jurisdiction over wildlife. That is to say, the states own wild animals, but only in trust for the American people (Freyfogle and Goble 2009); thus, the states assume responsibility for wildlife by way of issuing licences for fishing and hunting. But the federal government oversees the protection of wildlife at the national level – a result of the establishment of national parks in the nineteenth century and more recently in the era of cooperative federalism, which saw Congress pass a wave of national pollution statutes in the 1970s. Since biodiversity protection is a national issue, given that species occupy habitat in more than one state, it is predominately up to the national government to protect (Arha and Thompson Jr 2011).

US endangered species policy can be broken into three separate legislative efforts, all enacted within the past fifty years (see Figure 2.1). First, the Endangered Species Preservation Act of 1966 mandated the secretary of the interior to develop a program to conserve, protect, and restore species of native fish and wildlife (Vaughn 2011). Then came the Endangered Species Conservation Act of 1969, which replaced the previous act and defined types of protected wildlife, both domestically and internationally. Instead of focusing only on fish and wildlife, the new act included mammals, fish, birds, amphibians, reptiles, molluscs, and crustaceans. Finally, since the 1969 law did little to protect habitat, it was replaced by the Endangered Species Act of 1973.

The future of the ESA is unclear, but the central theme of this chapter – indeed, of the book – is that the act needs to be further amended and revitalized to work better and more cooperatively with landowners if the United States has any hope of reducing further biodiversity loss.

Figure 2.1. The History of US Endangered Species Legislation

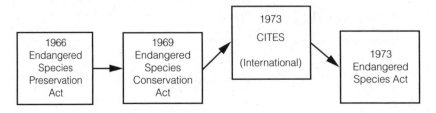

The Endangered Species Act of 1973

After signing the Convention on International Trade in Endangered Species of Fauna and Flora (CITES) in 1973, the United States was quick to introduce revised endangered species legislation. The ESA was designed to protect and recover imperilled species, whether plants, insects, or any other member of the animal kingdom. Such species are either "endangered" – meaning in danger of becoming extinct in all or a significant portion of its range; or "threatened" – meaning likely to become endangered. The regulatory power of the law is housed with the secretary of the interior, through the US Fish and Wildlife Service (USFWS), and the secretary of commerce, through the National Marine Fisheries Service.

The bill was introduced in the Senate by Harrison Williams (D-NJ) and passed unanimously; only four members of the House of Representatives had voted against John Dingell's (D-MI) bill in the lower chamber. President Richard Nixon signed the bill on December 28, 1973, and for two years it enjoyed unqualified support (Easley et al. 2001). The infamous snail-darter case, which saw a conservation group successfully bring suit against the Tellico Dam in the Tennessee Valley, was the first inkling of trouble for the ESA.

At its most basic level, the ESA is intended to identify, protect, and recover species at risk of extinction. The law protects only listed species, including the species' critical habitat. As originally defined in 1973, a "species" is "any subspecies or smaller taxa"; a 1978 amendment changed this definition to include "any distinct population segment of any species of vertebrate" (ESA 16 U.S.C.). This means that the ESA recognizes three taxonomic categories for vertebrates: species, subspecies, and distinct population segments – in contrast to Canada's legislation, which protects only full species. That said, species do account for about 75 per cent of the ESA's listings, with subspecies representing 21 per cent, and distinct population segments about 6 per cent (Scott et al. 2006).

An individual or group can petition to have a species listed, but most listings are initiated by the USFWS (for citizens' listings, see Biber and Brosi 2012). In both cases, the USFWS has twelve months to decide if a listing is warranted, "solely on the basis of the best scientific and commercial data available" (ESA 16 U.S.C., 1533(b)(1)(a)). And the Service is prohibited from considering the economic impacts of the listing. If twelve months elapse without a decision, the USFWS may determine the listing to be "warranted but precluded," and begin the twelve-month process over again. Due to budget limitations, this is often the fate of species on the waiting list (Easley et al. 2001, 50; see also Bean 2004; and Greenwald, Suckling, and Taylor 2006). Otherwise the twelve-month decisions, whether warranted or not warranted, must be published. If the listing is warranted, the secretary of the interior must give notice to professional scientific organizations, publish a summary of the proposed regulation in a newspaper where the species is believed to live, and hold a public hearing if any person files a request for one (Easley et al. 2001, 49–50).

The listing of a species requires the simultaneous identification and listing of its critical habitat, defined as "specific areas occupied by the species at the time it is listed whereby the physical and biological features of the area are essential to the conservation of the species and may require special management considerations or protection" (ESA 16 U.S.C. 1532(5)(A)). Geographical areas outside that occupied by the species may be deemed critical habitat if the area is determined to be essential for the conservation of the species. Critical habitat, however, is not necessarily all areas the species could potentially occupy – only that area essential to the conservation of the species necessary to preserve the status quo (Armstrong 2002). This means the USFWS does not consider recovery while listing a species (Easley et al. 2001). Finally, it is worth noting that designation of critical habitat can involve consideration of economic factors – although a certain core or essential area must be determined on the basis of science, according to a 1978 amendment of the act any critical habitat beyond that depends on a balancing test of costs and benefits (Easley et al. 2001, 67).

To protect a listed species, section 4(f) of the ESA mandates the development and implementation of recovery plans; these act as guidance documents and do not have the force of regulation. They include a description and history of the species, the reasons for the decline of the species, an estimated present-day population, a narrative that describes the actions necessary to promote recovery, and a target population at which point the species would be considered recovered (Easley et al. 2001, 72). Recovery plans are written either by a USFWS team or a team of independent scientists supervised by the USFWS during the process. A species can be delisted if it has become extinct, if it has recovered, or if the original data on the basis of which the species was listed contained an error. For a species to be delisted due to "recovery," it must be because "the best scientific and commercial data available indicates that it is no longer threatened or endangered" (ESA 16 U.S.C. 50 C.F.R. 424.11(d)(1)).

Although the ESA affects all land parcels in the country, since the federal government manages almost a third of the country's land, the act's main focus is federal lands and federal projects (Easley et al. 2001, 78). Section 7 requires all federal agencies to work pro-actively towards the conservation of listed species and to consult with the USFWS when considering a project or action, to ensure that it will not likely jeopardize the existence of any species or adversely affect critical habitat. That section also prohibits federal agencies, in their everyday work, or research and projects funded by federal agencies, from jeopardizing listed species or their habitat more broadly.

The ESA also prohibits any individual, organization, or business from taking – meaning to "harass, harm, pursue, hunt, shoot, wound, kill, trap, capture, or collect, or attempt to engage in any such conduct" (ESA 16 U.S.C. 1532(19)) – any listed species. And within that regulation, "harm" is taken to mean "an act which actually kills or injures wildlife," including "significant habitat modification or degradation where it kills or injures wildlife by significantly impairing essential behavioral patterns, including breeding, feeding or sheltering" (ESA 16 U.S.C. 50 C.F.R. 17.3). The notable and immediate exception to this prohibition is the taking of a species in self-defence, although not in defence of property or livestock (as was upheld in *Christy v. Hodel* in 1988).

Moreover, the ESA extends regulatory reach to private property. Although, unlike federal agencies, no landowner is required to take affirmative action to help a species, the act restricts land use by prohibiting the take of a species through habitat modification (Arnold 1991; Easley et al. 2001, 127). In 1982 the act was modified to allow individuals, businesses, and federal agencies to apply for incidental take permits via Habitat Conservation Plans, as discussed below. Finally, the penalties for violation are stringent, with fines ranging from $500 for transportation violations up to $3,500 for killing a species (for a first-time offence; for repeat offenders, the maximum penalty ranges from $1,300 for taking a species to $21,000 for fishing within the Stellar sea lion's designated buffer area in Alaska [ESA 16 U.S.C., 1561]).

The 1978 Amendments

The 1973 ESA originally was authorized for only five years, which set the stage for future reauthorization and/or amendments, which came in 1976, 1978, 1979, 1982, and 1988 (see Figure 2.2).

The 1976 reauthorization and amendment was minor, offering only clarifications of administrative procedures and exempting whale parts held lawfully before the date of the ESA's enactment. In the 1978 reauthorization, section 7 was the issue of contention, since it mandated that the federal government ensure that any action it took or for which it provided funding did not jeopardize the continued existence of an endangered species or cause destruction of its habitat. A few years prior, in 1975, an endangered snail darter halted the completion of the Tellico Dam on the Little Tennessee River. Since the dam would jeopardize the existence of the snail darter, section 7 prevented it from being completed, even though Congress repeatedly had granted money to the project because it was for the "economic rehabilitation of the entire region" (Easley et al. 2001). After legal appeals, in 1978 the US Supreme Court ruled, in *TVA v. Hill*, that the plain language of section 7 prohibited completion of the dam. The law's ability to stop industry in its tracks led the Senate to agree (in a vote of 94 to 3) that an amendment to the ESA was in order (Easley et al. 2001).

Rather than repeal or amend section 7, Congress created the Endangered Species Committee (more informally, the "God Squad") with the power to grant exemptions for ESA-halted federal projects, but only if the "economic benefits of those projects outweighed the benefits of conserving the endangered species" (Easley et al. 2001). Indeed, the newly empowered committee chose not to grant an exemption to the Tellico Dam project, finding instead that the benefits of the dam did not outweigh the value of protecting the snail darter.

The 1978 amendments also changed the listing procedure to require that the designation of a species' critical habitat be concurrent with its listing. The new procedure slowed down the listing process significantly, as the USFWS now had to identify habitat before a listing could

Figure 2.2. Summary of Major Amendments to the Endangered Species Act

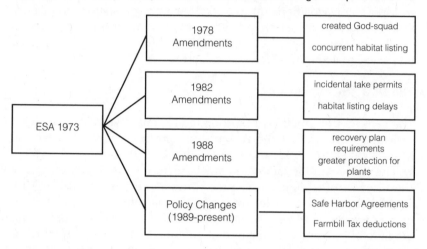

be considered complete. Moreover, the secretary of the interior was granted the authority to delay or withdraw a proposed listing if critical habitat was undeterminable, and to consider the economic effects of habitat listing, rather than just a scientific recommendation (Easley et al. 2001, 23).

The 1982 Amendments

Minimal changes to the ESA in 1979 altered the act's relationship with CITES and directed the USFWS to establish a prioritization system for listing species. More significant amendments were made, however, in 1982. These addressed the procedure for listing species and habitat by changing the standard for critical habitat identification to "the maximum extent prudent and determinable" (ESA 16 U.S.C., 1533(a)(3)). This made it easier for the USFWS to identify habitat and list species. Furthermore, Congress enabled the Service to list a species and delay habitat listing for up to a year. Thus, the listing process that was slowed almost to a halt by the 1978 amendments was brought up to speed in 1982. Related, this amendment also put the listing decision back into the hands of science, requiring that listings be made solely on the basis of biological, not economic, criteria.

The 1982 amendments also created "incidental take permits," which allow private landowners to apply for a permit to take (kill or injure wildlife) if "such taking is incidental to, and not the purpose of, carrying out an otherwise lawful activity" (ESA 16 U.S.C., 1539(a)). In conjunction with this change, section 10 was amended to create a process for obtaining such a permit through a Habitat Conservation Plan (HCP), in which the applicant details the potential impact of the proposed action on the species, steps the applicant intends to take to minimize such impact, the funding available to implement the first two steps, and any alternative actions that were considered and why they were rejected. The plan is submitted to the USFWS and then made available for public comment. If the plan is approved, the USFWS issues an incidental take permit. Few landowners apply for such permits, however; between 1982 and 1994 only twenty-one were granted (Easley et al. 2001).

The 1988 Amendments

The 1988 amendments were the last set of extensive changes to the ESA. Most notably, specific requirements were created for the secretaries of commerce and the interior to develop and implement recovery plans and to require a status report every two years on efforts to develop plans for listed species still lacking them (Vaughn 2011, 248). Minimum requirements for recovery plan content were also established, as well as a new protocol for public review of recovery plans (Svancara et al. 2006). The secretary of the interior was directed to use emergency listing powers to prevent significant risk to candidate species.

Greater protection was also extended to plants. Prior to 1988 it was only illegal to remove and possess listed plants (and then only on federal lands such as parks), but the new amendment prohibited malicious damage or destruction of listed plants on federal, state, or private lands. Moreover, the secretary of the interior was prohibited from favouring or prioritizing mammals for protection. A species' taxonomic classification was also not be considered in establishing recovery plan priorities, meaning charismatic mammals could not be bumped to the head of the line on account of their greater visibility and public appeal (Easley et al. 2001).

The ESA Today

The ESA officially expired on 1 October 1992, but Congress continues to fund the policy, as it can until the act is totally repealed (Vaughn 2011). Since the snail darter case in 1975, however, political opposition has been building against the ESA. The spotted owl controversy of the 1980s did little to help the act's proponents. When the USFWS refused to list the owl because its habitat included the timber industry's main source of income in the Pacific Northwest, environmental organizations dragged the agency through the courts. Ordered to list the owl, the USFWS finally did so in 1990, and soon after it also listed critical habitat, including three million acres of private land. The result was an almost decade-long battle in the courts over lands in the West. Since this case, issues of the present-day ESA have centred on private property. I take up this discussion in Chapter 4, but a brief synopsis of the political climate of the ESA is warranted here.

After the ESA expired in 1992, President George H.W. Bush put a moratorium on the listing of new species. Environmental groups then brought a complaint against the Bush administration through the trilateral agreement of Canada, Mexico, and the United States, which requires the three countries to enforce their own environmental laws. Under the moratorium the United States was not doing so, and although the complaint through the trilateral agreement was not directly responsible for the moratorium's lifting, it did bring international attention to the issue, which in turn helped create public pressure to repeal the moratorium in 1996 (Easley et al. 2001; Vaughn 2011).

During the Clinton administration the ESA came under fire numerous times. Both the administration and Congress agreed that the act was flawed, but no decision to repeal or amend it was made (Vaughn 2011). At the same time the "wise use" movement – a coalition of groups pushing for private property rights and a reduction in the regulation of public lands by government agencies such as the Bureau of Land Management and the Forest Service – created serious opposition to the ESA (Czech and Krausman 2001). Not surprisingly, the movement has its largest following in western states such as Arizona, Montana, Utah, Colorado, and Washington, where the federal government manages a considerable amount of land. These groups also seek to reduce funding for endangered species research in the expectation that a lack of information is a "formidable obstacle to conservation policy" (Czech and Krausman 2001, 5; see also Ehrlich and Ehrlich 1996).

In 1997, the Clinton administration, in response to such mounting opposition, developed Safe Harbor Agreements to ease tensions between the ESA and private landowners (Bean 2006; Colburn 2011; Wilcove et al. 2004). The agreements are intended to encourage landowners to take voluntary actions to protect or enhance populations of endangered species on their own land. Under an agreement between the USFWS and a private landowner, "a landowner voluntarily agrees to alter his property to benefit or attract endangered species in exchange for the assurance that USFWS will permit future takes above a pre-determined baseline" (Easley et al. 2001, 168). The ESA contains no economic incentive for a landowner voluntarily to improve or create habitat; instead the law only prohibits harm – meaning that as long as a landowner is not harming a species, he is obeying the law. There have been attempts, however, to increase voluntary stewardship among land-owners. Since the late 1990s the USFWS has operated Candidate Conservation Agreements encouraging private landowners to manage their lands to conserve species that are imperilled but not formally listed. Such agreements include "assurances" that landowners will not be subject to further conservation obligations if the species is eventually listed (Freyfogle and Goble 2009, 246–7).

In the past decade or so there has been an explosion in the number of HCPs, with more than 430 now approved and many more in the planning stage (Colburn 2011; Leonard 2009; Miller et al. 2002; Restani and Marzluff 2002; Thomson Jr 2006). According to the USFWS, most of the earlier HCPs approved were for planning areas of less than a thousand acres; now ten exceed half a million acres, and several are for more than a million acres. In some cases, there is more than one incidental take permit associated with a HCP. For example, as the USFWS (2012a) explains, "the Central Coastal Orange County [California] HCP was developed as an overall plan under which each individual participating entity received a separate incidental take permit. This suggests that HCPs are evolving from a process adopted primarily to address single projects to broad-based, landscape-level planning, utilized to achieve long-term biological and regulatory goals" (USFWS 2012a).

In another policy move to encourage landowners, a provision of the Food, Conservation and Energy Act of 2008 (the so-called Farm Bill) gave farmers a tax deduction for "expenditures paid or incurred from implementing actions benefitting the recovery of federally threatened or endangered (listed) species." To be eligible for the deduction, the expenditures must be for site-specific management actions recommended in approved recovery plans for listed species. The deduction for endangered species recovery expenses cannot be more than 25 per cent of a farmer's gross income from farming.

Although the ESA initially was rather rigid when it came to private property, it has evolved over time. Today the USFWS and the National

Marine Fisheries Service have five tools with which to work more effectively with landowners: HCPs, Safe Harbor Agreements, Candidate Conservation Agreements (with assurances), Recovery Credits, and Conservation Banking. The ESA thus has come a long way in terms of working with private property owners, but despite these efforts, public opposition, as Freyfogle and Goble note, "has been strong enough to keep the Fish and Wildlife Service from having enough money to carry out their many duties." As a result fewer species are being listed, fewer recovery plans are being written, and enforcement is weakening, leading the authors to observe that "[y]ear after year, the act becomes less of an obstacle to business as usual in America" (2009, 238).

The States and the ESA

Although not explicitly written into the ESA, it is widely recognized that "long term protection of endangered and threatened species in the United States has always depended on a partnership between federal and state agencies" (Niles and Korth 2006, 141). This is largely a matter of resources since state agencies collectively have more human and financial resource capacity than federal agencies. Currently, forty-six states have their own endangered species acts and manage their own endangered species lists, which include species that might be threatened within the state but not over the species' entire range (Arha and Thompson Jr 2011; see also Goble et al. 1999). Thus, state lists will differ significantly from one another as well as from the national list. Moreover, most states do not regulate habitat destruction or require state agencies to consult before taking action that could jeopardize a protected species (George, Snoops, and Senatore 1998).

The ESA does include provisions to work with the states – mainly through section 6, which instructs the Departments of the Interior and Commerce to "cooperate to the maximum extent practicable with the States" (ESA 16 U.S.C. 1535(a)). In practice, cooperation is less than ideal and there is much room for improvement (Arha and Thompson Jr 2011). One shining example of what could be accomplished, however, is the Cooperative Endangered Species Conservation Fund, which provides grants to states and territories to "participate in a wide array of voluntary conservation projects for candidate, proposed, and listed species" (USFWS 2011a). States must provide matching funds of 25 per cent (or 10 per cent each when two or more states are involved) for the projects. As of 2011, most states had entered into a cooperative agreement under section 6. Examples of grants for fiscal year 2011 range from a US$6 million grant for land acquisition as part of a multi-species HCP in California to a US$250,000 grant to support HCP development in Hawaii to conserve the hoary bat and numerous plants (USFWS 2011a).

Beyond section 6 grants, many states have also taken a proactive stance towards biodiversity conservation. In 1998 the International Association of Fish and Wildlife Agencies conducted a survey to gauge how much resources US states dedicate to conservation. It found that the states spend about US$135 million in aggregate and that, in contrast, the USFWS spends about $29 million each year on conservation (Niles and Korth 2006). State spending is very uneven, however, with a few spending a lot of resources and others almost nothing.

Since the creation of two new federally funded programs – state wildlife grants and the Landowner Incentive Program – state wildlife agencies are expanding their role in protecting state and federally listed species (Niles and Korth 2006). As well, the US Department of Agriculture oversees the Wildlife Habitat Incentive Program (WHIP), administered through the states, for private landowners who want to create habitat for wildlife on their property voluntarily. States also assume major responsibility for research and management programs, given the USFWS's limited resources and the availability of the scientific expertise of local state biologists and ecologists (Niles and Korth 2006).

Ultimately, however, the ESA is the law of the land, which means that, regardless of state law, the federal act takes precedent. Fortunately for some species this means two layers of protection. But, as I show in Chapter 8, it also comes with costs because overlapping bureaucracies sometimes stand in their own way.

Not directly related to the ESA itself, but germane to conservation in the United States, each state and federal territory recently completed a Comprehensive Wildlife Action Strategy that "assess[es] the health of each state's wildlife and habitats, identify[ies] the problems they face, and outline[s] the actions that are needed to conserve them over the long term" (see the Web site of the Wildlife Action Plan at http://www.wildlifeactionplan.org). The strategy is in part intended to prevent species from needing protection under the ESA: if states can do more now to protect habitat, fewer resources will be needed to recover species in the future. The various plans were completed in 2006, and although they are not legally enforceable, they do provide a comprehensive overview of each state's wildlife portfolio and signal a commitment by the states to protect biodiversity before it is too late.

Arha and Thompson Jr argue for more cooperative federalism under the ESA, whereby states assume a larger role in the protection and recovery of the nation's endangered species: "[states] enjoy a variety of advantages over the national government in protecting imperiled species, ranging from greater on-the-ground expertise in the needs of many local species to the ability to enlist local interest and pride in protecting native species" (2011, 3). But the authors are also quick to acknowledge that "biodiversity protection is a national issue that cannot be left to the states to address by themselves. Many species occupy habitat in more than one state" (4).

eNGOs and the ESA

The ESA has been bolstered by state efforts, but the role of the private sector cannot be overlooked, especially that of major environmental interest groups and non-governmental organizations (eNGOs) such as the National Audubon Society, Defenders of Wildlife, Sierra Club, The Nature Conservancy, the Wildlife Conservation Society, and the World Wildlife Fund, all of which rely on private donations and/or membership fees and "seek to protect natural communities and ecosystems, as well as species" (Kareiva et al. 2006, 176). These organizations are vital to conservation in the United States precisely because the ESA "is ineffective at preserving habitats that are found on private lands" (Adler 2011, 7). It is possible to argue that eNGOs are in the business of "supplying species habitat" since they are able to contract with landowners and acquire habitat through leases, easements, or outright ownership (Anderson and Watson 2011). For example, The Nature Conservancy "uses land acquisition as a principal tool of its conservation effort. The Conservancy helps to protect approximately 15 million acres in the United States" (Nature Conservancy 2012). It also prioritizes federally overlooked species and taxonomies in its conservation efforts (Kareiva et al. 2006).

A growing area of eNGO activity is land trusts, which focus primarily on the acquisition of private land. Land trusts have operated in the United States for more than a hundred years, but only in the 1980s did they begin to increase significantly in number (Gerber 2012); there are about 1,700 in existence today (see the Web site of the Land Trust Alliance, http://www.landtrustalliance.org).[5] Their use is somewhat controversial since they are associated with increased habitat fragmentation (Fairfax et al. 2005; Gerber 2012; Wright 1992). This is because different groups acquire land when it becomes available, and it might take years to acquire adjoining parcels. Also controversial is the notion of acquiring private land for conservation, especially when it is removed from the tax base by typically tax-exempt eNGOs (Gerber 2012).

Nevertheless, like that of the states, the involvement of eNGOs is both increasing and necessary to the greater US conservation movement. eNGOs provide public education and serve important watchdog functions. Organizations such as Defenders of Wildlife and The Nature Conservancy have the ability and know-how to work directly with landowners to enhance stewardship. Moreover, they often take leadership positions in drawing up the Habitat Conservation Plans that bring together landowners and the USFWS (Dana 2011). Finally, when stewardship is not possible, eNGOs, as noted, often have the controversial capacity to acquire land for conservation.

Criticism and Proposed Amendments

In a 2008 assessment of the ESA, Mark Schwartz concludes that thousands of species warranted listing but remained unlisted, critical habitat had not been designated for the majority of species, numerous recovery plans remained unfinished, funding for recovery plans was highly skewed, the USFWS had not had the staff resources to review species adequately, and voluntary landowner measures were not being assessed (2008, 289). Thus, the biggest debate about the ESA is whether the law should be further amended, or repealed and replaced by an entirely new law. I take up this issue in Chapter 5 in my review of the history of conservation in Canada and the United States, but for present purposes it is useful to note that the discussion centres on a number of key issues: critical habitat, recovery success, enforcement, incentives, and stewardship.

Despite forty years of implementation history, empirical data are still scarce about landowners – especially non-agricultural landowners – and incentives for stewardship. There is often a disjunction between conceptions of private property, ideas of stewardship, and endangered species management. The central purpose of this book is to provide empirical data to suggest that stewardship is possible, but that private property is an important institution that cannot be overlooked or pushed aside.

A major criticism of the ESA is that it is not successful at preventing extinction or recovering endangered species. Using extinction estimates of species considered critically endangered, it has been suggested that the ESA might have saved as many as 227 species from extinction (Schwartz 2008; Scott et al. 2006). On the recovery side, only twenty-three species had been delisted by the end of 2012 (USFWS [2013]). This is not an inspiring track record compared with the more than one thousand species that have been listed and the many more that are candidate species (Adler 2011; Ando 1999; Bean 2006; Davis, Scott, and Goble 2006; Doremus 2006; Langpap and Kerkvliet 2010).

Despite the poor recovery numbers, there is evidence that more species improve than decline as a consequence of protection (Schwartz 2008). For example, a 2007 USFWS study of all endangered species in the northeastern United States found that 93 per cent had increased or remained stable since being placed on the endangered list (Center for Biological Diversity 2007). The silver lining of the ESA cloud is that it is preventing extinction, although not necessarily recovering species (Scott et al. 2006). Nevertheless, one must acknowledge two things as we move towards the second half-century of the ESA's existence. First, the number of threatened and endangered species is much greater than the number listed (Wilcove and Master 2005); second, the record does not support the assumption that once a species is delisted it will thrive under existing regulations without species-specific interventions. More than 80 per cent of listed species are conservation reliant (Scott et al. 2010), which means they will require species-specific interventions for the foreseeable future.

Beyond its recovery track record, many of the ESA's problems centre on property rights. Some ranchers and farmers want the freedom to protect their economic interest on their own property, even at the cost of endangered species and other social goods. Developers do not want increased costs or bureaucratic red tape that limits development and decreases property values. Nor do they want the availability of land to decrease, particularly where demand for new developments is great. This has led to an increasing recognition by regulators and ESA supporters that it is essential to find a way to conserve endangered species in light of private property – that is to say, "safeguarding biodiversity requires addressing the divergent interests, backgrounds, and attitudes of private landowners" (Stern 2006, 555).

The diverse policy recommendations that I consider here deal with land-use issues; they do not cover the full range of ESA concerns, such as those relating to eco-system management. My goal is to illustrate some of the problems with the ESA as well as the inadequacy of some proposed policy reform strategies, and I argue that, regardless of the strategy or combination of strategies, policy makers need to understand the attitudes of landowners better before they can design and implement more effective approaches.

The Hammer Harder Approach

Freyfogle and Goble (2009, 238) point out that "pressures to gut the [ESA] have been nearly constant, along with recurring proposals to give the act more teeth and expand its coverage." According to such proposals, the reason for regulation's poor record of species recovery is that the ESA has never been enforced or funded adequately. In other words, the ESA is fine as it is – it just needs to be implemented properly. Elmendorf (2003) terms this the "hammer harder" approach. Houck claims that amendments have served only to weaken the act and, moreover, that "the pace of listing has reflected the pace of funding" (1993, 293) which has been all too slow. Thus, the solution to the biodiversity crisis is to reinvigorate the ESA and implement the law's regulations more aggressively. This would include increased funding, more effective administration, and more policing of violations. The problem with the "hammer harder" approach, however, is that regulation is ineffective when it comes to protecting biodiversity on private property (Bean 2002), mainly for three reasons: the lack of graduated sanctions, the lack of meaningful enforcement, and the creation of perverse incentives.

With respect to the first reason, as written by Congress and interpreted by the courts the ESA has very little room for leniency (Illical and Harrison 2007). This means that enforcers' decisions to sanction landowners often seem harsh, especially since they have no room to make deals or pacify violators except under the HCP provisions. Farrier (1995, 395) points out that "regulatory agencies faced with making case-by-case decisions on permissible land use are less likely to compromise where they have something to offer as a palliative for decisions that bear harshly on individuals." Essentially, this is to say that regulators would be more likely to hand out sanctions and enforce the ESA as needed, and intended, if the penalties were not so harsh and inflexible. Regulation does not work in this case because it is too strict. If the law were amended to create graduated sanctions, then hammering potentially could continue.

As for the second reason, enforcing or policing the ESA effectively would be extremely difficult given the manpower required. The enforcement of the ESA is the responsibility of the USFWS, but that is not its only one. The Department of the Interior, of which the USFWS is an agency, is in part a land manager with stewardship over a substantial percentage of the nation's federally owned land, most of it in the West. The USFWS is the principle federal agency responsible for conserving, protecting, and enhancing fish, wildlife, and plants and their habitats. The Service consists of eighty-one ecological services field stations, sixty-nine national fish hatcheries, and sixty-three fish and wildlife management offices nationwide. Its responsibilities boil down to seven areas: 1) managing wildlife refuges; 2) protecting endangered species; 3) protecting habitat; 4) conducting research; 5) enforcing wildlife laws; 6) providing recreational fishing; and 7) advising other agencies (Reed and Drabelle 1984). With so many responsibilities and so many private landowners in the county, it is unrealistic to expect that the USFWS could watch all landowners at all times, even with proper funding.

Moreover, enforcement of the law is difficult because legal sanctions require regulators to prove that a landowner has committed or is about to commit a violation. And criminal penalties must be supported by proof beyond a reasonable doubt (Polasky and Doremus 1998). This might be straightforward if the USFWS officer could produce a dead animal, but if the alleged "take" arose from habitat modification, proof of violation would be more challenging (Doremus 2006). For example, regulators likely would have to prove that the species lives on the landowner's habitat and requires it for some essential behaviour such as feeding or mating and, moreover, that the landowner's action adversely affects that essential behaviour (Polasky and Doremus 1998). To enforce the ESA to the point of applying sanctions thus would require a much larger number of "ESA-cops" out in the field constantly monitoring landowners' actions. Furthermore, even if regulators were able to enforce the ESA, "penalizing individuals is expensive, politically unpopular and creates negative attitudes toward environmental protection" (Stern 2006, 547). The conundrum is that, although regulators can increase compliance through the threat of punishment, they also risk losing public cooperation by creating resentment over penalties that are too harsh or given out too readily, as well as increasing distrust of authority.

Lastly, section 9 of the act has been accused of creating perverse incentives for what has become known as the "scorched earth" technique

(Bean 2002; Colburn 2005), whereby landowners destroy any potential species habitat (sometimes even before had intended to develop the land) to avoid restrictions that the ESA might later impose. In a study involving the red-cockaded woodpecker in North Carolina, Lueck and Michael (2003) found that landowners with potential forest habitat for the bird were significantly more likely to harvest the forest before it could be declared endangered species habitat protected under section 9. Paradoxically, "with the possibility of pre-emptive habitat destruction, the ESA might actually cause a long run reduction in the habitat and population of a listed species" (30). Full enforcement of the ESA would serve only to increase these perverse incentives. In sum, "hammering harder" with regulation will not solve the biodiversity crisis of conservation on private property. As Elmendorf says, "for those who prefer to hammer harder, I wish a sweet hereafter, in a land free of ecological monitoring and subversion problems, with a politics dominated by environmentalists" (2003, 451).

The Land Acquisition Approach

If hammering harder with the ESA is a non-starter, perhaps another approach, without amending or repealing the law, would be to reduce the reliance on private property for species and habitat preservation. Studies suggest that "ownership and jurisdiction over habitat influence the recovery of endangered species; those occurring entirely on private land fair worse than those found exclusively on federal lands" (Hatch et al. 2002, 691; see also USFWS 1994). If the problem is habitat fragmentation and destruction, then one obvious solution presents itself: acquire non-fragmented habitat for endangered species and conserve it from destruction. That is to say, government should buy all, or most of, the land that endangered species inhabit. This would allow government greater access to, and control over, the land endangered species need to survive.

Clearly, however, government cannot buy all such property; Defenders of Wildlife estimates it would cost between US$150 billion and $200 billion to purchase the amount of land necessary for a national habitat conservation system (George 2002; Shaffer, Scott, and Casey 2002). Although land trusts are on the rise, it is inconceivable that eNGOs would be able to raise such a sum even if the land were to become available. Further, there is political resistance to the concept of increasing the amount of public land, especially in the West, where much of the land is already federally owned. Many landowners feel that the federal government already has too much land and that government management of land is inferior to private ownership (Merrill 2002). The reasons for this are varied. Some feel that the government is too big and inefficient, while stewardship of land requires attention and a close relationship to the landscape (Peterson and Horton 1995). Others feel that what is owned in common, via public property, will suffer a "tragedy of the commons" (Hardin 1968). A related problem is that not all landowners are interested in selling their property. The government surely would have to invoke its power of eminent domain to buy some parcels and, as with strict land-use controls, eminent domain is a politically controversial concept (Cole 2002).

Thus, acquisition seems to be too expensive and too unpopular. But the notion is also extraordinarily cynical. To suggest that government must buy all the land necessary for conservation is to embrace paternalism. It also implies that landowners have no desire or ability to protect biodiversity – that they are motivated only by economic self-interest. Moreover, the proposal reflects a loss of faith in the democratic process. It suggests that, if landowners are not willing to obey property regulation laws, even those decided upon through the democratic process, they should not own the land. Surely this is a mistaken view.

Finally, land acquisition is undesirable because wildlife reserves are not a long-term solution to biodiversity loss. This is especially true when land is purchased solely for the purpose of establishing wildlife reserves with no public access. Reserves separate human beings from other species and do not provide the public with the understanding and appreciation of nature necessary for the cultivation of a conservation ethic. Essentially, a pure reserve strategy suggests that "humans and other species can and should inhabit separate ecological spheres" (Thompson Jr 2006, 103). This is not the best way forward for the ESA. With so many endangered species and people in the United States, the idea that they cannot coexist on the same land is unrealistic.

This is not to say, however, that "set-asides" or "reservation ecology" (Fischer, Lindenmayer, and Manning 2006), refuges (Davison et al. 2006), or land-sparing (Fischer et al. 2008; Green et al. 2005; Waggoner 1996) are not sometimes necessary. The debate over reconciliation ecology (Rosenzweig 2003, 2006) and "wildlife only areas" suggests that animals and humans sometimes have to cope with each other, while at other times humans have to leave wildlife alone. For example, land-sparing, or what Waggoner (1996) originally called "sparing land from nature" – where intensive agriculture is allowed on most of the land and permanent protection of species-rich areas takes place on nearby land – can be a balanced approach to agricultural practices (Fischer et al. 2008; Green et al. 2005). For its part, reconciliation ecology, or what Rosenzweig (2003) refers to as conscious human management of the land, might increase biodiversity in otherwise human-dominated areas such as urban centres, parks, cottage resorts, and so on. The idea is both to expand species' ranges and to change the way people think about the species they see (Rosenzweig 2006).

Thus, although preserving nature in wildlife refuges and creating more human-wildlife environments might work in the long run, the idea that through land-acquisition all nature can be saved is a faulty one.

The Incentive Approach

Hammering harder and acquiring land are unrealistic goals for the ESA. As Schwartz (2008, 293) points out, "with 80% of listed species occurring somewhere on private lands, the private landowner is unquestionably integral to the protection of biodiversity." Thus, a significant body of literature has grown around the role of incentives and compensation for landowners. Incentives can range from direct payment for conservation activity, such as planting trees or creating a pond, to indirect payment through tax credits, to cost-share programs where government subsidizes specific conservation actions, such as paying 20 per cent of the cost of protecting a floodplain. Incentives are popular among landowners, especially as many see them as consistent with the 5th Amendment of the US Constitution (Stern 2006), which establishes just compensation when private property is taken for public use.

Some notable incentive programs were mentioned above, including Habitat Conservation Plans with "no surprises" provisions, Safe Harbor Agreements, and Candidate Conservation Agreements with Assurances. In these programs, landowners agree to certain conservation measures in return for a guarantee from the USFWS that they will not incur additional conservation-related costs or restrictions in the future (Langpap and Wu 2004). It has been noted, however, that HCPs provide benefits only after sanctions have been levied or threatened against the landowner (Noss, O'Connell, and Murphy 1997; Raymond 2003). Furthermore, HCPs apply only to certain cases, and it is not entirely clear that they are making a serious ecological difference (James 1999). Lastly, as with other voluntary landowner agreements, the HCP process is heavily bureaucratic, making it both time-consuming and expensive for landowners (Bean 2006; Noss, O'Connell, and Murphy 1997). HCPs are, at best, only part of the solution.

A more successful voluntary landowner program is Partners for Fish and Wildlife, established in 1987 to provide technical and financial assistance to private landowners, including local governments and Indian tribes, willing to cooperate voluntarily on conservation. As of 2005, the Partners program had worked with over 37,700 private landowners to restore 753,000 acres of wetlands, 1.86 million acres of native grasslands and other uplands, and 6,806 miles of riparian and in-stream habitat, including the removal of 260 fish passage barriers (USFWS 2011b). The program may not seek out landowners, however, but must wait for landowners to approach it. Moreover, it cannot provide incentives in the form of direct payment to landowners, but only share the costs of specific projects landowners propose. Although the program exemplifies the possibilities of cooperative management, it is hindered by a lack of funding and a general lack of landowner awareness of the program's existence. As well, as reported to me in a personal interview with the director of the program in Ohio, landowners are often apprehensive about proposing a project because they fear involvement will lead to land regulation in the future.

Beyond voluntary programs, advocates of incentive-based approaches are quick to point out that incentives are "more effective at altering behavior than persuasion, education, or other efforts to change attitudes" (Stern 2006, 544). This is because incentives are premised on the belief that individuals will act in their own perceived self-interest. But some advocates are also willing to recognize the limits and complexities of such an approach. Stern points out that "changing behavior requires carefully structured, appropriately sized, and well-timed incentives" (545). There is almost a science to incentives and often a lot of uncertainty, which can be reduced only through an expensive process of trial and error. For example, with HCPs and mitigation banking (two incentive-based approaches), the critical issue is whether the correct terms are set for compensation: what type, where, and how much land will mitigate the loss of one unit of the designated habitat (Teal and Loomis 2000). The room for error is large since there is a risk of providing too much compensation for not enough land to help a species. This causes one to wonder if incentives are worth it. Indeed, are they necessary?

Moreover, incentive-based approaches do not always solve the problem of the "holdout," the private landowner who refuses to sell his or her property, even after most other landowners have done so, and who thereby might break up a migration corridor. This problem is especially pertinent in conservation areas, because holdouts can free ride so easily on the efforts of neighbours whose good deeds actually increase the value of the remaining private property (Elmendorf 2003). And in any case, whether or not it increases property values, when a conservation area is successfully returned to nature the remaining private landowners might find they prefer living in a pristine nature reserve (Raymond and Olive 2008). In fact, landowners might receive mixed incentives: intentional ones by the USFWS to encourage them to sell or increase their conservation behaviour, and unintended ones to stay in a beautiful and secluded nature preserve.

Finally, there is the risk that incentives end up paying landowners to do what they might have done anyway – say, plant more trees on their property or create areas of standing water, which would help create feeding areas for creatures such as bats – perhaps for free (Fairfax et al. 2005, see also Raymond and Olive 2008). But there is no sense in a policy that pays landowners for these activities. Such incentives are costly, especially when not well planned, and, some argue, unnecessary. Also, there is the concern that incentives become the norm – that landowners come to expect to be compensated and/or rewarded for any conservation effort (Farrier 1995; Stern 2006; Stone 1990). This is dangerous territory and a strong argument against the use of incentives as the primary strategy for conservation.

In summary, there are two main problems with pure incentive-based approaches: it is not clear that they work and, more important, it is not clear that they are always necessary. Part of the reason they do not work is that they do not obviate the need for monitoring and enforcement (Stern 2006). In fact, in some cases incentive programs might increase that need to ensure the landowner is holding up his or her end of the deal. For example, tax breaks or direct compensation for setting aside a certain amount of property for an endangered species requires that the USFWS monitor the property to ensure that the landowner is not receiving the incentive and then using the land as he or she wishes. Incentives are not a quick fix or a replacement for enforcement.

Nevertheless, what remains true is that American voters like incentive programs; non-regulatory conservation programs have political appeal. This is one reason Congress has expanded incentive-based agricultural conservation programs significantly in the past couple of decades – in contrast to the way Congress has been stalemated over ESA reauthorization (Shaffer, Scott, and Casey 2002). This suggests that incentives, in some form or another, will be part of the ESA for some time to come.

The Cooperative Management Approach

The last major policy recommendation within the scholarly literature is the idea of cooperative management, which combines regulation with the interaction and inclusion of landowners in policy decisions as well as incentives for stewardship. In this approach, which some politicians and a number of environmentalists tout, enforcement of the ESA would be complemented by the use of economic incentives as well as education and outreach campaigns. To a large extent, the 2008 Farm Bill exemplifies an attempt to move conservation policy in this direction. Through this legislation the federal government increased total spending on conservation programs by US$7.9 billion, and although some of the money is tied up in state government incentives and land easements, a substantial amount has been allocated to such programs as the Wildlife Habitat Incentives Program, which was designed to improve habitat on private property, usually that of farmers and ranchers, through direct payment to the landowner (as well as through cost-shared projects). The program, which is overseen by the Department of Agriculture and is not directly related to the USFWS (which, recall, is part of the Department of the Interior), is part of what Elmendorf (2003, 451) calls the "voluntarist school," as it favours economic incentives where each landowner is free to respond to the incentive if he or she so wishes.

The cooperative management approach is deeply complex. The idea is in part to make conservation in the economic interest of the landowner or, at the very least, to prevent compliance from being an economic burden. Moreover, it requires the right mix of regulation and incentives, as too many incentives will undermine regulation and lead to the kinds of problems I have addressed above. Conversely, however, too few incentives will fail to motivate cooperation and conservation. Benson, Steinback, and Shelton (1999, 72) argue for shared management of endangered species, whereby landowners are "respected for their knowledge and care of the land" and the government has "the structure and laws that allow them to work with rather than against landowners." The heart of the plan is to find a way in which landowners can maintain their private property rights while also benefiting economically from the conservation of their property. Examples of such an approach are the [Ted] Turner Properties in Montana and New Mexico[6] and the Irvine Ranch and Tejon Ranches in California.

Benson and colleagues also note, however, that, since ecotourism and recreational opportunities are not possible for each landowner (or in relation to each species), "when a landowner must lose income in order to maintain habitat, there should be adequate compensation programs available to replace that income" (Benson, Steinback, and Shelton 1999, 73). They propose tax relief, particularly a reduction in property tax, since the value of the property is reduced by the presence of a listed species. A program similar to this exists in parts of Ontario, where landowners who can prove that their land parcel is used mostly, or entirely, for conservation can request a tax deduction.

This approach walks a fine line between what a government can expect a citizen to do for the common good and what it asks too much of certain citizens (that is, landowners). Once government concedes that it is just and fair to pay landowners for conservation efforts, it will be much more difficult to return exclusively to command-and-control regulation. As I argued above, incentive programs create a potentially dangerous precedent. Before exploring the incentives aspect of cooperative management, it is important to look at a rarely addressed aspect of this approach: who are landowners and what do they want/need for conservation?

Conclusion

Created in 1973, the ESA was intended to identify, protect, and recover species in threat of extinction across all land types in the United States. As written, the law was stringent and uncompromising with private property and development. The snail darter case and the spotted owl ordeal, which I discuss in Chapter 4, challenged the public and lawmakers to rethink the law. Amendments in 1978, 1982, and 1988, as well as policies of the USFWS, have changed the law's relationship to private property and the public – the focus of Chapters 5 through 7.

In the epilogue to the second volume of *The Endangered Species Act at 30*, editors Goble, Scott, and Davis conclude that, with future ESA amendments, "some of the steps are clear" (2006, 290). These include confronting the backlog of unlisted but critically imperilled species; more measures to prevent endangerment; a system of protected natural areas representative of the ecological and geophysical diversity of the country; and reconciling human actions with biological needs of wild-life across all land parcels. "Ultimately," these authors conclude, "we need a new land ethic" (2006, 290).

One major problem with amending or writing new legislation is the lack of empirical research on the behaviours and attitudes of a variety of landowners. The "wise use" movement has been a loud opponent of the ESA, but not all landowners agree with its opinions. Individual cases like those of the grey wolf and the spotted owl also have made rather loud intrusions into ESA controversies. Extreme cases, however, obviously are not representative of American landowners. Farrier (1995) argues that US experience suggests that exclusive reliance on either land-use regulation or voluntary cooperation is inadequate; he advocates a model based on the integration of command and control with payment for stewardship. To a certain extent, this is the conclusion that lawmakers in Canada drew from the ESA.

3 Canada's Strategy for Species at Risk

In 1993 Canada became the first country to ratify the United Nations Convention on Biological Diversity (UNCBD). Implementation of the convention led to the development of a Canadian Biodiversity Strategy. Unlike the United States, where federal wildlife law takes precedent over state law, in Canada the provinces and territories have primary responsibility for wildlife species and for the lands upon which those species rely. The federal government has direct responsibility for migratory birds, aquatic species, and any species found on federal lands, such as parks or Aboriginal reserves.[7] This co-sharing of responsibility means that the conservation of species at risk requires a collaborative approach that respects the jurisdiction and responsibilities of each level of government.

The Canadian Biodiversity Strategy consists of six stated goals: conservation and sustainable use; ecological management; education and awareness; legislation; incentives; and international cooperation (Canada 2009a, 42). To meet these goals, the various levels of government developed a National Strategy for Species at Risk, consisting of three main components: the 1996 federal-provincial-territorial Accord for the Protection of Species at Risk, the 2000 Habitat Stewardship Program, and the 2002 Species at Risk Act (SARA).[8] Figure 3.1 illustrates the relationships among these initiatives.

The Accord for the Protection of Species at Risk (1996)

In October 1996 federal, provincial, and territorial ministers responsible for wildlife created the Accord for the Protection of Species at Risk. The

Figure 3.1. Canada's National Strategy for Species at Risk

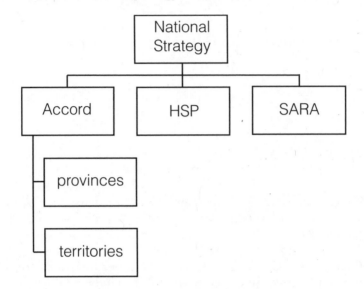

Accord is a set of fundamental principles of species conservation and an agreement to coordinate activities, to recognize the national Committee on the Status of Endangered Wildlife in Canada (COSEWIC)[9] as an independent scientific advisory board, and to establish complementary legislation and programs to protect species at risk. The Accord is non-binding; and rather than mandate standards, it recommends that any species at risk policy should include an independent (non-government) process for assessing the status of a species, means to designate and legally protect endangered and threatened species, protect critical habitat, develop recovery plans, ensure multi-jurisdictional cooperation, monitor the status of species, improve awareness, and include citizen participation. To administer the Accord, the Canadian Endangered Species Conservation Council (CESCC) was established in 1998. The CESCC coordinates the activities of the various governments and provides general direction on the activities of COSEWIC and the preparation of recovery strategies and action plans.

I describe below the degree to which actual legislation in Canada lives up to the goals of the Accord, but the federal SARA is certainly a cornerstone of the agreement. Of the ten provinces, however, only six have stand-alone species-at-risk legislation and only two have fully updated their legislation since the passage of SARA. Partly in acknowledgment of this void in the overall strategy, in 2006 the federal government, provinces, and territories endorsed a Biodiversity Outcomes Framework that advocates an "assess, plan, do, track" adaptive management approach (Canada 2009a). This was followed in 2007 by the National Framework for Species at Risk Conservation (NFSARC), to support the implementation of the 1996 Accord. The Framework's specific objectives are to "facilitate coordination and cooperation among jurisdictions," "encourage greater national coherence and consistency" in jurisdictional policies, and "provide context and common ground for federal/provincial/territorial bilateral agreements" (Canada 2009a, 4). The continuing need to create new "frameworks" and agreements speaks to the magnitude and complexity of the legislative process, but it also suggests an ongoing commitment by the federal, provincial, and territorial governments to work together.

Provincial Endangered Species Statutes

The 1996 Accord for the Protection of Species at Risk was signed by all the provinces and territories except Quebec (the territory of Nunavut did not exist at the time). As part of its responsibility for managing biodiversity, each province and territory has created legislation or policies for the protection of species at risk. Table 3.1 summarizes provincial and territorial efforts.

BRITISH COLUMBIA

British Columbia is home to almost two thousand threatened or endangered species, but the province does not have a stand-alone endangered species policy. Instead, the Wildlife Act (R.S.B.C 1996, c. 488) and the Forest and Range Practices Act (S.B.C. 2002, c. 69) include some provisions that designate and protect vulnerable species (British Columbia 2011b). In 2008 the Wildlife Act was amended to improve protection by addressing issues of possessing, breeding, release, trafficking, shipping, or transporting alien or exotic species. Prior to 2008, alien species such as alligators or tigers were not considered "wildlife"; under the amendments the minister is able to prohibit or regulate the keeping of listed alien species, making it an offence to acquire, possess, or sell them. The amendments also ensure that park rangers have authority to monitor hunting and fishing activities to ensure they are undertaken in accordance with the Wildlife Act (British Columbia 2011b).

Table 3.1. Summary of Canadian Federal and Provincial Government Policies for Species at Risk

Jurisdiction	Stand-alone Species-at-Risk Legislation	Wildlife Legislation that Includes Species at Risk	Independent Process for Assessing Species at Risk	Protection of Critical Habitat (Regulation of Private Property)
Federal	2002		yes	discretionary
British Columbia		1996	yes	none
Alberta		2000	yes	none
Saskatchewan		1998	no	none
Manitoba	1990		yes	mandatory
Ontario	2007		yes	mandatory
Quebec	2009		yes	discretionary
New Brunswick	2012		yes	discretionary
Nova Scotia	1998		yes	discretionary
Prince Edward Island		2004	yes	none
Newfoundland and Labrador	2001	2001	yes	discretionary
Yukon		2002	no	discretionary
Northwest Territories	2009	2009	yes	discretionary
Nunavut		2003	yes	discretionary

Note: For an updated summary of legislation across the country, see Ecojustice (2012).
Source: Author's compilation.

Beyond enacted legislation, British Columbia has a "Conservation Framework" that "provides a set of decision support tools to enable collaboration between government and non-government resource managers and practitioners using clearly defined criteria to: prioritize species and ecosystems for conservation; and determine the most appropriate and effective management actions" (British Columbia 2011a). The Framework is also intended to optimize allocation of resources, including staff time and dollars, to "adequately address British Columbia's stewardship responsibility for globally important species and ecosystems." The Framework approach also helps address the issue of jurisdictional rarity (where a species' range "drifts" across a jurisdictional boundary) and uses the best available scientific information to quickly and transparently prioritize species and ecosystems and assign them to appropriate management actions (British Columbia 2011a).

In addition to these initiatives, Sierra Club, joined by other conservation groups and citizens, spearheaded a Species at Risk Working Group that has launched a campaign for the province to enact stand-alone endangered species policy. Specifically the Working Group is lobbying the BC government to follow Ontario's lead and pass endangered species legislation that protects both species and their habitat. Thus far the Working Group has been unsuccessful, but pressure is mounting on the province to undertake such a policy change.

ALBERTA

Alberta also has yet to enact stand-alone endangered species policy, but its Wildlife Act (R.S.A. 2000, c. W-10) includes the designation and protection of endangered species. An Endangered Species Conservation Committee (ESCC) also serves as an advisory body and makes recommendations to the minister of environment on matters pertaining to endangered species (Fluker 2010). The law states that it is an offence to "willfully molest, disturb, or destroy a house, nest or den" of an individual endangered species (36.1), but there is no designation or protection of critical habitat under the law, and the minister is not required to prepare or implement a recovery plan for any endangered species.

However, the Alberta Division of Fish and Wildlife did develop a Strategy for the Management of Species at Risk, the goals of which include identifying "the relative security" of Alberta's wildlife, assessing the risk of extinction, and proposing the listing of these species in the provincial Wildlife Act. The strategy also proposes the development of recovery plans as well as preventive measures to keep other "at risk" species from being threatened or endangered (Alberta 2008). Nothing in the strategy is legally binding, and only when a species is listed in the Wildlife Act is protection legally mandated. Essentially, the Alberta approach is "such that most of the Alberta endangered species regime is government by policy" (Fluker 2010), as opposed to mandatory legal protections as offered by the US ESA, for example.

SASKATCHEWAN

Like the two provinces to the west, Saskatchewan does not have stand-alone legislation, but its Wildlife Act (S.S. 1998, c. W-13.12) mandates that at-risk plants and animals be protected from being disturbed, collected, harvested, captured, killed, and exported. There is no mandatory protection of habitat. Birds and grasslands, in particular, are not faring well in the province, and responding to opinion in favour of new legislation to protect species at risk, the provincial Ministry of Environment is currently preparing to move in that direction.

MANITOBA

Manitoba passed an Endangered Species Act in 1990 (C.C.S.M. c. E111, 1990 – Amended 1993). Its purpose is to "ensure the protection and enhance the survival of threatened and endangered species in Manitoba; enable reintroduction of extirpated species into the province; and designate species as threatened, endangered, extirpated, or extinct" (S.M. 1993, c. 3, s. 2). The law makes it unlawful to "kill, injure, possess, disturb or interfere with the species; destroy, disturb or interfere with the habitat of the species; or damage, destroy, obstruct or remove a natural resource on which the species depends for its life and propagation" (S.M. 1993, c. 3, s. 5). The law also provides, under an Order-in-Council regulation administered by the Wildlife and Ecosystem Protection Branch of the Department of Conservation and Water Stewardship, for the designation and listing of habitat in the province (Manitoba 2012). The province also has an Endangered Species Advisory Committee that advises the minister.

The law applies to all animals and fish, and is binding on the Crown and Crown agencies in Manitoba as well as other types of land in the province. This means the law extends discretionary protection to species and their habitat on private lands. Once a species is determined to be endangered, the minister may decide to protect its habitat, which could extend to private property. The law also permits the provincial government to expropriate land for conservation purposes and pay appropriate compensation. Once land is declared as habitat for an endangered species it is prohibited to "destroy, disturb or interfere with the habitat of an endangered species or damage, destroy, obstruct or remove a natural resource on which an endangered species, depends for its life and propagation" (S.M. 1993, c. 3, s. 8). Such prohibitions limit Manitoba landowners in ways similar to those that the ESA limits US landowners.

Manitoba's is a fairly stringent and progressive law, but it is not enforced fully in the province for many of the same reasons the ESA is not in the United States. Listing species is slow, and recovery plans are not written as quickly as needed since they are not required by law. Only about 60 per cent of the species listed in the federal SARA that are found in Manitoba are also listed in Manitoba, and 20 per cent do not have a recovery plan (Wojciechowski et al. 2011). Moreover, habitat is not automatically listed; often, rather than list private lands as habitat, the province works through incentive-based programs to increase landowner participation or finds ways to manage species on provincial and federal Crown lands. These programs include long-term conservation easements, a Wetland Restoration Incentive Program, and a Habitat Mitigation/Compensation Program (MHHC 2010). In many ways the Manitoba act is similar to SARA in that it offers discretionary protection to species while relying upon stewardship and incentive programs. The problem, therefore, is one of implementation and enforcement.

ONTARIO

Given its size, Ontario has a substantial share of Canada's at-risk species, but its Endangered Species Act, which came into effect on 30 June 2008 after a year of debate in the Ontario Legislative Assembly, is arguably the strongest of any province; indeed, the Legislative Assembly believed it was "the strongest law in North America" for conservation. The law prohibits the killing or harming of threatened or endangered species or the destruction of their habitat (S.O. 2007, c. 6). The law applies to private as well as public property, and it prevents landowners from using their own land in certain contexts if a threatened or endangered species co-habitats the property. In many ways the act takes the same "stewardship first" approach as SARA, but it also includes direct regulation of private property (as opposed to discretionary regulation under SARA). The act also established a Species at Risk in Ontario Stewardship Program, with C$18 million over four years to fund conservation and stewardship. Similar to the stewardship programs that exist at the federal level, this program is intended to foster individual or group stewardship across a variety of parcel types, including large and small private property parcels.

In May 2012 the Legislative Assembly attached "sweeping new powers" to the provincial government in Bill 55, a rider on a new budget bill (Leslie 2012), which, if passed, would have allowed the government to exempt private landowners from requirements to protect species and their habitat and might have permitted industry to push back deadlines for completing plans to protect species and submitting reports during projects. More than fifty environmental groups joined in protesting the planned legislation, and the provincial New Democratic Party led the charge against it in the Legislative Assembly. Ultimately, the budget bill passed without the controversial amendments, but changes could still come (Ecojustice 2012).

QUEBEC

In 1989 Quebec became one of the first provinces to pass endangered species legislation, An Act Respecting Threatened or Vulnerable Species (R.S.Q. c. E-12.01). This statute applies to all taxonomic groups of plants and animals, which can be listed as "vulnerable" or "threatened." The act does not define habitat, but it does allow habitat to be identified for each species. The act prohibits the possession, harvesting, exploitation, mutilation, destruction, acquisition, transfer, and genetic manipulation of plants, but these restrictions do not apply to habitat for wildlife. The act was updated in 2009 (R.S.Q. c. E-12.01), and in 2011 a companion bill, An Act Respecting the Conservation and Development of Wildlife (R.S.Q. 2011, c. C-61.1), was created. The purpose of the companion bill is "the conservation of wildlife and its habitat, their development in keeping with the principle of sustainable development, and the recognition of every person's right to hunt, fish, and trap in accordance with the law." The main focus of the bill is to protect the rights and obligations of hunters, fishers, and trappers while establishing various prohibitions related to vulnerable wildlife.

Although Quebec did not sign the Accord for the Protection of Species at Risk, the province still respects Canada's commitment to the 1993 UNCBD and has been a leader in the conservation of wildlife. An example of this – the Quebec version of the snail darter versus the Tellico Dam – occurred when the Quebec government permanently halted a hydroelectric project on the Chambly Rapids on the Richelieu River south of Montreal to protect an endangered fish species, the copper redhorse (Canada 2010a). This species of fish is unique to the river, and might be the only species capable of feeding on the infamous zebra mussel, which, since it was introduced into the St Lawrence, the Great Lakes, and their tributaries, has clogged drinking water supply and waste water disposal equipment (Bourdages 1996). The province's decision to protect this species, prioritizing it over an economic project, reflects its commitment to the UN convention.

NEW BRUNSWICK

In New Brunswick, the Endangered Species Act (S.N.B. 1996, c. E-9.101) was updated in April 2012 with a new Species at Risk Act (S.N.B. 2012, c. 6). Under section 4 of the 1996 law, it was illegal to "willfully or knowingly kill, injure, disturb or interfere with a member or any part of a member of an endangered species or regionally endangered species" or "willfully or knowingly destroy, disturb or interfere with the critical habitat of a member of an endangered species or regionally endangered species" (S.N.B. 1996, c. E-9.101). The law applied only to flora and fauna, and provided only one category: endangered.

The new legislation uses COSEWIC recommendations for listing species in New Brunswick as either threatened or endangered. It grants the minister of natural resources discretionary power to declare private property to be critical recovery habitat. However, if private land is declared habitat and endangered wildlife occupies that land during recovery, the land can be declared "survival habitat" in the long term only with written permission of the landowner. Similar to other provincial laws, the New Brunswick act does not extend mandatory protection to private land for conservation. Although the new law has not yet been implemented, it seems that incentive and stewardship programs will be the cornerstones of conservation in New Brunswick.

NOVA SCOTIA

Nova Scotia also has stand-alone endangered species legislation dating back to 1998. The Endangered Species Act (S.N.S. 1998, c. 11) protects species that have been assessed and determined to be at risk of extinction in the province. Under the law, it is illegal to kill or disturb a species at risk or to destroy or disturb its residence or core habitat. Penalties, both for individuals and corporations, can be incurred when the act is violated. The law extends to private lands, and it is up to the minister of natural resources to declare such lands "critical habitat." The law makes clear, however, "the importance of promoting the purposes of this Act primarily through non-regulatory means such as co-operation, stewardship, education and partnerships instead of punitive measures, including such preventative actions as education, incentives, sustainable management practices and integrated resource management" (section 1).

Species are listed under the act by the Nova Scotia Species at Risk Working Group, which assigns status based on an assessment of biological factors and rigorous assessment criteria, followed by classification into categories based on level of risk. Species determined as at risk are then approved by the responsible minister and included in the list of species at risk, which triggers their protection under the act (Nova Scotia 2001). The minister may declare private lands to be critical habitat and regulate the use of them. If the landowner is using the land – say, for farming or forestry – at the time of designation, he or she must be compensated for the loss of that use. This is unlike other such Canadian legislation, but similar to what some landowners and politicians have advocated for the United States (see Meltz 2011).

PRINCE EDWARD ISLAND

Like Saskatchewan, Alberta, and British Columbia, Prince Edward Island does not have stand-alone species-at-risk legislation. Instead, the Wildlife Conservation Act (R.S.P.E.I 1988, c. W04.1) includes provisions for the protection of species at risk and their habitats. Species at risk include plants, animals, and other organisms that are considered to be endangered, threatened, or of special concern because of sensitivity to human activities or natural events. A Species at Risk Advisory Committee advises the minister of environment, energy and forestry about which species should be listed as at risk, based on biological and scientific information. It also assesses the island's wildlife resources, particularly endangered or threatened species and species of special concern, analyses the effect of land use and environmental activities on wildlife and habitat, and makes recommendations about conservation of wildlife and habitat (Prince Edward Island 2011).

NEWFOUNDLAND AND LABRADOR

In 2001 Newfoundland and Labrador passed the Endangered Species Act (S.N.L. 2001, c. E-10.1), which provides "protection for plant and animal species considered to be endangered, threatened, or vulnerable." The legislation applies to species, subspecies, and populations that are native to the province, but not marine fish. Designation under the act follows the recommendations of COSEWIC and a provincial Species Status Advisory Committee on the appropriate assessment of a species (Newfoundland and Labrador 2011). About 85 per cent of SARA-listed species are also listed under the provincial act (Ecojustice 2012). The law can extend to private property, as it is at the discretion of the minister of environment and conservation to declare any land critical habitat. The province takes the stewardship-first approach of SARA, however, in that it "will endeavour to implement habitat protection on private lands for species at risk by working with the landowners through stewardship initiatives and/or conservation management agreements" (S.N.L. 2001, c. E-10.1). Similar to Manitoba, Newfoundland and Labrador avoids listing private property as protected habitat by using incentive programs or relying on Crown lands.

Unlike other such Canadian legislation, Newfoundland and Labrador's act "supports, as a guiding principle, that all species have the right to exist, therefore no species should become extinct or extirpated owing to human actions" (S.N.L. 2001, c. E-10.1). This is a strong statement about the eco-centric reasons to conserve biodiversity, an issue I take up in the case studies presented in later chapters.

THE TERRITORIES

The Yukon has no stand-alone legislation that specifically categorizes or protects endangered or threatened species. Instead, the Wildlife Act (R.S.Y. 2002, c. 229) lists certain species as "specially protected." I explore the management of species at risk in Nunavut at greater length in Chapter 8, but suffice it to say here that, like the Yukon, the territory does not have stand-alone species-at-risk legislation, but does have a Wildlife Act (S.Nu. 2003, c. 26, updated 2008) that pertains to species at risk.

The Northwest Territories passed the Species at Risk (NWT) Act in 2009, which protects and recovers species at risk. The act applies to any wild animal, plant, or other species managed by the territorial government; it also applies to both public and private lands, including private lands owned under an Aboriginal land-claims agreement. The act also created a Species at Risk Committee to assess the biological status of species that might be at risk in the territory. This assessment does not use COSEWIC data but instead relies on results from the territory's General Status Ranking Program, which is based on traditional, community, and scientific knowledge of the species. The committee includes members appointed by co-management boards and members from areas without settled land claims who are appointed by the territorial minister of environment. Members of the committee have significant traditional, community, or scientific knowledge about northern species and act independently from their appointing agencies. The committee makes recommendations about the listing of species and conservation measures, but does not consider socio-economic effects in its assessment. Responsibility for conservation and recovery of species is shared, however, among wildlife co-management boards established under land-claims agreements, the federal minister of the environment, the Tlicho First Nations government, and the territorial government (Northwest Territories 2009). As of 2012, no species had been listed under the act (Ecojustice 2012).

The Habitat Stewardship Program

The second prong in Canada's Strategy for the Protection of Species at Risk is the federally created Habitat Stewardship Program (HSP) for all species at risk in the country. The HSP allocates up to C$10 million per year to protect and recover species at risk and their habitats across Canada (see the HSP Web site at http://www.ec.gc.ca/hsp-pih/). The goal is to "contribute to the recovery of endangered, threatened, and other species at risk, and to prevent other species from becoming a conservation concern." Based on the COSEWIC designation of species at risk, the HSP assists "stewards" in projects that serve to protect species. Although individuals and groups can apply for monies, the activities must take place on private lands, provincial Crown lands, Aboriginal lands, or in aquatic marine areas. The program does not support projects on federal lands or in other countries.

Canada's decision to take a "stewardship first" approach (Smallwood 2003) to conservation comes from an almost decade-long experience with federal legislative attempts to pass species-at-risk policy. In 1996 Bill C-65, the Canada Endangered Species Protection Act, was introduced in Parliament. Its immediate rejection by industry came from concerns, partially founded on US experience with the ESA, that the bill would impose excessive costs on the private sector. Illical and Harrison (2007, 368) argue that "negative lessons from the US experience led both Canadian business and policy makers to shun the adversarial regulatory approach of the ESA in favour of co-operative stewardship." The provinces also objected to Bill C-65 on the grounds that it gave too much power to the federal government. The bill died in 1997 when a federal election was called.

In 1998 legislative initiative was rekindled by the creation of the Species at Risk Working Group (SARWG), a coalition of environmental and business organizations forged by Elizabeth May, the current leader of the national Green Party and its only Member of Parliament. The genius of SARWG was the recognition that environmentalists could create solid legislation without forcing industry to pay the costs. The group recommended that the federal government create financial support for voluntary stewardship programs as an alternative to regulation in the first instance (Illical and Harrison 2007). During this time, Ottawa went ahead and created the HSP without waiting for the passage of species-at-risk legislation. Although Canada had signed the UNCBD in 1993, it still had no federal policy by 2000. But this would not stop stewardship efforts.

A subsequent version of Bill C-65, C-33 (the Species at Risk Act), died with the calling of a federal election in 2000. A third version, C-5, was introduced in 2001 and passed in the House of Commons in June 2002, but it too died when Parliament was prorogued that year. The Senate then invoked a special parliamentary procedure to reinstate the bill without its having to go through three more readings in the House. The upper chamber finally approved SARA in October 2002, and the bill received Royal Assent on 12 December 2002 (Illical and Harrison 2007).

During the struggle to pass SARA, there was a lot of support for voluntary stewardship approaches, as eventually reflected in the legislation. The HSP stands outside SARA as a separate program, but, after the passage of SARA, stewardship funds have been streamlined into projects that directly address the recovery and/or protection of SARA-listed species.

The Species at Risk Act (2002)

The third element of the National Strategy for Species at Risk is the federal Species at Risk Act. Since the provinces enjoy jurisdiction over their natural resources, SARA applies only to federal lands, which are about 5 per cent of the country's total territory outside the North (Smallwood 2003). SARA is intended to recognize and protect all scientific classifications of species (and their habitat) that are at risk of becoming extinct in Canada or around the world. The act prohibits direct takes, making it an offence to "kill, harm, harass, capture, or take individuals of a wildlife species that is listed as extirpated species, an endangered species or a threatened species." Moreover, it is illegal to "damage or destroy the residence of one or more individuals of a wildlife species that is listed as an endangered species or a threatened species" (S.C. 2002, c. 29). These prohibitions automatically apply to all listed aquatic species, all birds listed under the Migratory Birds Convention Act of 1994, and all other species found on federal lands. No mandatory or automatic protection is guaranteed to species found on private lands.

One important principle that sets SARA apart from past legislation and its American counterpart is its precautionary approach to conservation. The preamble of SARA provides that "the Government of Canada is committed to conserving biodiversity and to the principle that, if there are threats of serious or irreversible damage to a wildlife species, cost-effective measures to prevent the reduction of loss of the species should not be postponed for a lack of full scientific certainty" (S.C. 2002, c. 29). This means that Canada is prepared to protect a species even when there is imperfect scientific information about its status in the wild. This is a serious commitment to endangered species and one that has been adopted by all signing parties to the UNCBD.

In SARA Canada also takes a stewardship-first approach to conservation. Since a lot of at-risk species live on private property, which is under the jurisdiction of the provinces, the federal government – unlike its American counterpart with the ESA – cannot regulate or pursue a command-and-control approach under SARA. What the federal government has been able to do through SARA is bolster the Habitat Stewardship Program.

The responsibility for implementing SARA is shared between the minister of fisheries and oceans, who oversees matters concerning aquatic species, and the minister of the environment, who is responsible for Parks Canada and oversees matters concerning all other terrestrial species on federal lands (Canada 2009a). Enforcement of SARA is the shared responsibility of wildlife enforcement officers, fishery officers, and park wardens.

Under SARA, species become protected once they are listed by the minister of the environment on the advice of COSEWIC. A species may be listed as "extirpated," which means the species no longer exists in the wild in Canada, but exists elsewhere in the world; "endangered," which means the species faces imminent extinction; "threatened," which means the species is likely to become endangered if nothing is done to reverse the trend; or "special concern," which means a species may become threatened or endangered because of identified threats (Canada 2009a, 6).

All COSEWIC species assessments that the minister of the environ-ment receives are posted publicly on the Species at Risk Public Registry. The minister has ninety days to publish (and make public) a response statement and provide timelines for action. Within nine months of re-ceiving the assessment, the governor in council, on the recommendation of the minister, must decide whether to accept or reject the assess-ment. Sometimes the governor in council will refer the species back to COSEWIC for further information. If no decision is made within nine months, the species is automatically added to the list in accordance with COSEWIC's recommendation (Canada 2009a, 6–7). Thus, the assess-ment for listing is a scientific decision made by COSEWIC, but the list-ing of the species for SARA protection is a political decision made by the governor in council on the recommendation of the minister of the environment.

Once a species is listed, Environment Canada assembles a recovery team to draft and implement a recovery strategy in collaboration with the appropriate federal, provincial, and Aboriginal entities. If a species is listed as threatened or endangered, then individuals of that species and their habitat become automatically protected on federal lands. For species listed after 2003, the minister has one year to complete a strate-gy for endangered species and two years for threatened species. For species listed that were grandfathered into SARA protection (automati-cally added to the list in 2002 when the act was created), the minister has five years to complete a recovery strategy.

In Canada the process is multi-step because each species is given a recovery "strategy" and then an "action plan." A recovery strategy is a planning document, similar to an American recovery plan, that iden-tifies what needs to be done to stop or reverse the decline of a species. It sets goals and objectives, and identifies the main areas of activities to be undertaken. All recommendations are made on the basis of the best available information (scientific as well as local and Aboriginal knowledge). But detailed planning is done at the next stage of the pro-cess: the action plan. In most cases one or more action plans will be developed to define and guide implementation of the recovery strate-gy. Nevertheless, directions set in the recovery strategy are sufficient to begin involving communities, land users, and conservationists in recovery implementation. This seems reasonable on the basis of the precautionary principle, in that cost-effective measures to prevent the reduction or loss of the species should not be postponed for lack of full scientific certainty.

Keeping the recovery strategy (plan) separate from the action plan (implementation) is meant to keep science separate from policy. Mooers et al. (2010) discuss the importance of separating the scientific "diagnosis" of what a species needs from political or socio-economic decisions about what to do about it. This separation arguably leads to greater transparency and accountability than if the science and the socio-economics are considered as part of a single process, which might make it more likely that the science will be mushed together with other considerations in a murky way, for which the American ESA recovery plan process might be criticized. Unlike US recovery plans, which state the full estimated cost of recovery, the Canadian recovery strategy cannot consider any socio-economic or political factors at all. Those decisions are all put forth in the action plan. The Federal Court upheld this distinction in *Environment Defence Canada v. Canada (Minister of Fisheries and Oceans)*, more commonly known as the Nooksack dace case. The Court sided with the applicant (Ecojustice on behalf of the David Suzuki Foundation) that the minister had a duty to designate not only the geographical components of habitat but also the biological and ecosystem components of habitat as spelled out in the recovery strategy for the Nooksack dace.

SARA includes a "safety net" provision that enables the federal government to act within a province that fails to protect an at-risk species. Although Ottawa has virtually exclusive authority over marine life and over most wildlife north of 60° north latitude, which has been delegated to the territorial governments, the provinces have near-comprehensive authority over terrestrial wildlife, lands, and resources. Thus, the safety net is a way for the federal government to provide "a residual power to protect species and habitat on non-federal lands" (Wojciechowski et al. 2011, 206). The law states that, "[i]f the Minister of the Environment is of the opinion that the laws of a province or a territory do not effectively protect a species or the residence of its individuals, he/she must recommend that the [governor in council] make an order applying the prohibitions to non-federal lands in the province or territory" (*Canada Gazette* 2009, 411). There are no clear guidelines in place, however, that establish when a province is considered to have "failed" or when it is appropriate for the federal government to act; the federal safety net is entirely discretionary.

For SARA to be successful, stewardship by Canadians is necessary. The Habitat Stewardship Fund provides millions of dollars to protect habitat, but other programs also bring together citizens, organizations, and conservation. The Endangered Species Recovery Fund is a joint program between Environment Canada and the World Wildlife Fund-Canada to support research and education. The Aboriginal Fund for Species at Risk provides funds to support projects on Aboriginal lands or projects carried out by Aboriginal organizations or communities. The Natural Areas Conservation Program "helps non-profit, non-government organizations secure ecologically sensitive lands to ensure the protection of our diverse ecosystems, wildlife, and habitat" (Canada 2007). Unlike the other programs just mentioned, the Natural Areas program works through an agreement between the federal government and the Nature Conservancy of Canada. This is to enable federal matching funds for Nature Conservancy projects, including those with non-governmental conservation partners such as Ducks Unlimited Canada.

In summary, various governance structures and advisory bodies support the implementation and monitoring of SARA, including COSEWIC, the Canadian Endangered Species Conservation Council (provinces and territories), the National Aboriginal Council on Species at Risk, and a multistakeholder Species at Risk Task Group, which advises the minister of the environment on SARA (Canada 2009a, 2). There are extensive enforcement powers and significant penalties for violators, including fines up to C$1 million and up to five years' imprisonment. In 2007 the budget committed $110 million over two years for the implementation of SARA. On average, since its passage into law, SARA has received $100 million per year in funding (3).

Challenges for Conservation in Canada

A 2010 Environment Canada study in collaboration with the provinces and territories of ecosystem status – the first assessment of biodiversity in Canada from an ecosystem approach – finds that "much of Canada's natural endowment remains healthy, including large tracts of undisturbed wilderness, internationally significant wetlands and thriving estuaries" (Federal, Provincial and Territorial Governments of Canada 2010, 1). The report also indicates areas of concern, however, such as loss of old-growth forests and wildlife habitat, declining bird populations, and shifts in marine, freshwater, and terrestrial food webs. Moreover, there are areas of critical concern, including failing fish populations, declining grasslands, fragmented forests, and dramatic loss of sea ice. Canada thus needs to take seriously its responsibility to safeguard biodiversity before it slips away.

Compared with the vast literature on the American ESA, very little scholarship exists in the area of endangered species policy in Canada, especially in the post-SARA period. Scholars who do write about SARA tend to focus on the listing of species (Elgie 2008; Findlay et al. 2009; Wojciechowski et al. 2011), the safety net (Wojciechowski et al. 2011; Olive 2011), critical habitat (Elgie 2008; Wojciechowski et al. 2011), or the overall slow implementation of the act (Findlay et al. 2009; Mooers et al. 2007).[10] I highlight these criticisms below, and offer a broader discussion of the challenges involved in regulating private property within the provinces.

VanderZwaag, Engler-Palma, and Hutchings (2011, 270) point out that "SARA provides a cascade of promises to protect Canadian wildlife" – commitments with respect to the independent scientific assessment of species using the best available science, the protection of individuals and their critical habitats, a formal ongoing recovery planning process, enforcement measures, and financial support for recovery activities – but it delivers on only a select few. Indeed, in a study of inner Bay of Fundy salmon the authors find that SARA failed on almost every promise: the recovery strategy was overly general, there was limited identification of critical habitat, a failure to extend legal protection to that habitat, and an uncertain and unwritten action plan. Moreover, no prosecutions or convictions of SARA prohibitions have been enacted with respect to the salmon. The result is "trickles of protection rather than a steady flow" (VanderZwaag, Engler-Palma, and Hutchings 2011, 305).

In addition, despite the uninspiring track record of provincial protection, SARA's safety net provision has been invoked successfully only once since 2002. In 2006, for example, a conservation group filed a complaint to the North American Commission for Environmental Cooperation, but after three years of delays and a legally narrowed scope of inquiry, the group withdrew its complaint (Wojciechowski et al. 2011). Subsequent lawsuits have been brought by environmental groups in Alberta and British Columbia to protect the woodland caribou and the spotted owl, but in both cases the minister of the environment deemed the claims to be insignificant, and no action was taken (Wojciechowski et al. 2011). Canada claims to take a precautionary approach to conservation, but the lack of protection granted to species across the country calls this commitment into question. Wojciechowski et al. (2011, 219) argue that "the threshold of plausibility required to trigger a precautionary obligation has been exceeded." In September 2013 the federal minister of the environment announced the safety net would be used to protect the greater sage grouse in Saskatchewan and Alberta. This is not an example of the precautionary principle, however, as the bird has declined more than 95 per cent since 1988. If anything, it is likely "too little too late," as opposed to "better safe than sorry." Moreover, as of November 2013 the federal government had taken no specific action to protect the bird in either province.

Some provinces are also lagging behind on their commitment with respect to the Accord for the Protection of Species at Risk. As VanderZwagg, Engler-Palma and Hutchings (2011, 295) note, "SARA cannot 'swim alone' in the protection of species at risk." The result is non-current listings across the country. Wojciechowski et al. (2011, 210) find that the number of SARA-listed species that are also listed in provincial or territorial species-at-risk legislation varies dramatically "from 100 percent in Ontario and Newfoundland [and Labrador] to zero percent in all three territories and [Prince Edward Island]," and only 33 per cent of SARA species are listed in all the jurisdictions in which they occur. This means that 77 per cent of species are not listed or do not have their habitat listed in parts of their range, and thus they remain unprotected.

Another critical finding is that species are less likely to be listed if the jurisdiction in which they occur does not have stand-alone species-at-risk legislation. Elgie (2008) finds that 77 per cent of the species recommended by COSEWIC had been listed under SARA but only 37 per cent had been listed under provincial endangered species laws. This is largely because, under SARA, a COSEWIC-recommended species automatically becomes listed unless the federal cabinet decides not to do so within nine months, in which case it must publicly provide written reasons. Most provincial laws have no such time limits or accountability requirements.

As Table 3.1 illustrates, the provinces provide a patchwork of conservation for species at risk: in Ontario, Manitoba, and Quebec, species are afforded protection, while in Alberta, British Columbia, and Saskatchewan, species have little hope of protection and recovery. Although all the provinces and territories agree in principle that species-at-risk legislation should include an independent (non-governmental) process for assessing the status of species, designating and legally protecting endangered and threatened species, providing protection of critical habitat, developing recovery plans, ensuring multi-jurisdictional cooperation, monitoring the status of species, improving awareness, and including citizen participation, very few actually deliver on these goals. In most places there is no mandatory protection for endangered species and their habitat. Dearden (2001, 90) argues that "one of the most fundamental weaknesses in the Canadian approach to resource management is the general antipathy between the different levels of government and the challenges in getting them to work together cooperatively for the good of all Canadians and the Canadian landscape." The Ecojustice (2012) report, *Failure to Protect*, which grades species-at-risk legislation across the country, awards the three westernmost provinces and the Yukon each an F, and no province does better than a C+ (which Ontario is awarded). The report concludes that, "across the board, Canada's federal, provincial and territorial governments are doing an abysmal job protecting our species and the habitat they need to survive and recover" (Ecojustice 2012, 23).

In 2009 and 2010, SARA underwent a review of its first five years by the House of Commons Standing Committee on Environment and Sustainable Development. The committee examined the implementation of the law and gathered feedback in the form of parliamentary testimony by a number of organizations and experts in the field. During the meetings, while industry representatives narrowed in on the ambiguities of the permit process and compensation issues, environmental activists concentrated on the federal government's refusal to define concepts such as "critical habitat," "residence," "recovery," "damage," and "destroy." These words, phrases, and ideas had been debated during the initial consideration of the act, but were never made clear in the language of the bill. For example, section 58 defines "critical habitat" as "habitat that is necessary for the survival or recovery of a listed wildlife species and that is identified as the species' critical habitat in the recovery strategy or action plan for the species." Thus, the critical habitat designation happens only during recovery – a process that can take years after a species has been listed. And it is not clear what is protected in the time between the species' listing and the finalization of a recovery plan. The process is supposed to take nine months, but in practice it takes much longer. There is currently a major lag in the development of recovery strategies, which is problematic not just for a species that needs its habitat protected, but also for landowners who need to know exactly how far legal reach extends around the endangered species.

This lack of precision also makes it difficult to decide if a province is protecting critical habitat, because often that habitat is not defined. As a Nature Canada representative has pointed out, even though SARA clearly indicates that, "if the laws of a province or territory do not effectively protect a federally listed species ... SARA provides the federal government with the authority to take action," the act never clearly defines "effective protection" (Wren 2009). Like other environmentalists, she fears this might be a reason the safety net provisions have never been implemented. Neither the federal government nor any provincial government has a clear conception of what protection is necessary before the safety net can be invoked.

Over the year of House of Commons committee meetings, no private landowners or landowner groups testified, likely due to no private landowners' having been adversely affected in the seven years since the act was fully implemented. In fact, there are no examples of the law's having been applied to private property anywhere. As Rachel Plotkin of the David Suzuki Foundation said, "we haven't seen any instances where that has even begun to happen" (Plotkin 2010). Julie Gelfand, appearing on behalf of the Species at Risk Advisory Committee, claims: "we're barely getting listed species approved. We have very few recovery plans or strategies in place" (Gelfand 2009; see also Olive 2011, 2012b; and Wojciechowski et al. 2011).

The only groups related to landowners to testify formally before the House committee were the Canadian Cattlemen's Association (CCA) and the Ontario Federation of Anglers and Hunters. The CCA recommended that the federal government provide more financial support for good management practice, education, and awareness for landowners, clearly define "critical habitat," and devise clear guidelines on how to implement fair and reasonable compensation to landowners (Strankman 2009). The Federation recommended that landowners be included on recovery teams (the groups that devise recovery plans for individual species) and that, overall, SARA needs fewer sticks and more carrots for landowners.

The law's implementation has been slow, and the role of private landowners has not yet been fully determined. It is too soon to judge the effectiveness of SARA, but one should note that it has not yet come under public criticism in the way the ESA has in the United States in recent years.

SARA and eNGOs

As in the United States, a number of dedicated environmental organizations in Canada focus on endangered species conservation. The largest of these are the David Suzuki Foundation, the Canadian Nature Federation, Nature Conservancy Canada, Sierra Club Canada, Ecojustice, Ducks Unlimited Canada, and World Wildlife Canada. Unlike American eNGOs, however, Canadian groups face a number of institutional barriers, of which McKenzie (2002) focuses on three. First, in Canada's parliamentary system, there is strict party discipline, so lobbying individual Members of Parliament is less useful than lobbying congressmen who can cross party lines. Second, since federalism divides jurisdiction over natural resources and private property among different levels of government, eNGOs must lobby federal and provincial governments to affect endangered species policy. Third, the Canada Elections Act limits third-party advertising; moreover, unlike their US counterparts, Canadian groups are disinclined to use electoral strategies such as block voting or campaign contributions (McKenzie 2002, 72–3).

Land trusts are also less prevalent in Canada than in the United States – there were only eighty-two in 2000 (Watkins and Hilts 2001), and no national statistics are available about the number at present (Gerber 2012). It is likely that land trusts are less widespread because, under Canada's common law, landholders have land tenure rather than land ownership, so relatively fewer actual land *owners* are legally able to enter into a land trust.[11]

Canadian eNGOs nevertheless are making an important contribution to endangered species policy. In fact, SARA might not exist without their participation. In 1994 six major environmental groups and over one hundred other regional and national organizations created the Canadian Endangered Species Coalition (Elgie 1995; see also Amos, Harrison, and Hoberg 2001). Although the attempt in 1996 to pass Bill C-65, the Canada Endangered Species Protection Act, failed, the environmental movement once again sparked the SAR legislation process in 1998 when Elizabeth May brought the Species at Risk Working Group into existence. Today, key Canadian eNGOs such as the David Suzuki Foundation and Ecojustice (formerly Sierra Legal Defence) continue to be advocates and watchdogs on behalf of Canada's species at risk.

Canada and the US Approach

Reflecting upon thirty years of ESA history, Canada decided to take a stewardship-first approach to species-at-risk conservation. The Habitat

Stewardship Program, created before SARA, provides funds and resources to help landowners, Aboriginal organizations, and industry carry out conservation projects. Since the passage of SARA, the program has prioritized species listed under the act, and it awards funds regionally to help raise awareness, create and implement recovery and action plans, and collaborate with private landowners to protect habitat.

How does the Canadian legislation compare with its US counterpart? In 2001 David Anderson, Minister of the Environment, told the House of Commons: "Let me assure the House that the proposed Canadian species at risk act is fundamentally different from the American act and, I might add, dramatically better" (Anderson 2001). Table 3.2 summarizes the approaches of the two laws on key issues, but Illical and Harrison (2007) note three major differences between them. First, the costs of species protection are borne by government under SARA, rather than by the private sector as under the ESA (via regulation). Second, non-discretionary language in the ESA provides the USFWS with little choice but to go to great lengths to protect species, whereas SARA's discretionary language give the federal government flexibility to determine what actions to take and when. Third, under SARA, Ottawa defers to the provinces; under the ESA, Washington claims primary responsibility.

The reason Canada chose a different approach to solve a similar problem is partly institutional: provinces have jurisdiction over their own natural resources, including wildlife and land. The original version of SARA, Bill C-65, attempted to regulate land within the provinces, but this was immediately rejected in Parliament. Thus, Canada could not take the same command-and-control approach that the United States did. Context is another factor. The political climate in Canada during the 1990s differed significantly from that in the United States at the height of the environmental movement in the early 1970s. Canada's ratification of the UNCBD also set it upon a different path than the United States, committing itself to the precautionary principle as well as to the inclusion of Aboriginal peoples and their traditional knowledge in the conservation of biodiversity (see Chapter 8).

Despite their differences in legal approaches, both countries rely on private landowners to steward endangered species on private property. The regulation of private property, particularly as it concerns the designation of critical habitat, presents a significant challenge to Canadian conservation efforts. Although SARA offers only discretionary

Table 3.2. The Approaches of the ESA and SARA on Key Issues

The Endangered Species Act	The Species at Risk Act
Federal law (1973)	Federal law (2002)
Aimed at recovery and protection of individual species	Aimed at recovery and protection of individual species
Applies to all land parcels in all fifty states	Applies only to federal lands
USFWS makes decisions about listing species and their habitat	Independent scientific review board that makes recommendations about listing species
Listing decisions based on "best science" available	Listing decisions based on "best science" available
Habitat is listed at time of species listing	Habitat is listed at the time of recovery strategy
Works with states through section 6 grants	Includes a "safety-net" to regulate within provinces

protection to species on private lands, the provinces are left to sort out the logistics of mandatory protection. And, as we have seen, the provinces have done so to varying degrees.

Conclusion

Canada was the first country to ratify the UN Convention on Biological Diversity. It also created a National Strategy for Species at Risk, which involves a three-pronged approach: a collaborative accord with the provinces and territories to create legislation across all lands; the Habitat Stewardship Program to fund stewardship efforts by all Canadians; and the federal Species at Risk Act. Through this approach, Canada has begun to address its UNCBD obligations. Each part of the overall strategy affirms Canada's commitment to the anthropocentric and eco-centric worth of other species, and advocates for voluntary stewardship of the nation's biodiversity.

It is important to keep in mind, however, that SARA applies mandatory protection only to federal lands and its discretionary power to regulate inside provinces has never been used in the law's more than ten years' existence. As with the ESA, SARA can be tough on paper, but in practice the law is weakened. This has led one critic to claim that "the government's performance in implementing the Act has been under-whelming to say the least" (Elgie 2010, 210).

Moreover, only six of the ten provinces and one of the three territories have stand-alone species-at-risk legislation. Only Ontario, Quebec, New Brunswick, and the Northwest Territories have updated their policies since SARA was passed in 2002. Other than on federal lands and all lands in Ontario, species are afforded only discretionary protection, which often means little to no protection. The provinces are not forced or even incentivized to create and update legislation, and the process is moving slowly as a result. British Columbia and Alberta have created policies (without the full force of law) for species at risk. Manitoba has stand-alone legislation, but the province continues to seek ways to avoid property regulation by addressing biodiversity needs on public lands. In short, Canada's patchwork of approaches pales in comparison with US policy on habitat protection and the consistent identification and listing of species.

It is possible that, in having to face new challenges in protecting the biodiversity of the North, Canada will shift the National Strategy towards a more stringent regulatory approach. Its Arctic territory is enormous – only Russia's is larger – and makes up almost 40 per cent of Canada's total land mass. Climate change, pollution, tourism, and increased naval and shipping traffic in the North are placing a large strain on that bioregion. From Alaska to Labrador, species from ice worms to polar bears are suffering. If Canada takes its commitments to the UNCBD and those made under the Arctic Council through its Northern Strategy seriously, then "environmental stewardship" in the Arctic will require more than SARA and the Northern Wildlife Act.

4 Willingness to Cooperate

In his seminal work *Why People Obey the Law*, Tom Tyler (1990) points out that "Americans are typically law abiding people." He goes on to say, however, that compliance is never complete and that everyone breaks the law sometime. Why individuals obey laws and comply with public policy is not always straightforward. In fact, there are a myriad possible motivations for both compliance and non-compliance. In this chapter I explore these motivations and pose theoretical expectations about why landowners are willing to comply or cooperate with the US Endangered Species Act (ESA) and the Canadian Species at Risk Act (SARA) or provincial policies. Understanding the ways in which individuals think and make decisions about compliance is important to designing effective policies and effective enforcement strategies (May and Winter 1999). The case studies in Chapters 6 and 7 examine willingness to cooperate among urban and suburban landowners in both Canada and the United States.

The exact relationship between attitudes and individual behaviour remains uncertain, but there is general agreement that the two are significantly related (Dietz, Fitzgerald, and Shwom 2005). For example, research on property owners has found that landowner attitudes generally predict behaviour (Kraus 1995). And more broadly, research on individual compliance with environmental regulations also indicates a significant link between attitudes and actions to obey legal requirements (May 2005). This relationship is far from perfect, and there is clearly some disconnect between personal values and behaviour in some settings, as anyone can recognize the difference between wanting to do something and actually doing it (Egan and Jones 1993). Nevertheless, the idea that personal values are relevant to explaining a host of personal actions, including compliance with public policy, is not in serious doubt.

Based on citizens' attitudes and interests, two main theoretical models, the deterrence model and the accommodative model, are used to explain compliance (Murphy 2003; Tyler 1990; Tyler and Darley 2000). The deterrence model, based primarily on the idea of punishment, is as old as government itself. In 1651 Thomas Hobbes argued that a central government was necessary to overcome man's fear of death and ensure the safety of the people. According to Hobbes, all human motivation is based on two movements: appetite, or movement towards objects; and aversion, or movement away from objects. Essentially, what compels people to act is desire and fear and, therefore, a government must be seen to create laws that manipulate fear and desire for the greater good of society. That is to say, any theory of compliance "must start out accepting the fact that the threat of punishment tends to deter," and, more generally, "people want what is pleasant and rewarding and they avoid costs, punishments and pains" (Friedman 1975, 2).

In the social sciences the deterrence model is particularly popular in the rational choice literature, as it assumes that individuals are rational, profit-seeking actors (motivated by financial desire). Kagan and Scholz (1980) refer to these actors as "amoral calculators," since they disobey laws when the probability of being caught and the subsequent sanctions are small in relation to the potential profit gained via non-compliance. The model leads to the belief that actors will comply with a law or policy only when confronted with the reality of harsh sanctions and penalties (Murphy 2003). Olson (1965) referred to this as "opportunistic obedience," since it fully explains compliance due to fear of sanctions or promise of reward. However, the idea that deterrence is a complete explanation for compliance was put in doubt later in the 1960s, especially among sociologists, when the relationship between crime and punishment, particularly capital punishment, seemed dubious (Friedman 1975; Grasmick and Bursik Jr 1990).

Furthermore, research has shown that the use of threats and legal coercion, particularly when perceived as illegitimate, can produce the opposite behaviour from that which is sought (Murphy 2003). In practice, sanctions can undermine the sense of duty to comply (May 2005) and rouse resentment in citizens, making them less likely to comply, or at least more willing to try to get away with non-compliance (for example, by cheating on their taxes in retaliation for harsh parking tickets). Stone (1990, 265) points out that negative inducements, such as fines or tariffs, "create a climate of conflict and divide the two parties [government and citizens]." Similarly, in social psychology, "labelling theory" suggests that the actions of lawmaking and law-enforcement officials are a primary source of deviant behaviour when government disrespects citizens (Kagan and Scholz 1980). For example, if government arbitrarily raises fines for speeding without public support in an attempt to encourage drivers to obey speed limits, citizens might resort to radar detectors and radio call-in shows to report speed traps. Thus, the outcome might be an increase in speeding, the exact opposite of what was intended by regulation.

Nevertheless, fear of punishment (fines or incarceration) remains an accepted and widely used deterrent against non-compliance with social regulation. But the way deterrence is used in combination with other policy tools is an area of increased investigation. This is particularly true of the relationship between laws, sanctions, and enforcement strategy (Church and Heumann 1989; May and Winter 1999; May and Woods 2003). Friedman argues that, when the relationship between laws and enforcement is weak, it signals to citizens that "people in authority do not take the rule very seriously" and, thus, both the threat and the legitimacy of the rule are weakened (1975, 95). The situations in which enforcement style and public interaction affect policy compliance bear further scrutiny, particularly in regard to the importance of perceived procedural justice in the policy process. I discuss this in detail below.

Beyond fear of punishment there are other deterrents or "negative motivations" (Tyler 1990) for complying with a law or policy. These include guilt and shame (Blake and Davis 1964; Briar and Piliavin 1965; Grasmick and Bursik Jr 1990; Grasmick, Bursik Jr, and Kinsey 1991; Reckless and Dinitz 1967). When actors violate norms, especially those endorsed by people they respect or value, they run the risk of being embarrassed or suffering a loss of respect. The difference between shame and embarrassment is straightforward: shame is a self-imposed punishment whereas embarrassment is socially imposed (Grasmick and Bursik Jr 1990). The most immediate adverse consequence of shame is psychological discomfort, but more long-term effects might include depression, anxiety, or damaged self-concept, which could impede normal function in one's social environment. The consequences of embarrassment might include a loss of valued relationships and perhaps restrictions in opportunities to achieve other valued goals over which significant others have some control (Grasmick and Bursik Jr 1990;

Grasmick, Bursik Jr, and Kinsey 1991). In short, these motivations, although difficult to document empirically, have real consequences that affect individuals' decision to comply.

Grasmick, Bursik Jr, and Kinsey (1991) conducted a study of the "Keep America Beautiful" anti-littering campaign in Oklahoma City in the 1980s. Nationally, the campaign was an appeal to citizens' conscience and community pride to reduce littering. In 1982 an initial sample of Oklahoma City residents was interviewed about environmental attitudes, including littering. Another sample was interviewed in 1989, two years after the campaign began. Grasmick, Bursik Jr, and Kinsey found that, after the campaign, people were more likely to report feelings of guilt and shame in regards to littering. Specifically, 39 per cent of the 1982 respondents said they would feel guilty if they littered, while 67 per cent did in 1989. Only 8 per cent of those interviewed in 1982 believed they definitely would lose the respect of others if they littered, compared with 21 per cent in 1989. The Grasmick, Bursik Jr, and Kinsey study has methodological limitations,[12] but overall it suggests that the campaign's attempt to increase the threats of shame and embarrassment for littering was successful. More important, this had consequences for potential behaviour: in 1982, 39 per cent said they probably would litter in the future, compared with 31 per cent in 1989. I do not examine the role of shame directly in this book because too few landowners know about the law or about endangered species for shame to be an effective enforcement strategy. However, if outreach and education are able to inform enough people about the importance of biodiversity, then shaming people into conservation efforts might be a method to achieve changes in desired public behaviour.

Lastly, the deterrence model includes the other side of punishment: incentives and rewards. Although incentives are likely considered "positive" by those receiving them, this type of inducement is included as a negative motivation in the literature because incentives originate from an external source (usually government) and can be used to deter people from taking specific actions. In fact, government can entice compliance through incentives in an abundance of ways. Like punishment, the point of incentives is to "bring individual motivations into line with community goals" (Stone 1990, 264). Incentives do this by altering the consequences of individual action such that "what is good for community is also good for the individual" (ibid.). For example, the Wildlife Habitat Incentives Program, run by the US Department of Agriculture, provides financial incentives to landowners who are willing to establish or improve wildlife habitat on their own property. Thus, the community benefits from improved environmental conditions while the individual actors (landowners) benefit from personal rewards.

Grabosky (1995) explores the use of rewards and incentives as instruments of regulation, including grants and subsidies, bounties, commissions, tax credits, loan guarantees, prizes, patronage, and praise. He acknowledges that one major advantage of incentives is that "the promise of reward is more freedom-enhancing, and thus more just, than is the threat of punishment" (271). This is because one can refuse the offer of reward and forgo the activity entirely, but one cannot refuse punishment – as Grabosky says, "positive incentives allow freedom of choice; penalties do not" (262). For example, landowners can choose to accept incentives or tax credits for establishing habitat on private property under the Wildlife Habitat Program, but they are not required by law to take any action at all. Conversely, under section 9 of the ESA, landowners are forbidden to harvest trees that are the habitat of endangered species. Thus, Grabosky's point is that landowners are freer under the Wildlife Habitat Program than they are under the ESA, which is important given the significance of basic freedoms and freedom of choice to Americans.

From a regulatory standpoint, however, incentives, which might be freedom enhancing for the public, are more time intensive and require a lot of monitoring by regulators. As Stone (1990) points out, punishments and penalties do not have to be given out to be effective, but incentives always have to be paid. This means that regulators have to keep track of actors' behaviours and be sure to distribute the promised rewards, otherwise the "alliance and spirit of good-will" (Stone 1990, 265) that incentives create will break down. Another related drawback to incentives is their financial cost, which must be weighed against their possible effectiveness as a policy tool.

Related to the issue of cost is the idea of paying citizens to change their behaviour, since, over the long run, this could set a dangerous and costly precedent. Once government starts paying its citizens to behave in a certain way, they will come to expect payment for that behaviour, and it becomes difficult to remove the incentive or reward later on. For example, a small landowner who learns that he or she can receive a tax benefit for, say, planting more trees will come to expect the benefit and likely become agitated if government tries to remove the benefit while still expecting the landowner to plant trees. Other strategies, particularly enforcement, can also be expensive and time consuming. So, although this criticism is important, it is not unique to incentives.

Finally, there is the argument that positive reinforcement to induce a certain behaviour that would unlikely occur otherwise is manipulative and more devious than the straightforward prohibition of undesirable conduct (Church and Heumann 1989; Stone 1990). People are assumed to be rational and their decision to act in a certain way is predicated on conscious goal seeking. Government use of incentives thus implies that it is appropriate to "alter people's self-propelled progress toward their goals by changing the opportunities they face" (Stone 1990, 264). It seems, however, that, in many instances, the use of punishment suffers from the same criticism, since it can easily manipulate people to act in ways other than they would naturally. Rules might be more straightforward than incentives, but both types of inducements are manipulative and justified on the basis of public interest.

Punishment and incentives are both promising strategies for dealing with a common problem where there is a "divergence between private and public interest" (Stone 1990, 264), since they can alter individual behaviour to benefit the common good. But inducements are only half of the compliance story, as Tyler points out: "if rewards and punishments alone produced sufficient compliance for society to function effectively, the authorities would find their task simple and straightforward" (1990, 18). That is to say, the ESA or SARA would have solved their country's biodiversity crisis already. Tyler goes on to claim that in democratic societies the legal system cannot function if it can influence only by manipulating rewards and costs, because the system then would consume large amounts of resources and society would be in constant peril of instability (1990, 22).

Society thus needs to foster other reasons for complying with the law – namely, "affirmative motivations," which emanate from good intentions and a sense of obligation to comply (May 2004). Tyler breaks affirmative motivation into two types: normative commitment through legitimacy and normative commitment through morality. Commitment through legitimacy means obeying a policy or law because one feels that the authority enforcing the law has the right to dictate behaviour; commitment through morality means obeying a law because one feels the law is right. In the latter case there is no feeling of obligation to an external political authority, but a desire to follow a law because it is consistent with one's personal sense of what is morally right (Tyler 1990, see also Monroe 1996). For example, most people obey the legal prohibition of premeditated murder because of their own sense of morality, not because of fear of punishment or because they think the police are a legitimate source of authority. Internal values are a sense of what is and what is not legitimate and what is or is not worth obeying, according to personal ethics or religious doctrine as opposed to furthering one's personal gain or the interests of others (Friedman 1975). On the other hand, commitment through legitimacy is bound up in external conditions – namely, procedural justice. Citizens need to believe that laws were created in a fair and democratic process that included public discourse.

Voluntary compliance, however, might be encouraged through education, technical assistance, and other inducements associated with democratic processes such as feedback mechanisms and voting opportunities. Voluntary compliance is desirable because incentives and punishment, and the associated monitoring of individual behaviour, are burdensome, requiring enforcement officers and a large judicial system. Moreover, punishment is effective only to the point of diminishing returns, as too much punishment will create resistance to a law. Although the threat of punishment is much less expensive and requires less monitoring, it can also be less effective if individuals realize the threat is not backed up by actual punishment. Thus, approaches based on voluntary compliance, such as cooperative management, seem much more practical and potentially more effective for compliance and cooperation with the ESA and SARA. These laws do have regulatory powers, but, for reasons I explained in Chapters 2 and 3, the laws rely by and large on self-enforcement and, ultimately, require voluntary stewardship for species recovery to be successful.

Cooperative management, however, likely requires procedural justice if it is to inspire willingness to cooperate. Commitment through legitimacy as an affirmative motivation for voluntary compliance works only when there is procedural justice. Citizens will comply with a law if they support and believe in the system that made it. As Levi (1997, 23) points out, "in most cases citizens are willing to go along with a policy they do not prefer as long as it is made according to a process they deem legitimate." In a review of sixteen studies examining the relationship between legitimacy and willingness to cooperate, Tyler (1990, 33) finds that "citizens with higher levels of support for the authorities are less likely to engage in behavior against the system." Murphy (2003) tests Tyler's theory in the area of taxation compliance and finds some support for an emphasis on procedural justice.

One can readily see how the two commitments, morality and legitimacy, might conflict. For example, a person might consider euthanasia immoral for personal reasons, but have no objections to its legalization so long as a democratic majority supports the law. The individual would not practice euthanasia personally, but would not prevent other individuals from doing so.

The literature tends to focus on commitment through legitimacy, rather than morality (Levi 1997; Tyler 1990), since "legitimacy is the normative factor of greatest concern to authorities" (Tyler 1990, 161). Issues of morality are often pushed aside because, in pluralistic societies, there is supposedly no accepted single moral code and so manipulation of a commitment through morality could be deemed illiberal. The consequence of focusing only on legitimacy, however, is that it blurs the relationship between the two motivations. It seems reasonable to suggest that actions accepted as moral by citizens (such as laws permitting abortion) would more likely be accepted as legitimate (such as abortion laws). This relationship also might work in the other direction, but further research is required. Here it is relevant because it might be possible that landowners consider stewardship to be moral or ethical (an obligation to one's religious principles or to society) and, therefore, are likely to accept conservation policy as legitimate. SARA and, to a greater extent, Newfoundland and Labrador's Endangered Species Act suggest there is a moral element to conservation, and they thereby potentially increase the legitimacy of the law.

De Young (2011, 1) argues that a conservation aesthetic, theoretically drawn from Aldo Leopold's land ethic, can be "viewed as a form of intrinsic motivation" and "provides an affirmative strategy for encouraging environmental stewardship." The idea is for landowners to react to the satisfaction they derive from the "benefits embedded in responding to, and living within, biophysical limits." He is quick to point out that such a motivation is often overlooked both in the literature and in the real world. That is to say, the US Fish and Wildlife Service (USFWS) is not trying to teach landowners to note the level of satisfaction felt in living in balance with nature. Similar to my own argument, De Young stresses that more attention should be given to affirmative motivations and the degree to which they increases landowner cooperation with "the very same activities we often try to manipulate them into doing" (2011, 2). Often we assume that individuals need to be bribed or tricked into a desired behaviour when they might already want to behave that way. In Chapters 6 and 7 I attempt to acknowledge the existence, importance, and potential of affirmative motivations for stewardship. As will be evident, landowners sometimes want to steward species on their property, and for them no bribe is necessary.

Thus far we have explored the basic reasons individuals might comply with a law. These actions can be broken down into two main motivations: negative motivations (punishment, incentives/rewards, shame and embarrassment); and affirmative motivations (legitimacy and morality). To help clarify individual motivations, the issue of plagiarism among college students illustrates the model of compliance well. Why do students comply with plagiarism policies? If they fear being caught and expelled from university, then deterrence can be said to be influencing their behaviour. If they fear disapproval from their friends and classmates, then the negative motivation of shame/embarrassment is motivating behaviour. If they refrain from plagiarizing because they believe school policies ought to be obeyed, legitimate authority is influencing behaviour. Finally, if they do not plagiarize because it violates their personal convictions, morality is the motivating factor (see Tyler 1990 for other examples).

All of these motivations are independent, but each can influence an individual's willingness to comply with the law. For an individual, some motivations might be more powerful than others. For example, some might be influenced by peer pressure while others might have little regard for the opinions of others. One student might not care if his friends and classmates know he cheats on exams, whereas another would be so embarrassed by such a revelation as to never cheat. Many people might be influenced by a combination of negative and affirmative motivations. Thus, moving to the realm of conservation, a landowner might wish to comply with the ESA because he or she values other species (an affirmative motivation) and also because the USFWS has offered a specific financial incentive (a negative motivation). In this instance it is the combination of moral support for a law and incentives that shapes behaviour.

Tyler (1990) argues that a commitment to the law via legitimacy motivates citizens to comply with the law. He tests this idea through panel surveys of Chicago residents regarding laws about theft, littering, and traffic. Although Tyler does not deny the role of negative motivations, particularly fear of punishment, he focuses more on the style of enforcement and the public's perception of the justice system. For him, affirmative motivations are an important part of understanding compliance, and he illustrates that commitment through legitimacy works for most citizens.

Levi (1997) develops an alternative model of compliance known as "contingent consent" to explain the role of consent in governance and democratic theory. Contingent consenters are "those individuals who want to act ethically, who like to contribute to the collective good, all things being equal, but who will do so only under certain contingencies" (1997, 20). Her model explains compliance by the trustworthiness of government and the norm of ethical reciprocity, which states that individuals in a given population cooperate with government demands only as long as others are contributing (24). Her model is essentially a subset of Tyler's notion of procedural justice. She does consider other possible explanations, such as peer pressure, incentives and opportunity costs, and maintains these options as competing hypotheses, but she is dismissive of two other explanations – habitual obedience and ideological consent – since the possibility that citizens comply with the law out of habit or custom is not "readily susceptible to investigation through case studies" and "not directly subject to falsification" (29). Levi leaves habit as a kind of null hypothesis (although she does not refer to it as such). She argues that, if her theories and competing theories do not capture the motivations for compliance, then the explanation is likely due to habit. Ideological consent or moral commitment to a policy, Levi explains, is too difficult to measure and falsify. Thus, it too is a residual explanation and not part of her overall compliance model. In my examination of landowners and the ESA and SARA in Chapters 6 and 7, I challenge Levi's model and add to Tyler's work on the importance of affirmative motivations.

Non-compliance

Although motivations for compliance have been established, it is important to consider why an individual might not comply with a law or policy. The answer is not just the absence of specific reasons to comply. In addition, non-compliance can involve a breakdown in communication between policy makers or regulators and citizens. Citizens cannot obey a law they do not know about or cannot understand. For example, obeying parking laws near Wrigley Field in Chicago is problematic because signs are confusing, poorly worded, and occasionally even contradictory. It is not that a baseball fan (especially a non-resident) intends to park illegally, but that he or she cannot understand where to park at what times and on what days of the week with or without a local parking sticker. The problem is neither deterrence nor affirmative motivation, but communication.

Second, individuals might not comply with a law because they lack the resources for compliance. As Coombs says (1980, 891), "there are times when target individuals understand perfectly well what a policy demands of them but simply do not have the wherewithal to comply. If carrying out a policy demands unavailable funds, talent, time or energy, then the probability of compliance will be low." The problem here, however, is distinguishing between a lack of resources and a self-proclaimed lack of resources. Safety and occupational health regulations might be good examples, since such policies have high expectations that firms will monitor safety conditions and provide proper equipment for employees, but firms might claim that they cannot afford to do so.

Non-compliance can also be explained by the lack of affirmative motivations. This leads to a consideration of the relationship between citizens and the bureaucracy, where there are two fundamental concerns: the enforcement style (behaviour) of regulators and the effect of the relationship on citizens' commitment to legitimacy. Enforcement style and compliance are intimately bound together, as the threat of punishment can be communicated in a variety of ways, some more effective than others. May and Woods (2003) investigate the extent to which the enforcement style, or the character of day-to-day interactions, of building code inspectors influences compliance with regulations among contractors. They define "formalism" as the rigidity with which rules are interpreted and applied and "facilitation" as the willingness of inspectors to help and be forgiving. They hypothesize that inspectors who are too formal and rigid will influence contractors to see rules as unreasonable, and that repeated interactions and consistent signals are necessary to foster shared expectations about compliance (2003, 128). They are unable, however, to detect consistently a relationship between enforcement style and compliance. Instead, they conclude that knowledge and cooperation are the two key aspects of bringing about stronger voluntary compliance.

May and Winter (1999) study how the behaviour of regulators affects compliance in Danish agro-environmental policy. They expect that compliance will vary according to the amount of formalism and coercion in day-to-day interactions between regulators and regulated, where low degrees of each are relatively ineffective, high degrees of each are expected to be more effective but potentially problematic, and a mix of the two is the most effective. In other words, both formalism and coercion are important for encouraging compliance – the key is finding the right balance between the two approaches. The authors' results largely support this hypothesis as well as the related expectation that the use of sanctions is effective up to a point when it becomes overbearing and loses effectiveness. Both May and Winter (1999) and May and Woods

(2003) suggest that the behaviour of regulators and the interactions between citizens and regulators can affect compliance levels as well as public perceptions of policy.

In a similar vein, Kagan and Scholz (1980) argue that unreasonable behaviour by regulators generates resistance to compliance, where "unreasonableness" might involve disrespect for citizens or arbitrary refusal to take their concerns into account in the enforcement process (see also Murphy 2003). That is to say, citizens need to see the enforcement process as legitimate: what matters is not so much the law itself as the process of lawmaking and the behaviour of government during both that process and the enforcement of the law. For example, Opotow and Brook (2003) find that ranchers in western US states see regulatory rules, such as those under the ESA, as disrespectful because they establish the government as experts and demand that ranchers conform to rules. What makes these landowners unwilling to comply is a perceived lack of governmental legitimacy.

Therefore, it is possible to argue that, when it comes to bureaucratic and government influence on compliance, there are two important values. First is the general belief that legal authorities are legitimate and ought to be obeyed; second is the belief that following the law is important (Tyler and Huo 2002). These values are important to root in society because they foster affirmative motivations and voluntary compliance. The expectation is that "increased levels of trust and perceptions of legitimacy of the regulations enhance affirmative motivations" (May 2004, 65).

Willingness to Cooperate with Conservation Policy

Given what we know about compliance, why would a landowner be willing to comply or cooperate with the Endangered Species Act or the Species at Risk Act? Although most of the literature involving citizens and the law focuses on actual compliance, my focus in this book is on "willingness to cooperate."

A central component of the success of the ESA and SARA is voluntary cooperation and stewardship. The ESA and SARA are neither well known nor well understood, even by the landowners they directly affect (Brook, Zint, and De Young 2003; see also the data I present in Chapters 6 and 7), so one difficulty with measuring actual compliance is knowledge.[13] To the extent that landowners are found not to be complying with the law, it would be difficult to determine if their non-compliance was driven by ignorance or attitudes about conservation and private property. Without talking to landowners about the law, including about their awareness of specific legal requirements, and their motivations for specific actions (or inactions) – in short, without knowing or understanding the reasons for compliance – measurements of compliance can be misleading.

Moreover, there are no records of legal compliance to consult: unlike other areas of compliance literature (Tyler 1990), neither the USFWS nor Environment Canada keeps such public records, and since landowners rarely receive sanctions, the record of non-compliance would be virtually empty in any event. Therefore, since simple compliance with the legal specifics of the ESA and SARA is difficult to measure and less meaningful without a thorough understanding of individual motivations for non-compliance, my study focuses on willingness to cooperate with the law through voluntary efforts.

In my case studies I asked landowners a myriad questions about their views on the morality of conservation and the legitimacy of conservation policy. In half the cases I also asked landowners if they would carry out certain, strictly voluntary, actions, to gauge how willing they were to cooperate with conservation law. To comply with the ESA or SARA, very little is required of small landowners, especially in Canada, where SARA does not regulate private property. Mainly, they must refrain from intentionally killing, harassing, or otherwise harming the species.

In 1995 the USFWS established a "small landowner exemption" that includes activities conducted on residential properties and lots five acres or less as well as other activities that the USFWS determines have negligible effects on a *threatened* species. Essentially, small property owners are exempt from section 4 of the ESA unless there is direct evidence of intentional harm to a threatened species. But the USFWS does reserve the right not to extend the exemption to landowners in cases where the risk to the species is too great. Moreover, the exemption does not apply if a small landowner lives on *endangered* species habitat. In such a case, all the landowner's activities are open to scrutiny, and attempts to alter habitat by cutting down trees or putting in a backyard pool, for example, could be considered a violation of the ESA. Therefore, for all intents and purposes, for US small landowners compliance mostly amounts to adhering to section 9 and avoiding the intentional "take" of a threatened or endangered species. Likewise, in Canada, SARA requires very little of private landowners or even other citizens, since the law extends only to federal lands. All citizens are expected to comply with SARA at all times (by not taking a species or harming habitat) on public federal Crown lands. And landowners are expected to steward endangered species found on their own property or otherwise voluntarily cooperate with incentives.

In trying to determine why a landowner would be willing to cooperate as opposed to simply complying with legal requirements, I pose two main theoretical expectations. Affirmative motivations – a commitment through morality and legitimacy – are of primary concern in my work. I consider negative motivations – punishment and incentives – but they are not of central importance. In this sense, my model is similar to Tyler's work except that I focus on legitimacy and morality as well as willingness to cooperate.

Implicitly, I expect the motivations for cooperation to be similar to those for compliance, even though the two sets of behaviours are distinct. The models in the literature are based on theories of willingness to comply, and posit that negative motivations are key to enticing compliance. Since my model tests willingness to cooperate, I expect punishment to be less motivating since non-cooperation is not punished. It is also important to understand, however, that landowners in Canada and the United States lack an understanding of their respective country's endangered species law and in most cases do not know what the law requires of them. Thus, they did not know if the actions I inquired about were related to compliance or cooperation. In this sense, their willingness to cooperate might overlap with their willingness to comply, since they were not able to make a distinction. Moreover, the ESA and SARA are so ambiguous at times that it is not clear which actions constitute compliance and which cooperation. It is in this sense that my model deals with both compliance and cooperation, while ultimately focusing on willingness to cooperate. My two main expectations are:

Landowners will interpret conservation policy as consistent with their own sense of morals.

Landowners will interpret conservation policy as consistent with their idea of legitimacy.

By "conservation policy" I mean specifically the ESA or SARA and any provincial policy that might be in effect. Again, my aim is not to disprove the importance of other motivations, but to explore the existence and possible influence of affirmative motivations, which have been understudied and overlooked in work on US and Canadian endangered species policy. To the extent that cooperative management is a promising strategy for conservation reform, it is essential to establish the extent to which landowners are willing to cooperate with the law – otherwise one risks providing too many or too few incentives (either in the form of punishment or payment). My expectations are limited in the sense that they are not directional. In this study I am looking for empirical evidence that affirmative motivations exist at all. I am less concerned with a measurable influence on willingness to comply. That is to say, I am not suggesting that a one-unit increase in moral affirmative motivation leads to a two- or three-unit increase in willingness to comply. Rather, I mean to illustrate that landowners have moral affirmatives, to link those attitudes with beliefs about stewardship and property, and to explore the relationship between morality and legitimacy. Future work needs to delve deeper into the complex issues of increasing (or perhaps manipulating) affirmative motivations for optimal levels of cooperation.

The case studies in Chapters 6 and 7 wade into murky waters. Levi's model of compliance, as discussed above, relegates moral commitment to a residual explanation or null hypothesis. She does this on the basis that principled commitment is "a hard variable to measure since it is an internal motivation" and "attitudes and values, even when captured by surveys and the like, do not always correlate with behavior" (1997, 30). I agree that moral beliefs are difficult to measure, but this is largely why I have opted not to confine myself to a survey method, but also to engage in longer interviews that allowed citizens to express their moral commitment, if any. And while I agree that values do not always correlate with behaviour, this is a poor reason to exclude them from study. The theory of reasoned action (Ajzen and Fishbein 1980) posits that core values give rise to basic beliefs, which provide the foundation for higher-order beliefs, attitudes, and norms, which then become the basis of behavioural intentions that, under the right conditions, result in specific behaviour (Vaske et al. 2001).

If it is true that affirmative motivations exist and influence landowners' willingness to cooperate with the ESA and SARA, the implications are plentiful. First, recognition that landowners possess strong moral affinity for other species would provide a foundation for government and other non-governmental actors to build upon. SARA and other Canadian laws assert the morality of conservation, but there is mixed empirical support as to whether citizens feel this way. Second, results that suggested landowners are not morally opposed to government regulation of private property and, moreover, that they would accept such regulation as justified for the sake of conservation would be compelling. In the United States the ESA stands at a reauthorization roadblock because politicians believe landowners' value property rights more than conservation (or more than virtually anything else for that matter). Thus, part of my goal is to show that Americans might be Lockean, but there is room for Leopold on private property, too. Third, perception of legitimacy is often assumed to be important in compliance, but it is not often tested empirically. This is surprising, since, "if legitimacy is an important concept, it should lead citizens to behave in ways not always consistent with their own self-interest" (Tyler 1990, 29). The importance of private property and the protection of the associated rights might be trumped by the values of morality and legitimacy.

My study is specific to a willingness to cooperate with the ESA and SARA. One could apply a similar model to other public and environmental policies, but commitment through morality might be less important in the case of other policies, since the ESA and SARA specifically involve other living creatures. For example, compliance with gun registration laws might have little to do with commitment through morality but more with fear of punishment or legitimacy. On the other hand, policies such as the Toxic Substance Control Act or the Clean Water Act would make excellent case studies, since commitment through morality might still play a role through feelings of moral obligations to the Earth, other species, and future generations of human beings.

Conclusion

Citizens comply with policy for many reasons, which one can summarize as two main models: deterrence (negative) and accommodative (affirmative). Citizens also choose not to comply for a variety of reasons, including a lack of information or resources or a perceived lack of procedural justice in lawmaking. Understanding the relationship between motivations and compliance or non-compliance is central to policy formation and implementation. Effective policy making and enforcement hinges on citizens' willingness to comply. And, in the case of the ESA, effective policy making also hinges on citizens' willingness to cooperate and voluntarily steward. Recognizing that compliance and cooperation can be explained through personal affirmative motivations as well as deterrence requires a focus on peoples' internalized

5 Private Property Meets Conservation

It has been said that "to be an American is to own and control private property" (Jacobs 1998, 36). When the county was being settled, land, so plentiful and expansive, was given to men and their families to grow crops and build homes. In turn, these landowners helped build America. However, America looks much different today. As a democratic country with liberal institutions and more than 300 million people, it has to face certain realities about scarcity and social goods. Landowners might own a parcel of property, but they also safeguard the resources, such as water, air, soil, and wildlife, that flow into and out of that property. These resources are public goods that benefit all Americans, not just property owners. But what kind of responsibility do US landowners have to the social good? Does property ownership create an obligation to protect the country's natural resources? Should it be illegal for landowners to destroy resources on their own land? Why would a landowner be willing to comply or cooperate with laws protecting a social good on his or her own property? These questions have no simple answers.

It is perhaps not surprising that "the dominant issue in contemporary environmental policy concerns the collective interest in private land" (Bromley 2000, 23). It is estimated that between 80 and 95 per cent of endangered species rely on private property for survival in the United States (Bean 1998; Shogren and Tschirhart 2001; USFWS 1997), with 20 per cent relying solely on private lands (Wilcove et al. 1996). It is in this sense that endangered species conservation poses the quintessential environmental policy conundrum: how to protect a public resource on private property. The US approach, via the Endangered Species Act (ESA), is heavy-handed, top-down regulation by the federal government. The Canadian approach, via the Species at Risk Act (SARA), is discretionary regulation that relies on provincial and territorial regulation.

The commonality is that both countries rely heavily upon individual stewardship by landowners (and, to a lesser extent, other citizens). But why would landowners cooperate willingly with a policy that directly conflicts with their own economic self-interest?

The strategy of stewardship relies on an ethos that has never been proven empirically to exist in either country. In this chapter I briefly examine the institution of private property in the United States and Canada. I provide the theoretical foundations of a "Lockean" conception of property before moving on to empirical evidence, which I present in Chapters 6 and 7. John Locke, the seventeenth-century English philosopher, suggested a conception of private property based on an absolute individual right that cannot be infringed upon by any legitimate government. I also explore in this chapter the concept of stewardship. By briefly examining the development of conservation practices at the turn of the twentieth century, I look at two different schools of thought, "wise use" conservation and wilderness conservation, both of which played an important role in property debates throughout that century. This history is predominately American, but one can hardly deny the influence of the US conservation movement on Canada. As MacEachern (2003, 9) points out, "it was only natural that the two nations should travel along similar paths: they shared much the same social, intellectual, and environmental conditions that fostered conservation." Their environmental histories, indeed, are woven together by the lives of a few civil servants who have had a lasting impact on policy in both countries.

To be effective, the ESA and, to a greater extent, SARA require stewardship by private landowners. It is not the "wise use" mentality of conservation, however, that is most desirable to this end. Public lands can be important, and arguably should be used wisely for conservation purposes, but conservation on public lands alone cannot suffice. Instead, policy makers hope that landowners accept and practice the idea of a "land ethic." As developed by Aldo Leopold, the land ethic promotes the "intrinsic worth" of other species and rejects the extinction of any species for material gain. Ultimately, I argue that a balance between a Lockean norm of private property and a Leopoldian norm of stewardship is possible on the same parcel of land.[14]

Property in North America

As British colonies, the histories of Canada and the United States are deeply intertwined. It was not until the Treaty of Paris 1763 that Europeans even began drawing up divisive lines on the North American map. Thus, from the time of the last ice age to the mid-eighteenth century, species and ecosystems stretched freely across the Northern American continent without regard for borders or government jurisdiction and regulation. But in 1776 when thirteen colonies declared their independence from Britain, they also declared independence from other British colonies that did not join them, and so borders were created across North America – borders that served the interests of power with no thought given to the wildlife living there. The United States, in claiming independence, also declared dominion over its own natural resources. The Canadian and US landscapes were forever altered as different governments assumed responsibility (in varying degrees) over the flora and fauna of their respective nations.

Many of the ideas that exemplified intellectual trends in Europe during the eighteenth century eventually took root across North America. For both the United States and Canada, the story of private property begins with John Locke (1632–1704) and Adam Smith (1723–1790). For Locke, as he described in his *Two Treatises on Civil Government*, natural law sets the foundation for a society in which "government's role is to help convert natural resources into private property, and then protect that property" (quoted in Roush 1995, 2). Essentially, Locke argued that individuals have a natural right to ownership, and anything not owned in nature is free to be appropriated by individuals. Through mixing human labour with objects in nature, an individual becomes the owner of the object whereby "no government action is required" (Raymond 2003, 44).

This view went hand-in-hand with Smith's *Wealth of Nations* (1776), which convinced colonists, or at least the statesmen among them, that "sharply defined, readily transferable, and lawfully protected property rights would ensure the optimum allocation of resources" (Czech and Krausman 2001, 129). Thus, Locke argued for a pre-political, or natural, right, which Smith desired government to protect. Together these ideas "legitimize[d] possessive individualism over land" (Bromley 2000, 25). Applied in the British colonies, they meant that land would not be passed down through the bloodlines of feudalism, but would be free for ownership by the hard work of freemen. Government then would protect this natural right. The Homestead Act of 1862 is the first evidence of the institutionalization of Lockean notions of private property in the United States (26). Long before, however, Thomas Jefferson had been convinced by this line of thinking and, through the Declaration of Independence, gave Americans this basic right, otherwise known as "the pursuit of happiness." This was based on Jefferson's creed that farmers have "a right to use the land as they believe and that society's and individual property owners' interests are one and the same" (Sullivan et al. 1996; see also Bultena et al. 1981).

The Lockean notion of property is the basis of an "intrinsic right" to property that is now prevalent in Canadian and US law. Today it means "a secure right to do with one's property as one wishes without the threat of government interference" (Raymond 2003, 44). In both countries, however, the common law and legislation recognize that private property rights are limited – essentially, by liability under tort law and under land-use planning regulations that restrict the permissible uses of real property and that sometimes impose use requirements. Importantly, property is also limited by the concept of public interest that forms the basis for the law and practice of expropriation.

The point here is that, in both countries, some interests and parties are more sympathetic than others to limitations on these rights. The Lockean conception of property can be found, for instance, in the Republican Party's 1994 "Contract with America," which introduced a "property rights" clause based on compensation to private landowners when public action reduces property values. The notion was that Americans have an intrinsic right to private property, and if government wants to interfere, then the public must compensate the landowner – in essence, pay to intrude upon the right to ownership. The idea failed to gain traction at the national level, but a few states passed laws mandating such compensation (Bromley 2000, 24).

In Canada Prime Minister Stephen Harper has made the Lockean concept the centre of the debate over Arctic territory. His famous "use it or lose it" attitude about the North sums up the Canadian attitude towards property: the doctrine of prior use as discussed by Locke – that use denotes ownership – is the principle underlying exploitation of Canada's North. In August 2011 Harper visited the northern territories to encourage mining development projects under the auspices of "job creation" and "economic benefit," but at a larger level the issue is really one of use. Canada is making a claim of "effective occupation" (Grant 2010) of the Arctic, and needs to secure a "use claim" on the territory. This is akin to arguing that, "if we are using it, it must be ours," or, "if we don't use it, someone else will." It is not enough to claim ownership: we must use it to ensure ownership. This has led to a policy of "putting more boots on the Arctic tundra" (Canada 2009b, 3). In short, Canadians are mixing their labour with land and so securing their property rights. This is acceptable, justifiable, and the right course of action, according to the Stephen Harper government.

Perhaps surprisingly, this Lockean idea has also appeared in predominately French-speaking Quebec. When former Quebec premier Robert Bourassa tried to justify the development of hydro-electricity in the James Bay region, he relied upon the argument that nature is wasted until mixed with labour and improved, or made valuable, through ownership. In his view, Aboriginal peoples were wasting the water by not mixing their labour to improve its value; thus, the Aboriginals did not legitimately own the water (see Desbiens 2004). This is how the province of Quebec believed it could claim ownership and establish hydro-electricity on otherwise "native lands."

There is, therefore, some theoretical ground for the existence of a deeply held normative belief in a property owner's intrinsic right to control land with limited political interference (Olive and Raymond 2010). Moreover, anecdotal evidence exists that this norm, which dates from the eighteenth century, is still prevalent today. It is hard to find a book about property and the environment in the United States or Canada that does not mention Locke. His labour theory of property has withstood attack because of its appeal to American and Canadian values of individualism and reverence for hard work (Bromley 2000, 26).[15] This norm has made it difficult to regulate property for the sake of species conservation – or for any other reason, as debates over eminent domain make clear. The history of the ESA is rife with property conflicts, as many Americans see the law as a direct affront to their intrinsic right to private property. SARA avoided this fate by not regulating private property – a deliberate decision that speaks volumes about the sanctity of property in Canada.[16]

As I argue next, however, there are also grounds for another deeply held normative belief: a duty to care for land responsibly and to avoid contributing to the extinction of species (Olive and Raymond 2010). Landowners in both countries struggle to reconcile these norms and, as the next chapters show, often support both ideas. SARA and the ESA would never have been possible without the existence of a desire to steward the North American landscape. From a policy standpoint this means conservation policy must respect both norms.

Stewardship Potential in Canada and the United States

Feudalism did not travel to Britain's American colonies; in fact, the colonists adamantly rejected it as it applied to property ownership. Yet the concept of Crown wildlife found its way to the colonies in the eighteenth century. Freyfogle and Goble (2009, 22) note that "[t]he legal rule in medieval England was that game species were owned by the Crown, not by landowners or other private citizens." These animals, however, were owned by the king only in a sovereign capacity whereby the king was obligated to manage wildlife in the interests of the entire kingdom; Parliament was responsible for enforcing this obligation. This English precedent held after the American Revolution, in the sense that the states now owned wild animals, but only in trust for the people and, thus, had a duty to manage wildlife for the benefit of everyone (Freyfogle and Goble 2009). Today, in both Canada and the United States, subnational governments assume responsibility for wildlife, including issuing licences for fishing and hunting. Over time, however, each country's federal government has become increasingly involved in wildlife management, a development that began in the latter half of the nineteenth century with the establishment of the first national parks.

The assumption of the US presidency by Theodore Roosevelt after the assassination of William McKinley in 1901 changed the conservation movement in both countries. As president, Roosevelt was "instrumental in pressing for legislation to protect large tracts of land" and "his wisdom and leadership set the stage for acquiring state and federal parks, wildlife refuges, forests, rangelands and recreation areas" (Benson, Steinback, and Shelton 1999, 11). Perhaps it was fate, or just some larger reflection of public opinion at the time, that Teddy Roosevelt was president at the same time that Wilfrid Laurier was prime minister of Canada. Roosevelt was well known for his nature studies during his formative years and for his cowboy persona, which persisted during his time in the presidency (Roosevelt 1913). Laurier was an amateur ornithologist and an advocate of wildlife protection (MacEachern 2003, 8). Together these men, along with the policies and institutions they created and the people with whom they surrounded themselves, initiated actual moves towards conservation in North America.

It was not until the turn of the twentieth century that Canadians and Americans awoke to the reality that natural resources were not limitless. The buffalo was near extinction and the passenger pigeon had already suffered that fate. Moreover, "the seemingly endless Canadian forests were showing signs of overcutting and urban areas were polluting the air, land and water" (MacEachern 2003, 1). Environmental scholars normally invoke John Muir, Gifford Pinchot, and Aldo Leopold as the founding fathers of environmentalism. The Canadian fathers are less well known, but arguably equally as important. These men include Clifford Sifton, William Little, Henri-Gustave Joly de Lotbinière, Gordon

Hewitt, and Howard Douglas. As different as all these men were from one another, together they left a lasting mark on the environmental consciousness of Americans and Canadians. Their brief stories merit discussion here in order to sketch the development of "stewardship" as it is understood today.

Even before John Muir (1838–1914) founded the Sierra Club, he was considered the "father of National Parks" for his dedicated petitioning of the US Congress in 1890 to pass the National Park bill, crucial to the establishment of Sequoia National Park and Yosemite National Park. Muir's approach to nature was "purely aesthetic, his beliefs well grounded in the transcendentalist philosophy of Emerson and Thoreau" (Foster 1998, 33). He was not interested in conserving parks for hunting or recreation, but for the simple purpose of the park itself. He had an eco-centric conception of nature, and for him "love of nature – nature untouched, unused and unspoiled – was a form of religious worship" (ibid.). This was not, however, the variant of conservation that Roosevelt tapped into during his time in office, nor was it the kind that took root in America's West at the turn of the twentieth century.

When Roosevelt came to office, he made Gifford Pinchot (1865–1946) his chief of the Bureau of Forestry in the Department of Agriculture. Pinchot knew Muir personally and was familiar with his concept of conservation, but it was not an ideal that Pinchot shared. The literature sometimes distinguishes between "preservation" and "conservation," with the former reflective of Muir's idea of preserving wilderness for its own sake. The schism is sometimes described as "non-use" preservationists versus "wise use" conservationists (Foster 1998, 33). At the time, however, Roosevelt, Pinchot, Sifton, and others used "preservationist" and "conservationist" interchangeably. In the strict sense, Pinchot "[was] not a preservationist. Forests were of no use to him unless they could be effectively and economically used; he cared little for the aesthetic aspects of nature" (32). Pinchot was a conservationist: one who believed in conserving the forests so they could be used sustainably for the purposes of human development. This idea was the main thrust behind forest conservation at the dawn of the twentieth century.

Pinchot is less famous, although equally important, for shaping Canadian forestry practices. His ideas deeply influenced Canadian politician Clifford Sifton (1861–1929). Sifton was minister of the interior in Laurier's government from 1896 to 1905, a proponent of effective occupation of Canadian territory and responsible for immigration policy that encouraged the colonization of Canada's West and North. Sifton presided over the creation of the new provinces of Saskatchewan and Alberta in 1905, and helped establish the Commission of Conservation in 1909 to provide up-to-date scientific advice on the conservation of human and natural resources for Canadian governments (Hall 1985). At this time, the problem of exploitation of natural resources in both the United States and Canada was widely admitted and the conservation movement was gaining momentum. Sifton was the Commission's chairman and "guiding spirit" from 1909 until 1918. For Sifton, as for Pinchot, conservation ultimately was about utilitarianism: natural resources should be used in ways that would generate the greatest benefit for all Canadians (Hall 1985).

In 1908 Roosevelt called for collaboration with Canada on the conservation of forests, and proposed the creation of a bilateral Commission of Conservation. Pinchot accordingly wrote to Canada's governor-general, Lord Grey, to request "cooperation between Canada and the United States in a common and joint endeavor to safeguard the interests of posterity and guard from further reckless waste and wanton destruction and to protect that great inheritance of natural resources" (*Ottawa Citizen*, 30 December 1908, quoted in Gillis and Roach 1986, 172). Ironically, Roosevelt's idea of a commission did not bear fruit in the United States, but Canada's Commission was able to work directly with US organizations and the federal government in Washington to bring about noticeable change. The two countries established many bilateral fish and game laws at the time and signed a Migratory Bird Treaty in 1916. In 1918, however, the Commission was replaced by a growing bureaucracy that formalized the Commission's role in different branches and departments of the federal government (Dorsey 1998).

The individuals I have mentioned were important not because they valued biodiversity in itself but because the concept of conservation in the United States and Canada originated with them. When history looks back upon environmentalism in the two countries, the story always begins with the conservation of forests and the creation of national parks. Although it would be quite some time before Americans would turn their full attention to the conservation of biodiversity, many of the ideas and practices of "stewardship" over nature were founded in the early conservation movement. There are also direct links between national parks and the stewardship of wildlife. This is clearly evident today in places such as Yellowstone and Banff, but it dates much further back. For example, Pinchot and Muir had a profound effect not just on Clifford Sifton but also on Howard Douglas and James Harkin, two

Canadian Dominion Parks commissioners. Harkin became the first commissioner of the National Parks of Canada and established the foundation for park and wildlife preservation, while Douglas was appointed superintendent of Rocky Mountain Park in 1898 and was among the first in government to comprehend the role and importance of wildlife in a park (Foster 1998, 55). Douglas personally travelled to the United States to bring buffalo back to Canada and place them under protection in Banff National Park.

Not all conservationists at the time were proponents of economic exploitation of the land. The youngest "father of environmentalism" is perhaps the most well known today; his work, especially A *Sand County Almanac*, stands above the rest as emblematic of conservation ethics in the United States. Aldo Leopold (1887–1948) was one of America's first professionally trained foresters. Rather than follow in the footsteps of Pinchot in promoting the wise use of land tracts, however, Leopold advocated wilderness preservation in national forests (Minteer 2006, 118). By 1939 Leopold had developed his theory of the "biotic community," in which "the biota as a whole is useful, and the biota include not only plants and animals, but soil and waters as well" (Leopold 1949, 240). His work focuses on "land health," and he actively and publicly encouraged Americans to "assume personal responsibility for conservation of the land" (Minteer 2006, 125). For Leopold an ecological conscience meant the recognition of an ethical obligation to promote the "integrity, beauty, and stability" of the community (ibid.). This idea – or land ethic – took hold in the minds of some American landowners and is "all but worshipped among environmental ethicists today" (126).

During the first half of the twentieth century these men shaped the North American landscape and created the management and conservation practices of Canadian and US governments. Their lasting legacy is two strands of conservation philosophy: wise use conservation and preservation of the intrinsic worth of nature. Men like Pinchot and Sifton thought of conservation as primarily about economics, or what we would call today "sustainable development." The idea was to conserve forests so that society could continue to extract resources from them over the long run.

By the time the Second World War began, both Canada and the United States were moving towards a period of unprecedented growth and resource extraction. It was a time that has been dubbed the "dawn of conservation diplomacy," when stewardship relied on the "relationship between Canadian senior civil servants and their American counterparts"

(Foster 1998, 15). Conservation was not an executive decision in either country. Instead, senior bureaucrats worked collaboratively to promote forestry and parks. How remarkable, then, that today, when cooperation is required more than ever, so little diplomacy exists between the two countries for the purposes of biodiversity stewardship.

From Forestry to Biodiversity

By the 1960s it became clear that the world's environmental problems could not be solved by sustainable-use practices alone. Nuclear weapons, toxic chemicals, species extinction, air quality, water pollution, and oil spills were salient. Concerns about wildlife became prevalent enough to initiate federal action. The United States passed the Endangered Species Protection Act in 1966, followed quickly by the Endangered Species Conservation Act of 1969, the ESA of 1973, and the signing of the Convention on International Trade in Endangered Species of Fauna and Flora in 1975. Canada was slower to act, but pressure on wildlife was less significant in a less industrially developed and urbanized country. In 1992, however, Canada signed the UN Convention on Biological Diversity and in 2002 passed SARA.

In both countries, however, the legislation that eventually passed relied upon an "intrinsic worth" argument. Congressional witnesses testifying in 1973, for example, spoke of the intrinsic worth of plants and a "genuine respect" for all forms of life. In fact, eight out of twenty-two speakers at hearings on the ESA bill referred directly to a moral argument for species preservation (Olive and Raymond 2010). Similarly, Canada's SARA states in its preamble that, "wildlife, in all its forms, has value in and of itself." And when the Minister of the Environment, David Anderson, reintroduced SARA in the 37th Parliament in 2001, he said, "We have a moral obligation to protect this precious diversity so that it can be enjoyed by generations of Canadians to come" (Anderson 2001). Moreover, as discussed in Chapters 2 and 3, both laws eschew economic costs of protection. The thrust of biodiversity conservation is rooted not in sustainable development, but in Leopold's public interest "premised on the goal of land health," which is a "pragmatic appeal to the intrinsic value or good of the land and its flora and fauna" (Minteer 2006, 150).

In short, there is evidence of a second normative belief: an intrinsic duty to take care of the land and to steward natural resources (Olive and Raymond 2010). This norm finds its origin in the thought and work of Leopold, and numerous modern writers – among them American philosophers J. Baird Callicot and Mark Sagoff and legal scholar Eric Freyfogle – have discussed the importance of Leopold's land ethic. If it is difficult to find a book about private property and the environment that does not mention Locke, it is equally surprising if the book does not also discuss (or at least quote) Leopold.

Sagoff (1988) also brings together Leopold and Locke, and adds Pinchot, pointing out that classical liberalism supports "Pinchot's view that individual welfare is what matters in policy choices." Sagoff connects this with the way in which Locke's conceptions of property "might justify the idea that perfectly competitive markets define the best or most valuable uses of land," in contrast to Leopold's assertion that "nature, as an object of reverence, love and respect, itself has a moral worth and therefore should be protected for its own sake" (149).

In Canada the modern-day incarnation of Aldo Leopold is most likely scientist, author, and environmental activist David Suzuki, who has been tapping into, and advocating for, many of Leopold's ideals for the past forty years. Suzuki has captured the land ethic through what he calls "the sacred balance." From Suzuki's perspective, human beings are part of the biotic community and must find a way to live in balance with it. Similar to Leopold's acknowledgment that human beings are part of the same community as the land, Suzuki writes that "land denotes places or context – it means the nation or the region we belong to, as well as the part of it that belongs to us; it is also a place of safety – we long for dry land, we look for a landing place" (2007, 116). Suzuki thus invokes Leopold's claim that "a land ethic changes the role of Homo sapiens from conqueror of the land-community to plan member and citizen of it" (1949, 204).

We thus have two separate norms: the Lockean norm of private property and the Leopoldian norm of stewardship. Often, as with the ESA, they are in conflict. Those who possess a conservation and sustainable development ethic akin to Pinchot's often align with those who argue for the protection of property rights. Those who argue for stewardship, cooperative management, and regulation often support Leopold's land ethic. In the literature on the environment and private property this creates "a mythical fixed pie" (Bazerman 1983) in which Lockeans and Leopoldians make completing claims on a single parcel of land.

When Property and Conservation Collide

In hindsight it is clear that the snail darter changed everything. The Committee on Endangered Species' refusal to grant an exemption to the

Tellico Dam woke the American public to the power of the ESA. The public perception of the law changed, and it "became clear that protecting species would not in all cases be a cost-free proposition" (Easley et al. 2001, 24). The environmental opposition movement, if one may call it that, started to gain momentum in the late 1970s and early 1980s in the western states, where a tradition of opposition to federal authority dates back to the nineteenth century. Ronald Reagan was elected president in 1980 as part of the "widespread anti-regulatory sentiment" in the country. Reagan called himself a "Sagebrush Rebel," and promised a "Sagebrush solution" to the nation's environmental problems (Easley et al. 2001, 24; see also Graf 1990). By this he meant devolving federal power to the states and reining in the power of the Bureau of Land Management in the West. As part of this plan Reagan appointed James Watt as secretary of the interior because of Watt's opposition to the environmental movement. Watt was able to halt ESA implementation and enforcement almost completely. In Reagan's first year as president, not a single species was added to the ESA list (Easley et al. 2001).

In 1988, at the end of Reagan's second term, the country witnessed the birth of the "wise use" movement, where some Americans began to target the ESA as an infringement of their intrinsic right to property. The movement's focus is the "promotion of a wise-use alternative" to "the radical, restrictive focus of mainstream environmental policy," which illegitimately fosters "an anti-property and anti-people focus" (Jacobs 1998, 31). More cynically, the movement's mission has been summarized as "whatever mainstream environmentalists support, wise-users oppose" (Elmendorf 2003, 447).

The movement has continued to gain in popularity, particularly in the West, and has succeeded in reining in a number of environmental regulations. Its goals include opening more public lands to commercial mineral and energy production and rewriting the ESA to weaken it substantially. In 1993, for example, the coalition attempted to have the act amended to ensure financial compensation to a landowner for any government action that decreased property value, arguing that landowners should be compensated for the public use of private property (Jacobs 1998).

The Reagan era passed, however, and in the 1990s land and private property rights once again took centre stage in ESA politics – but this time "wise use" arguments would not win the day. The US Supreme Court's 1995 decision in *Babbitt v. Sweet Home* upheld the ESA's version of "take," concluding that it was reasonable for the regulatory definition of harm to include habitat modification. These conceptions of "harm" and "take" have allowed environmental activists success-fully to sue private commercial landowners[17] for altering habitat, as in the case of the spotted owl in California. These court cases have played out on the assumption that "society as a whole has a collective property right to biological diversity, where ever it is found" (Elmendorf 2003, 456; see also Farrier 1995). Landowners, in other words, are not the true owners of biodiversity, since that is a public good. This gives the public claim to the stewardship of the land, regardless of the property regime in place. It is a battle of rights in which the ESA has become the "front line in the conflict between advocates of private property rights and activists promoting the common good" (Parkhurst and Shogren 2003, 1099).

It is important to understand, however, that the ESA is not techni-cally a land-use law at all, even though that is how many landowners and some scholars have come to understand it (see, for example, Sax 1983). Such an interpretation is not without good reason, since each list-ing under the act includes the protection not only of the species but also of its habitat, and a landowner cannot destroy the habitat of an endan-gered species. With almost five hundred species now listed with critical habitat in the act, this amounts to a lot of land.[18] It is also a difficult real-ity for some US landowners, for whom the ESA is a violation of the Lockean norm of private property.

The confrontation between the law and private property is a big part of the reason Congress has been deadlocked over ESA reauthorization since 1992, when the law officially expired. Congress continues to re-new the act on a yearly basis, but it has yet to make a final decision about its future. The policy's political story since 1990 had been about flexibility and certainty, in an attempt to reconcile conservation with economic development (Scott et al. 2006). Politicians and environmen-talists, as well as lawyers and economists, are trying to create an ESA for the future that will be flexible enough to work with landowners and developers, while making real headway towards species recovery.

Numerous attempts have been made to reform the ESA. For exam-ple, when the Republicans gained control of both the House and the Senate as a result of the 1994 mid-term elections, one of their announced goals was to revamp and significantly weaken the ESA by decreasing its tight grip on landowners' behaviour (Doremus 2006). Of particular importance to the ESA story is Dirk Kempthorne, a Republican senator from Idaho from 1993 to 1999 and who served as governor of Idaho from 1999 to 2006 before becoming secretary of the interior in the George W. Bush administration. Kempthorne made it no secret that he was not a friend of the ESA, and as a senator introduced Bill S.1364, the Endangered Species Conservation Act of 1995, which together with a companion bill in the House of Representatives, sought unsuccessfully to redefine "endangered," "threatened," and "critical habitat" so as to render them almost be ineffectual in the legislation and far removed from private property issues (Powledge 2009).

Through a combination of environmental and religious groups and aggressive executive branch efforts under President Bill Clinton, the ESA survived the Republican-dominated Congress (Doremus 2006), but attempts to redefine the act came again during the George W. Bush administration. Most of the proposed legislation was championed by Republican leaders from western states who promised to strengthen the use of science[19] when determining critical habitat[20] and to ensure fairer treatment of property owners (Davis, Scott, and Goble 2006). For example, in October 2007 the Senate Committee on Finance considered a bill (S.2242) that included amendments to the Internal Revenue Code to provide a tax credit to individuals who enter into agreements to protect habitat for endangered species. Similar proposals have been floating around for the past several years, with many politicians seeming to favour economic incentives as a way to appease landowners (and voters).

In April 2007 the Bush administration attempted to weaken the ESA without going through Congress. A ninety-page Interior Department proposal included limiting the number of protected species and the acreage of habitat preserved for them, as well as shifting power and funds from the federal government to the states, a move that would have granted local officials veto power over which plants and animals would be protected (Knickerbocker 2007, 7). Democrats and environmental lobbyists were quick to attack the document, which has since disappeared from the political radar. The listing of endangered species nevertheless slowed considerably during the Bush administration; as Knickerbocker (2007, 7) noted, "it's a fraction of the number his father made in four years (58 new listings compared with 231 by the senior Bush), and most of those were court ordered." Moreover, new funding for the protection of species was cut significantly during the Bush presidency.

Despite reduced listings, the ESA and endangered species are often featured in newspaper articles and mainstream media. Most popular are articles about lawsuits, disgruntled developers, unhappy landowners, and political confrontations. Recently the species most often featured have been the bald eagle, the grey wolf, and the polar bear. Even a cursory review of the roughly 250 articles published in 2011 and 2012 in major US newspapers reveals the most common storyline: environmentalists versus developers/landowners. For example, in February 2008, when grey wolves were taken off the ESA (due to recovery), environmental groups were reportedly "dismayed by the decision, calling it shortsighted and a political concession to ranching and hunting interests" (Abdollah 2008, A17). There was concern that delisting the wolves so quickly would lead to their demise as ranchers and hunters opened hunting season with a vengeance. Thus, after environmentalists sued the government in 2011, a federal court judge reauthorized the listing of the wolves in parts of Montana (federal lands and parks). Immediately following this decision, Montana's governor Brian Schweitzer encouraged ranchers and hunters to kill endangered wolves that prey on livestock in direct defiance of the legal protections. He also advocated for USFWS and park rangers to kill wolves that stalk elk herds (Zuckerman 2011).

Adding to media attention on the ESA, a scandal surfaced in November 2007 when the USFWS revised seven decisions on species status after concluding that a Bush administration appointee "may have improperly influenced" listing decisions and "overruled agency scientists' recommendations" (Eilperin 2007, A03). In March 2007 the official in question, Julie MacDonald, resigned after USFWS employees complained that she had "bullied, insulted, and harassed the professional staff ... to change documents and alter biological reporting" (Knickerbocker 2007, 7). The episode was "a blemish ... on the scientific integrity" of the USFWS, according to H. Dale Hall, the USFWS director (Eilperin 2007, A03). In 2005 the Union of Concerned Scientists released the results of a survey of 450 USFWS scientists, two-thirds of whom said they knew of cases where Interior Department political appointees had interfered with scientific reports and decisions; 84 said they had been ordered to remove or change technical information from scientific documents (Knickerbocker 2007).

When Barack Obama was elected president in 2008, environmentalists undoubtedly breathed a sigh of relief. In his first four years in office, however, very little had changed in the politics of the ESA. The Obama administration has cleared surprisingly few species – just 59; in contrast, the previous Democratic president, Bill Clinton, declared 522 species during his eight years in office, while George W. Bush saw only 62 species listed in his two terms (Harkinson 2011). While 251 species are waiting on a final decision, the Obama administration is actually proposing to cut the USFWS budget by 5 per cent or $20.9 million (Harkinson 2011).

The shared "mythical fixed pie" (Bazerman 1983) discourse that permeates scholarly literature and media accounts about the ESA attempts to solidify actors as competitors. The myth of the fixed pie leads to a "failure of negotiators to find mutually beneficial trades as a result of the myth that what is good for one party is bad for another" (Hoffman et al. 2002, 830). Often, the literature sets up debates with environmentalists on one side and landowners on the other. For example, in his critique of the ESA, Colburn (2005, 447) claims that "the high stakes of virtually all ESA decisions drive participants to consistently extreme, strategic positions. No disputant has a real incentive to trust and cooperate with their opponent." The critique assumes that "participants" are "opponents," a type of discourse that reinforces the myth that environmentalists think "no tree should ever be cut in a national forest, whereas landowners take the view that no one has the right to tell what can be done on their land" (Hoffman et al. 2002, 831). This is Muir against Pinchot, or even Leopold against Locke. The story is as old as America itself.

Compromise is made problematic from the outset by establishing the scenario as zero-sum. There is no doubt that the ESA is a conflict-ridden policy, and that at least some participants view the conflict as "us against them." The history of the ESA shows that media, politicians, and scholars alike often paint the conflict as insoluble, focusing on the most extreme views on either side. In this discourse, everyone loses. But is there a way out? How can the ESA move beyond the conflict? Is the conflict real or has too much attention been given to conflict-ridden cases?

Collision in Canada

Private property and endangered species conservation have not collided in Canada to the same extent as in the United States. This is largely because of the "negative lessons" legislators drew from the American ESA experience during the development of SARA in Canada. Illical and Harrison (2007, 388) argue that Canadian parliamentarians purposely avoided regulation of private property because the "US Endangered Species Act cast a large shadow." By invoking stewardship norms and avoiding private property, Canada has yet to posit a Locke v. Leopold dichotomy. But the fact that Canada did not regulate property might suggest that Locke has already won the debate and forced government to stay off the land.

In introducing the bill in the House of Commons, its sponsor, environment minister David Anderson, stated that "the proposed bill will cover all birds, fish, mammals, plants or insects as being at risk nationally. These species and their critical habitats will be protected whether they are on federal, provincial, territorial or *privately owned land*, in the air or in the water" (Anderson 2001). Thus, it is evident that the law was originally intended to apply to private property. Anderson anticipated opposition from the outset, and went on to argue that

> anecdotal evidence on severe economic losses by landowners in the US because of the American endangered species act has generated concern and fear in some parts of Canada. Let me assure the House that the proposed Canadian species at risk act is fundamentally different ... while it does give the government the power to protect endangered species and their critical habitat on private lands, we have gone a long way to meeting the concerns of landowners. (Anderson 2001)

The minister was referring to the past thirty-five years of debate and disagreement on the ESA. As negative lessons started to sink in, however, the regulation of private property was taken out of the bill. For example, during debate in the House, Bob Mills, environment critic for the Official Opposition party, the right-wing Conservative Alliance,[21] suggested that Canada should learn from America's mistakes and "have the landowners on side." He argued that "we cannot expect landowners to absorb all of the cost of protecting something that 100% of us want to protect" (Mills 2001). Similarly, Joe Comartin of the left-wing New Democratic Party declared that "landowners must be assured that they are not facing personal losses if a species is designated on their property" (Comartin 2001). Jon Herron of the centre-right Progressive Conservative Party also agreed that "it is imperative to encourage, recognize and reward stewardship by offering more carrots and resorting to fewer sticks" (Herron 2001). Numerous politicians felt strongly that the ESA approach was not ideal because it was unfair to landowners.

Through an analysis of House of Commons and Senate hearings, Illical and Harrison show that business and agricultural witnesses who referenced the ESA during their testimony were unanimously critical of the US approach and thought that if SARA mimicked the ESA it would lead to a "loss of jobs, decline in land values, and excessive litigation" (2007, 388). During the final rounds of debate before the passage of SARA, even the environment minister had changed his regulatory tune, contrasting the "Canadian, co-operative approach" with the US confrontational "them versus us" approach (Duffy 2000).

By the time the bill reached the Senate in October 2002, it was clear that SARA's strategy "depends upon an effective federal-provincial-territorial working relationship" wherein stewardship is the cornerstone of protection on private lands (Banks 2002). Senator Mira Spivak of the moderate-centrist Liberal Party, who opposed the bill, acknowledged how the House had changed the bill from one that protected all species on all land to one that protected those species who "have, by chance, made their way to federal lands – about 5% of our country." She argued that "this bill imposes no legal obligation on the government to do anything off federal land for any species on the verge of extinction, unless it lives in water or is protected by the Migratory Birds Convention Act" (Spivak 2002). In the end, her complaint that this "will clearly be an ineffectual act" fell mostly on deaf ears; the Senate passed the bill in October 2002 and the law received Royal Assent on 5 June 2003.

In the relatively short history of SARA there has been little in the way of property conflict. As noted in Chapter 3, during the act's five-year review in 2009–10 no private landowners or landowner groups chose to offer testimony to the House of Commons Standing Committee on Environment and Sustainable Development, likely because no private landowners had been adversely affected by SARA since its implementation and the role of private landowners has not yet been fully determined (Gelfand 2009; Olive 2011; Plotkin 2010).

While SARA is based on the principle of "stewardship first," provincial legislation is potentially less kind to private property, as I discuss in Chapter 7 with respect to Ontario's Endangered Species Act. The first piece of post-SARA provincial legislation, it regulates private property in ways similar to the ESA. Other provinces are in the midst of drafting new legislation, and each is facing the issue of how to regulate private property. A collision of private property and habitat might be in the offing if provinces decide to regulate property in the command-and-control style of the ESA.

From Collision to Collaboration

Interestingly, neither the ESA nor SARA defines "stewardship" despite the heavy reliance of each on the concept. No standard or widely accepted definition exists, but after purveying the stewardship literature,

Earl, Curtis, and Allan (2010) conclude that the most commonly invoked and understood notion is that of Bryden and Hart (2000): "stewardship is about looking after something not for oneself, but for another or others." It is not clear if this is what SARA or the ESA intends, but if the intent is similar then we need to know if landowners are willing to look after endangered species for other Canadians and Americans. It could be that landowners are not willing or that they simply are not good stewards. The literature cannot answer these questions adequately because the empirical evidence is lacking, especially in Canada.

That said, we do have numerous empirical studies of farmers and ranchers in the United States (Brook, Zint, and De Young 2003; Erickson and De Young 1992–3; Reading, Clark, and Kellert 1994; Stern 2006; Sullivan et al. 1996; Vogel 1996). By and large these studies suggest, in line with Kellert's extensive work in the field, that landowners have a utilitarian and somewhat negative attitude towards the environment. It is almost assumed in the literature that farmers, particularly western farmers and ranchers, are known for "their individualism, self-reliance, and strong anti-government sentiment" (Inman and Mcleod 2002, 92). Thus, these studies often examine the economic aspects of regulation and conservation, where landowners' material interest in the land is assumed to be at odds with endangered species conservation. For example, in a study of ranchers in the southwestern United States, Opotow and Brook (2003) find that, while ranchers describe themselves as responsible stewards of the land, they consider regulatory burdens of conservation unfair and tend to have a negative attitude towards the federal government. Similarly, Hoiberg and Bultena (1981) show that farmers in Iowa who distrust the government are most likely to oppose government regulation.

Unfortunately, some studies do not link attitudes towards private property with those towards stewardship or environmental decision making, leading them to conclude, for example, that, "if people believe in private property rights, they are likely to be hostile to outside intervention on land management issues" (Brooks, Zint, and De Young 2003; see also Napier and Camboni 1988; Reading, Clark, and Kellert 1994). Although farmers are often depicted as encompassing American values of rugged individualism and self-sufficiency, Peterson (1991) challenges this idea by illustrating that farmers consider themselves to be both stewards with a duty to care for the land and pioneers or frontiersmen with a responsibility to control the land. Picking up on this line of argument, Sullivan et al. (1996) suggest two distinct yet conflicting streams of thought regarding agriculture. The first, they argue, is "rooted in

Thomas Jefferson's concept of a stable democracy of yeoman farmers," while the second questions the ethics of gaining dominion over nature. The latter was "initiated by de Tocqueville and Cooper, justified by Darwin, articulated poetically by the transcendentalists, and refined to a science by Aldo Leopold" (124). Through a comparative study of organic and non-organic farmers, Sullivan et al. conclude that "no single pattern of beliefs characterizes the farmers," and "we are left with a tension at the level of individual farmers that mirrors the broader cultural and philosophical debate over the interaction of environmental and agricultural values and beliefs" (140).

In a study documenting the complex and varying perceptions of private property by landowners, Jackson-Smith, Kreuter, and Krannich (2005) find that rural ranchers and farmers view increasingly restrictive land-use rules as an attack on their rights. Just over half of the landowners surveyed felt strongly that their rights to property were "absolute" and should not be constrained by society or government. This is a reflection of Locke's influence. The authors also find, however, that landowners felt a "stewardship obligation based on a desire to care for the land and leave it in better shape than when they acquired it" (596). A surprisingly high proportion of landowners appeared "ready to balance their own individual freedoms against the impacts of their actions on the greater good of society" (606). In short, without relinquishing their rights to property, landowners are open to the idea of conserving the land and endangered species.

Conclusion

When Bruce Babbitt, US secretary of the interior from 1993 to 2001, declared the peregrine falcon recovered, he exclaimed, "[t]he Endangered Species Act is working. It's a part of our American spirit and heritage" (Vaughn 2011, 257). That heritage dates back to the beginning of the twentieth century, when President Theodore Roosevelt and Prime Minister Wilfrid Laurier oversaw civil servants such as Muir, Pinchot, Sifton, and Douglas. The desire to create national parks and conserve tracts of land for forestry wove itself into the national fabric of both the United States and Canada. It was also during this period that the governments of both countries looked across their shared border and began an era of conservation diplomacy.[22] Roosevelt said, "it is evident that natural resources are not limited by the boundary lines which separate nations, and that the need for conserving them upon this continent is as wide as the area upon which they exist." This is still true today. But in the twenty-first century there is not much diplomacy for biodiversity, even though citizens of both countries look to the same spirit and heritage of private property as an individual right and stewardship as the "right thing" to do because it "preserves the integrity, stability and beauty of the biotic community" (Leopold 1949).

The existence of these two norms, or widely shared values, has caused tensions in the policy and politics of the US Endangered Species Act and, to a lesser extent, the Canadian Species at Risk Act. For the past forty years US lawmakers, developers, landowners, and environmentalists have been pulling the ESA in different directions. The result has been an ebb and flow of protection of species and their habitat. Over time, the law has loosened its grip on private property and the use of incentives and compensation for landowners has become more commonplace. The spirit of stewardship and the moral responsibility lawmakers felt is still present and carried on through the work of contemporary activists and scholars. This spirit surfaced in Canada in 2002 when lawmakers recognized the intrinsic value of non-human species and created SARA. Since that law does not regulate private property, or violate the Lockean norm of absolute ownership, less confrontation and fewer lawsuits have taken place in Canada.

One major difficulty of assessing the success of both the ESA and SARA is the lack of empirical data on landowners' ideas and beliefs about private property as opposed to conservation and government regulation. A great deal is known about the views of western US farmers and ranchers, but positing the economic self-interest of landowners against the conservation of endangered species is too easy a dichotomy. As I show in the following chapters, the Lockean norm of private property is prevalent among landowners – more so than a social or instrumental notion of property – but this reality is not incongruent with the existence of stewardship.

Czech and Krausman (2001, 139) argue that "there will be no easy legal solution to the ESA-property rights conflict." This might well be true, but it certainly will be true if landowners' knowledge, attitudes, and values are understudied and potentially misunderstood. The implication of coexisting values is that public policy can work if a balance can be found between developing the stewardship muscle and respecting the property norm. But does stewardship really exist? Are there affirmative motivations for cooperation and stewardship?

6 Indiana, Utah, and Saskatchewan Case Studies

Urban landowners are underappreciated in the endangered species conservation literature. In this chapter I present three case studies that I conducted of urban and suburban landowners' attitudes towards conservation, private property, and government regulation. Their attitudes are important because urbanites represent the voting majority and because endangered species increasingly are appearing in urban areas. Patterns of ownership are shifting as family farms dwindle and urbanization increases. The result is that endangered species no longer live just on farms and ranches, but also on a variety of land parcels, including small, single-family parcels. In fact, 22 per cent of endangered species in the United States live in urban areas, which are only 8.4 per cent of the US landscape but where half of all Americans live (Brosi, Daily, and Davis 2006; Schwartz, Jurjavcic, and O'Brien 2002). As Jacobs argues, "America is changing. As it changes, ownership changes. We are becoming a more (sub)urban and less rural nation" (1998, 37). Engaging only ranchers and farmers in endangered species conservation is thus insufficient. Without the input and voices of the full range of property owners, the "discourse of environmental policy lacks vigor and depth" (Peterson and Horton 1995, 147), particularly as there is good reason to believe that the values of people living in suburban areas differ from those of people who make a living off the land (Jackson-Smith, Kreuter, and Krannich 2005).

The first case study involves a conservation management area for the endangered Indiana brown bat where, in 2007, I and my colleague Leigh Raymond conducted twenty-two interviews with landowners. The second case study comes from a rapidly growing suburban area in Utah where the endangered desert tortoise makes its home. There,

I interviewed thirty-five landowners. The third case study occurs in the prairie province of Saskatchewan, which does not have stand-alone species-at-risk legislation. In 2011 I surveyed 1,000 registered voters by mail in the province's four largest cities.

These are "hard cases" for conservation. I specifically selected areas of the United States and Canada that are not especially liberal politically or obviously environmentally conscious (like the West Coast). Simply arguing that citizens and landowners in those states or provinces care about endangered species and are willing to steward private lands would not be an adequate response to the "wise use" movement or other public opposition to the ESA or SARA. Moreover, I did not choose as cases charismatic creatures to which individuals might attach themselves emotionally and wish to conserve at high cost. Instead, the landowners in these cases who were willing to steward their land indicate a deeper commitment to biodiversity. I discovered that, in all three places, both John Locke and Aldo Leopold appear to have influenced individual conceptions of property and stewardship. Conservation policy in both Canada and the United States needs to acknowledge the tension between these two norms and to try to exploit the stewardship potential while working within the bounds of established property norms. The challenge will be not only to work bilaterally to conserve species and ecosystems, but also to work with the diverse set of landowners who own the habitat where more and more endangered species live.

Indiana

In 1991 the Indianapolis International Airport Authority (IAA) began planning an expansion. The land eyed for the new United Airlines Center, however, was home to the Indiana bat (*Myotis sodalis*), listed since 1967 as an endangered species.[23] In compliance with the Clean Water Act and the ESA, the Airport Authority agreed to create for the bat a Conservation Management Area (CMA) that is one of the largest mitigation and private conservation areas in central Indiana. The tract is 1,890 acres of land and water, 23 per cent of which is forested wetland for Indiana bat habitat, 16 per cent is existing bat habitat to be preserved, 12 per cent is buffer areas, 17 per cent is airport-owned parcels (including barns and hayfields), and the remaining 33 per cent is privately owned (American Consulting 2002). Since 1991 the IAA has implemented a program to purchase and preserve bat habitat within the

CMA that has given the area the feel of a wildlife preserve: in my dozen or so visits to the CMA I was always surprised by the lush green beauty of the place.

In the Western world, especially in pop culture, the uncharismatic bat is too often associated with vampires, witches, and the infamous antics of Ozzy Osborne. The Bible refers to the bat, among other "unclean" animals, as an "abomination" (Leviticus 11: 13–20). The Indiana bat hibernates throughout the US Midwest (Kentucky, Indiana, Illinois, and Missouri) from October to April. During the summer, the bat lives in specific areas, including near the Indianapolis airport, where it can roost and forage. Bats are usually found in trees with thick bark, such as shagbark hickory trees, that have recently died and are suitable for roosting (predominantly under loose slabs of bark). Roost trees tend to be large trees in shady areas close to a water source, such as a river or a creek. From 1992 to 1996 the IAA built and monitored more than three thousand bat houses in the CMA, and through studies with Indiana University, more than seven hundred were observed using the structures. In the fall of 2007, I co-conducted a study of attitudes towards endangered species conservation in a sample of twenty-two private property owners drawn from the Indiana bat's CMA (see Raymond and Olive 2008).[24]

Utah

The desert tortoise, one of only four remaining tortoise species in North America, inhabits areas of California, Arizona, and southwestern Utah. It is arguably the most charismatic of the three species in these case studies. Most Americans and Canadians are probably familiar with the fable of the "tortoise and hare," and might consider the creature to be patient and wise. To Native Americans, tortoises are sacred creatures that symbolize the Earth. Reptiles, however, are not favoured species (Czech and Krausman 2001); drivers of all-terrain vehicles and automobiles often run over the tortoises intentionally. Tortoises are not cuddly or especially cute, and serve no immediate purpose for human beings. They are the kind of creature that an individual would steward for unselfish reasons.

The desert tortoise has a long life span, up to fifty years, and is slow to adapt to change. Its population has been dwindling rapidly since the 1980s, and the USFWS listed the creature as threatened in 1990. Southwest Utah, however, is one of the fastest-growing areas of the country, and its rapid urbanization is wreaking havoc on the tortoise. In 1996 Washington County created a twenty-year countywide Habitat Conservation Plan (HCP) for the tortoise. Under the HCP, about 1,500 acres of habitat have been legally cleared of tortoises (by relocating them to a tortoise reserve) and are in various stages of commercial development. A total of 161 tortoises have been legally "taken" (Owen 2000). The HCP has established a 62,000-acre reserve area known as the Red Cliffs Desert Reserve, but less than two-thirds of the land in the larger HCP is federally owned, since it also includes the communities of Hurricane, St George, and Washington City.

As part of the American West, Utah and its farmers and ranchers have been the focus of numerous landowner studies. Kreuter et al. (2006) find that farmers and ranchers in the state generally disagree with being required to provide habitat for threatened or endangered species without receiving compensation. Jackson-Smith, Kreuter, and Krannich, in a study of Texas and Utah ranchers, note that most people "assume that virtually all private property owners – particularly landowners in the Western states – have similar perspectives regarding the importance of private property; that is, they favor strong protection of private property rights" (2005, 588). What the authors find, however, is less stringent attitudes about private property among Utah ranchers than among those in Texas. Recent books such as *American West at Risk* (Wilshire, Nielson, and Hazlett 2008) also focus on land-use battles and conservation problems in states like Utah, but no published scholarly studies to date, save for my own prior work (see Olive and Raymond 2010), have focused on non-agricultural landowners in that state. How these landowners think and feel about conservation on property used for residential and recreational purposes is virtually unknown.

Beyond its contribution to the diversity of landowner studies, part of what makes Utah an interesting sampling location is that the long history of western alienation makes the state fertile ground for the "wise use" movement. In Utah, federal agencies manage two of every three acres of land – the most anywhere in the country except Nevada and Alaska. And despite the large Red Cliffs Tortoise reserve, which sits on Bureau of Land Management property, there has been no shortage of battles between the tortoise and developers who would like to use that land for new subdivisions and commercial lots. For example, there is draft legislation to authorize the construction of a freeway by-pass as well as water developments in the reserve. Environmentalists, the USFWS, the oil and gas industry, and the Bureau are also caught up in arguments over the endangered prairie dog and property development. If one expected animosity towards government regulation of private property anywhere, it would be in Utah. In an attempt to understand the political and regulatory context of the case, I interviewed bureaucrats in the state.[25] Although obtaining a sample of landowners in Utah was more difficult than in Indiana,[26] in the end I interviewed, either directly or by phone, thirty-five private landowners in a designated habitat area for the tortoise.[27]

Saskatchewan

Saskatchewan is covered mostly by boreal forest in the north and grassland prairie in the south, and has a population of just over one million people, residing mostly in the southern part of the province. The major industries are agriculture, mining (potash and uranium), forestry, and oil and gas. Saskatchewan is an excellent case study for species-at-risk policy for three primary reasons.

First, Saskatchewan is one of four provinces with no stand-alone endangered species policy. It is likely that the province will develop such legislation in the upcoming years as part of its commitment via the 1996 federal-provincial-territorial Accord for the Protection of Species at Risk, but it has been slow to move, and there are virtually no independent empirical studies of landowners in the province (see Bruyneel 2010). Saskatchewan has a vast wealth of wildlife and plants that are of critical importance to Canada and the rest of the world. Of particular international interest are birds. The Important Bird Areas (IBA) program, an international effort of more than one hundred countries to identify and conserve bird populations, has identified 597 IBAs in Canada, 53 of them in Saskatchewan (Nature Saskatchewan 2010). Saskatchewan is also home to native grasslands, but only 20 per cent remains, which is wreaking havoc on grassland birds; according to the North American Breeding Bird survey, "grassland birds show the most consistent widespread and steepest decline of any group of birds in North America" (Nature Saskatchewan 2010). One prominent example is the burrowing owl, whose population has declined 93 per cent in the past twenty years, largely due to changes in the prairie landscape that have resulted not just in the disappearance of much prairie grass but also a 40 per cent decline in wetlands (Nature Saskatchewan 2009).

Saskatchewan's 1998 Wildlife Act (S.S. 1998, c. W-13.12) does have some provisions for species at risk. Fifteen species are now covered under the act, although three are already extirpated (the greater prairie chicken, the black-footed ferret,[28] and the plains grizzly bear).[29] The act mandates the protection of these plants and animals from being disturbed, collected, harvested, captured, killed, and exported, but there is no mandatory protection of habitat. Seventy-six SARA-listed species also live in Saskatchewan, but no recovery plans have been created for any of them, even though, "if species do not have a provincial recovery strategy, it is more likely that critical habitat is not being protected" (Wojciechowski et al. 2011). Thus, Saskatchewan's endangered species and their habitat are not being protected effectively by either the province's own Wildlife Act or SARA.

This leads to the second reason Saskatchewan is an important case study – namely, that land in the province is predominately privately owned or managed by those who have leased Crown lands from the province or federal government. In southern Saskatchewan, about 80 per cent of the land is privately managed. This land is mostly farmland – 46 per cent of the province's total land is devoted to crops and pasture, and only 8 per cent to national or provincial parks and wildlife habitat areas. Nature Saskatchewan (2011) correctly points out that "the health of the prairie ecosystem depends on the good stewardship of landowners across Saskatchewan." Even though urban landowners do not take up a lot of space – less than 5 per cent of the province's total land – more than 85 per cent of the population lives in urban areas. The voting power of urban areas thus makes the attitudes of urban landowners and residents important for two reasons: they vote lawmakers into office and they own land that is shared by endangered species. It also means that policy affecting the land and communities of Saskatchewan's rural residents is dictated largely by urban voters.

Finally, Saskatchewan is an important case study because of its demographics. Canada's *4th Report to the UN Convention on Biological Diversity* (Canada 2009a) raises a number of challenges to conservation in Canada, including the country's rapid urbanization. It recognizes that stewardship is an idea more familiar to rural peoples, and notes that

> Canadian society is shifting, and our values are changing simultaneously. Despite our history as a nation of rural communities separated by distance, time and language, we are now a largely urban society highly concentrated along our southern border … Canada's population is also aging. Most of our population growth is due to immigration, primarily to large urban centres in the south. In part as a result of these trends, visitation to

protected areas is in decline in many jurisdictions across the country. These shifts pose new opportunities and challenges. If Canadians do not feel a deep personal connection to their natural world, they won't understand its importance, take the opportunity to experience its beauty or care about its stewardship. This in turn will impoverish not only our natural world but our society. (165)

Saskatchewan has long been an agrarian society, settled mostly by Germans, Ukrainians (longing for a bread basket outside the Russian Empire and later the Soviet Union), British, and French, and before them by Aboriginal and Métis people, who now account for almost 12 per cent of the population (Saskatchewan 2012) and are the fastest-growing demographic in the province. With the recent boom in the province's oil and gas and potash industries, however, Saskatchewan's economy is growing, its demographics are shifting, and the values of its people might be changing.

In winter 2012, I mailed surveys to 250 randomly sampled registered voters in each of Regina, Saskatoon, Moose Jaw, and Swift Current, together with a brief explanatory letter and a self-addressed stamped envelope. I received 369 responses, a 37 per cent rate. Although their attitudes as voters are important, I excluded respondents who lived in a condominium or apartment since they are not responsible for land-management decisions that might affect endangered species.

Together, Saskatchewan, Indiana, and Utah present a new set of land-owner case studies in conservation. The Indiana bat and the desert tortoise are not the poster species of World Wildlife calendars and serve no immediate self-interest of human beings. No specific species is of interest in Saskatchewan since no privately owned habitat is being protected in urban or suburban areas, and those that are in considerable threat of extinction include such unglamorous species as prairie grass, the burrowing owl, and the sage grouse; the province has no charismatic large mammals save the bison, which exists only in National Parks. Thus, in all three cases the species that live on private lands and require stewardship are less popular, less friendly, and perhaps less charitable. In each case, small private landowners in a somewhat politically and socially conservative area of North America would have to be willing to steward species on their own land. The bar might be high, but if landowners prove willing for such species as these, there is hope for almost any creature.[30]

Measuring Attitudes

The interview instrument I designed for the Indiana case study was the template for both the Utah and Saskatchewan studies. My intent was to probe landowners on a number of issues related to private property, conservation, endangered species knowledge, and government regulation. In this book, my focus is predominately on two themes: Lockean attitudes towards property and Leopoldian attitudes towards stewardship – both in the context of willingness to cooperate with public policy. Landowners' affirmative motivations for cooperation, stemming from morality and legitimacy, are shaped by how they feel about private property and about other species. The expectations, or hypotheses, here are, first, that *landowners will consider private property to be more an intrinsic right than an instrumental and changing social right*; and, second, that *landowners will support the stewardship of endangered species*. In fact, I expect the landowner to hold both these somewhat contradictory beliefs. Respondents have multidimensional views of property, and even those whose attitude towards it is Lockean will support stewardship. This is not to argue that the Leopoldian norm is stronger or more prevalent, but to point out that the two norms are not opposites, or even necessarily in conflict. The expectations I present here are in conjunction with those in Chapter 4 – namely, that *landowners will interpret conservation policy as consistent with their idea of legitimacy*; and that *landowners will interpret conservation policy as consistent with their own sense of morals*.

To examine the extent to which landowners support a Lockean conception of private property and to probe their views on the legitimacy of land regulation, I asked six different questions at different points in the interview or survey (see Table 6.1). Three are related and stem from Bromley (2000), who argues that the problem is that, for some Americans, "the idea of land – and property rights – is a static and durable idea," while for others, "property rights are the socially recognized rules of control," and when "social circumstances change, property rights must also change" (30–1). Thus, I asked landowners if they agreed that land is a natural and unchanging absolute right or more a changing and instrumental right. I then asked respondents to place themselves on a continuum between these conceptions of property. I also invited respondents to express their attitudes about the fairness of the regulatory burden, the idea of limitations on property, and their trust in government to protect property.

Table 6.1. Landowners' Attitudes towards Private Property, Indiana, Utah, and Saskatchewan

Question	Location	Agree	Disagree	Don't Know
		(per cent)		
Some people think of private property as a right created by government that can be changed over time according to the changing needs to society. What do you think of this view?	Indiana	28	68	5
	Utah	40	45	15
	Saskatchewan	48	20	32
Some people think of private property as an absolute or "God-given" right that must be respected by a legitimate government. What do you think of this view?	Indiana	64	31	5
	Utah	54	37	9
	Saskatchewan	18	56	26
Do you think it is unfair to expect landowners to bear the cost of protecting endangered species on their property?	Indiana	41	36	23
	Utah	54	23	23
	Saskatchewan	61	18	21
Do you agree that it is okay to set limits on private rights for protection of endangered species?	Indiana	41	27	33
	Utah	67	25	8
Do you trust the government to protect your private property rights?	Indiana	50	50	0
	Utah	72	28	0
	Saskatchewan	n.a.	n.a.	n.a.

Note: Rows do not always add to 100 due to rounding.

Relatedly, I asked landowners in Utah and Saskatchewan about their attitudes towards government regulation (see Table 6.2). The literature on farmers and ranchers suggests that landowners do not want regulation and, moreover, that those who are hostile towards government are likely to reject the idea of federal regulation of private property entirely, even for a public good like biodiversity conservation. Accordingly, I asked respondents if they thought the government should be involved in protecting endangered species, if they knew that the government was making laws to protect endangered species, and if they thought the government should fine landowners who have harmed endangered species on their own private land. The intent of these questions was to elicit attitudes about the legitimacy of the ESA and SARA, and I hoped answers to all nine questions would provide insight into the ways landowners understand private property and government regulation.

Table 6.2. Landowners' Attitudes towards Government Regulation of Private Property,
Indiana, Utah, and Saskatchewan

Question	Location	Yes/Agree	No/ Disagree	Don't Know
			(per cent)	
Are you familiar with the	Indiana	18	82	0
Endangered Species Act/Species	Utah	29	71	0
at Risk Act?	Saskatchewan	22	64	14
Do you think that the government	Indiana	n.a.	n.a.	n.a.
should be involved in protecting	Utah	78	19	3
endangered species?	Saskatchewan	96	4	0
Do you think the government	Indiana	n.a.	n.a.	n.a.
should make laws to protect	Utah	72	28	0
endangered species?	Saskatchewan	90	4	6
Do you think the government	Indiana	n.a.	n.a.	n.a.
should fine landowners who	Utah	55	36	9
harm endangered species	Saskatchewan	60	19	22
on their own property?				

Note: Rows to do not always add to 100 due to rounding.
n.a.: This question was not asked in Indiana.

To examine the extent of a Leopoldian norm, in Indiana and Utah I asked four separate questions (Table 6.3) and presented a series of hypothetical stewardship activities to test willingness to steward (Table 6.4). In Indiana I asked landowners if they would be willing to build a bat house, plant trees, reduce night lighting, and reduce pesticide use on their property for the sake of bat conservation. In Utah I asked landowners if they would allow the USFWS on their property to monitor the desert tortoise and if they would be willing to avoid soil disruption and reduce pesticide use for the sake of the tortoise. Essentially, I asked landowners how important it was for human beings to protect other species and whether or not they felt it was ever acceptable to allow human action to cause the extinction of other species. Although these questions do not necessarily speak specifically to a duty to care and steward the land, I hoped they would illicit attitudes towards the stewardship of nature and affirmative motivation through morality. Pushing further, I asked landowners to consider whether or not other species had a right to exist. In the interviews, I left this question open ended, to allow for a more reflective answer. As the qualitative data show, landowners did grapple with the question, defining "right" in different

Table 6.3. Landowners' Attitudes towards Leopoldian Conceptions of Species, Indiana, Utah, and Saskatchewan

Question		Agree/ Important	Disagree/ Not Important	Don't Know
	Location		(per cent)	
How important would you	Indiana	55	41	5
say it is for human beings to	Utah	63	29	9
protect endangered species?	Saskatchewan	90	3	7
Some people argue that	Indiana	45	45	10
all species have a right	Utah	54	31	15
to exist. What do you think	Saskatchewan	81	12	7
of this idea?				
Some people argue that	Indiana	40	50	10
sometimes it is okay for	Utah	37	49	15
human activities to result	Saskatchewan	15	71	14
in the extinction of a				
species. What do you				
think of this idea?				
Some people say that	Indiana	77	14	9
private landowners have	Utah	67	17	17
an obligation not to harm	Saskatchewan	69	7	24
endangered species found				
on their property. Do you agree?				

Note: Rows do not always add to 100 due to rounding.

ways. In the surveys I did not leave the question open ended and added no explanation, which might explain the low rate of "don't know" responses, as illustrated above. Lastly, I asked landowners if they thought they had a responsibility to take care of endangered species found on their own land.

All my questions were a way to measure values and attitudes. I did not monitor behaviour, and I examined only "willingness" to carry out specific actions. However, "there is consensus across a broad literature that values are a reasonable way of conceptualizing how we make decisions about the environment" (Dietz, Fitzgerald, and Shwom 2005, 12:31). The idea is that values influence individual decisions; in turn, those decisions shape behaviour, and, ultimately, the environment. A one-to-one correlation is not expected whereby all landowners act on the beliefs they express. Nevertheless, a moderately strong relationship

Table 6.4. Landowners' Willingness to Steward, Indiana and Utah

Action	Yes	No	Don't Know	Total Number
Indiana				
Plant more trees?	15 (67%)	6 (28%)	1 (5%)	22
Reduce night lighting?	7 (35%)	12 (65%)	0 (0%)	19
Reduce pesticides?	5 (27%)	12 (58%)	3 (15%)	20
Build bat house?	5 (25%)	12 (75%)	0 (0%)	19
Utah				
Give the USFWS access to property?	9 (50%)	9 (50%)	0 (0%)	19
Reduce pesticides?	4 (21%)	9 (52%)	5 (27%)	18
Avoid soil disruption?	5 (30%)	13 (70%)	0 (0%)	18

between values and land management decisions is reasonably expected (12:4). What I am examining is the degree to which Lockean and Leopoldian norms influence affirmative motivations for cooperation with conservation policy.

At heart, both the ESA and SARA are about the conservation of other species, and both laws recognize moral, political, and economic reasons for protecting them. I argue that landowners who feel conservation is morally the right course of action will accept the ESA as a morally sound policy. Although such a connection does not prove de facto a willingness to comply or cooperate with the law, it certainly establishes a foundation for such willingness. Individuals probably are more willing to act in accordance with their sense of right and wrong than go beyond their moral limits. Landowners who do not feel that species conservation is a moral question, however, will lack the moral motivation to comply or cooperate.

Landowners who accept the regulation of private property as the morally right course of action will also possess affirmative motivations to comply with the law. Save for a few notable exceptions (such as Jackson-Smith, Kreuter, and Krannich 2005) the scholarly literature and the mainstream media suggest that US landowners have a strict and limited notion of property that stands in opposition to the needs of the ESA. The small amount of research involving predominantly larger landowners suggests that many perceive property to be a natural or God-given right. For them, property is a moral institution, and if they believe the regulation of private property is wrong, they will lack a commitment to the ESA through morality. Yet a landowner might believe that conservation is moral because other species have a right to exist, but also feel that government regulation of private property is wrong because human beings have a God-given right to private property. The larger point, however, is determining if the landowner is willing nevertheless to comply or cooperate with the law. The landowner does not have to believe that conservation and regulation of private property are both moral to have an affirmative motivation to comply, although the combination of both likely would increase such willingness.

Results and Discussion

The Saskatchewan case study has a large sample (369), while the Indiana and Utah samples are much smaller samples (22 and 35, respectively), so a quantitative statistical analysis is not possible. I therefore present qualitative results in the form of frequencies from the interview and surveys as well as quotations from the interviews. I present the cases side-by-side instead of in the aggregate. Although the cases are similar enough – small, non-agricultural landowners in conservative jurisdictions – they are sufficiently distinct that comparison is valuable. I divide the findings into those relating to Locke and private property and those with respect to Leopold and stewardship. I then pull together the themes from the three case studies and suggest policy directions for a new species-at-risk law in Saskatchewan.

Locke and Private Property

In each case fewer than half the respondents agreed that property is an instrumental right that can change as society's needs change. As Table 6.1 shows, only 28 per cent of Indiana landowners agreed with the claim, while 40 per cent in Utah and almost 50 per cent in Saskatchewan did so. In Utah and Indiana more than half (54 and 64 per cent, respectively) agreed with the more Lockean conception of property, that land-ownership is an intrinsic right that stands outside of government. In Saskatchewan, however, 55 per cent of respondents disagreed with that notion and another 26 per cent were not sure what they thought. To both questions – whether property was an intrinsic or an instrumental right – a high percentage in Saskatchewan responded "don't know," perhaps not surprising considering the abstract nature of the concepts. Interviews offered greater opportunity for clarification of the concepts, but even so, only 48 per cent of Saskatchewan respondents agreed with the instrumental Leopoldian concept and only 17 per cent with the more intrinsic Lockean conception. These responses highlight a difference in attitudes in Saskatchewan, Indiana, and Utah; as I discuss below after I present the results from a second Canadian case, they suggest that Canadians might not be the direct descendants of Locke.

In all cases it was possible for a landowner to disagree or agree with both concepts. A possible explanation of this apparent contradiction is that a landowner might feel one is a reflection of reality while the other is a normative statement. For example, a landowner could feel that, although property is an instrumental right in today's society, ideally it should be a Lockean right. During the interviews, when asked if property is an instrumental right, some landowners interpreted that to mean "does property function as an instrumental right in America today." But when asked if property is an intrinsic right, some landowners responded by normatively grasping the idea as their dream for property rights in America. In Utah one landowner said about the absolute notion of property, "I would very much like to support that view of property and if I had a chance to in terms of voting for it, I would … I think it is the way things ought to be." The same landowner agreed that property is an instrumental right because that is how he thinks property functions in society today (Raymond and Olive 2008).

To clarify attitudes towards private property I asked landowners to place themselves on a continuum with the absolute/Lockean notion at one end and the instrumental/Leopoldian notion at the other. In this instance, as Figure 6.1 shows, most Saskatchewan landowners placed themselves towards the Leopoldian end, while most Indiana landowners were towards the Lockean end; perhaps surprisingly, respondents in Utah, the most western state and home to the "wise use" movement, had a slightly more balanced view of property than those in Indiana. Overall, these landowners had diverse conceptions of property, and while there was some support for the more Lockean notion of absolute property, it was not overwhelming and quite lacking in Saskatchewan, where landowners did not seem to agree with either sense of property. This suggests that the Lockean notion is either less prevalent in Canada than in the United States or perhaps less prevalent in a predominately urban area than in the more suburban acreages outside Indianapolis. I pick up this discussion again in Chapter 9 after I present results from Ohio and Ontario. Suffice it to say here that I found only a little support for the expectation that landowners consider property more an intrinsic than an instrumental right.

Figure 6.1. Landowners' Attitudes towards Private Property on a Continuum from an Intrinsic to an Instrumental Right, Indiana, Utah, and Saskatchewan

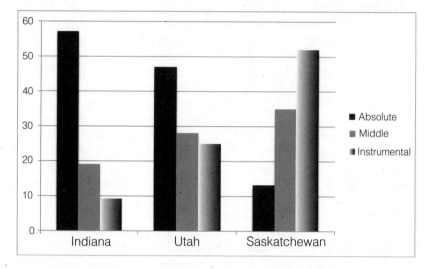

Whether they agreed with an intrinsic notion of property or not, many interviewees in Utah and Indiana drew a connection between property and America and between property and democracy. These connections seem to be deeply entrenched in the US property system. As one landowner in Indiana put it, "that is part of what the US is about itself. The fact that we have the ability to own private property and no one can basically tell you what to do with that property. And that is one of those basic inalienable rights that we have." This was echoed in Utah, where a landowner claimed "this whole country was founded on property rights. That is why they left England to come here." This type of deeply held connection between America as a country and private property is more emblematic of a Lockean norm and more akin to what the literature suggests landowners believe.

Despite their views on private property, however, the respondents in all three cases felt relatively similarly about sharing the burden of endangered species management, with the majority (41 per cent in Indiana, 54 per cent in Utah, and 61 per cent in Saskatchewan) believing it is unfair to expect them to shoulder the cost of endangered species conservation. One Indiana landowner felt that anything above his taxes would be asking too much. Only 18 per cent of respondents in Saskatchewan thought it is potentially fair for landowners to bear the cost, even though they also rejected the Lockean notion and accepted that property is a social right. This implies that compensation or cost-sharing programs might be necessary for some landowners. But the question also focuses on the financial costs of conservation, where there is often little or no cost associated with voluntary stewardship. There is a middle ground between doing nothing for free and paying thousands for conservation.

For example, when asked if they felt comfortable with the government's placing limitations on their land and property rights for the sake of conservation, 67 per cent of respondents in Utah and 41 per cent in Indiana were willing to accept some type of limit on what they could do with their property for the sake of conservation. In Indiana 33 per cent of respondents were not sure how they felt about this question, many saying it was too abstract. It was common to hear a landowner say "the government should tell me what not to do to hurt the little turtle and I won't do it anymore" or "I could probably not do this or that, like use pesticides for a month or two, if it would make a difference." But other landowners wanted more certainty: "I would have to know 100% that the limit would help otherwise [the government] can't ask me." So long as the request was not monetary, landowners were willing to accept limits. Such a finding is illustrative of the overall paradox: landowners consider property more an intrinsic right and they also support the stewardship of endangered species. To accept limits on their property rights, landowners want to know that the species is legitimately in danger and that exacting limitations will assist legitimately in its recovery. An affirmative motivation for cooperation with conservation is evident. It mighty not be the only motivation or even the strongest one for compliance and cooperation, but it is present in the decision-making schema of landowners.

Turning to government regulation, it is important to note that the vast majority of respondents were not familiar with federal endangered species policy: only 29 per cent of respondents in Utah and 18 per cent in Indiana knew about the ESA, while only 22 per cent of Saskatchewan respondents had heard of SARA. This is highly telling, and has numerous implications for compliance and cooperation, as I discuss below. It is important here because the series of questions I asked about government regulation should be seen in the context of individuals who do not already realize that their land is regulated, that laws are in place, and that fines are possible. In Saskatchewan, where SARA does not apply to private land, 60 per cent of respondents said they had heard of the provincial Wildlife Act, which in any case does not protect habitat. Moreover, 30 per cent believed the law does not apply to their property but 50 per cent thought that SARA does. This reflects a misunderstanding and general lack of knowledge of endangered species policy.

As Table 6.2 illustrates, support for government involvement in the regulation of conservation was high but it faded when sanctions were introduced. In Saskatchewan and Utah, where landowners were asked if the government should be involved in protecting endangered species, a surprising 96 per cent in Saskatchewan agreed while 78 per cent in Utah did. When asked if the government should make laws to protect species, the support dropped only a few percentage points to 90 per cent and 72 per cent, respectively. In Utah landowners' responses included, "actually I do think it is one of the proper uses of government," "somebody has to," "I don't know how else it would be done or carried out," and "they are the only ones that can." Even factoring in possible response bias, there was still overwhelming support for government involvement in conservation and strong support for conservation laws.

When asked if the government should be able to fine landowners who harm endangered species on their property, only 60 per cent of Saskatchewan respondents and 55 per cent of Utah respondents agreed. Similar to the question about fairness, this result suggests that landowners were hesitant, but not totally unwilling, to accept government regulation of private property for endangered species conservation. At the same time, it is important to keep in mind that more than half of landowners in both cases were willing to accept sanctions for violations of species-at-risk legislation. One Utah landowner said, "if there is a law then there must be consequences," while another claimed that "if you have good laws, then a good citizen ought to obey those laws. And if you don't, there are fines."

Some respondents did feel, however, that punishment for violating conservation laws "is wrong" or "stupid." And landowners were careful to point out that the government should not decide unilaterally to make a law without public input. One respondent said that a law is acceptable "if that is determined by the [democratic] process"; another cautioned that "there needs to be more on the level where the people can voice their opinion too and not just have the government making all decisions." Procedural justice and legitimacy thus are the linchpins of government regulation for these respondents, who would respect laws and sanctions that are created in a democratic and legitimate way.

This is an affirmative motivation through legitimacy for cooperation and compliance.

Overall, respondents expressed attitudes towards private property that suggest a fungible notion of property and a general willingness to accept, sometimes grudgingly, government regulation of property for overall social and environmental well-being. Respondents did not exhibit the hard stance on private property so often depicted in the media and in much of the literature. Instead, like Jackson-Smith, Kreuter, and Krannich (2005) and demonstrated in earlier work (Olive and Raymond 2010; Raymond and Olive 2008), I found that landowners possess a multidimensional notion of property and are sometimes quite open to government involvement for the greater social good. Only a few respondents placed themselves at the intrinsic end of the continuum, and even most of these remained sympathetic to the instrumental view. Moreover, this less than entirely Lockean concept of private property sets the foundation for landowners' accepting regulation for conservation as appropriate, as the right thing to do because conservation is important, and because social goods must be held in balance with private interests.

Leopold and Stewardship

Even though the Lockean property norm is prevalent and the regulation of property somewhat unpopular among respondents in Indiana and Utah, acceptance of the need for stewardship is still apparent. In all three case studies the majority of landowners felt that it is important to protect endangered species; in Saskatchewan the number rises to 90 per cent (see Table 6.2), which might suggest a response bias, but even so it is reasonable to assume that most landowners agree it is important for society to protect other species.[31] The reasons landowners felt species protection is important fall into two categories: web-of-life arguments and moral/religious stewardship obligations. According to one Indiana landowner, "the ecology of the planet depends on the cause and effect of animals and insects and it has evolved for millions of years. It has a kind of balance written into the genetic make-up." In the religious dimension, an Indiana property owner said, "I think that is how God made us. I think that ... everyone has a purpose on this earth – every creature." Similarly, a Mormon interviewee in Utah said, "I believe [conservation] is a responsibility because it is what God has asked us to do. My basic core belief is religious."

What is interesting here is that, regardless of their geographic location or religious orientation, most respondents felt that at a basic level it is important for human beings to take care of other species. I did not ask Indiana respondents about their religion, but the state is predominately Protestant. In Utah 63 per cent of interviewees were Mormon, 3 per cent were Catholic, 14 per cent Protestant, and 6 per cent Christian non-denominational; the remaining 14 per cent chose not to answer. In Saskatchewan 42 per cent of respondents were Protestant, 21 per cent Catholic, 1 per cent Mormon, 17 per cent Christian non-denominational, and 19 per cent other or no answer. In neither case could I find a significant correlation between religious affiliation and attitude towards other species. It seems that those who invoke moral reasons for valuing other species come from varied religious backgrounds, with no particular religion expressing stronger views.

Among the 41 per cent of respondents in Indiana and the 29 per cent in Utah who felt conservation is not important, the reasons they gave had other than a moral basis, and often concerned money. Most felt that too much is being spent on conservation – that the cost is too high when there are so many other important problems in society. A Utah landowner admitted, "I don't know that it is important as all the money being used [for conservation]." These respondents did not reject the importance of conservation as a policy goal, but questioned the cost of attaining it. Very few reported feeling that it is not important for human beings to protect other species.

It is somewhat surprising that in all three cases many respondents – 45 per cent of those in Indiana, 54 per cent in Utah, and 81 per cent in Saskatchewan – agreed that other species have a right to exist. One Indiana landowner felt that "certainly all species have a right to exist" and "we shouldn't be killing another off." Carried to its logical conclusion, the implications would be astounding. The idea that a bat or tortoise could have a right to exist is a strong claim, and certainly consistent with Leopold's concept of a biotic community where "we see land as a community to which we belong" and we thus treat it "with love and respect" (1949, ix). Moreover, it is consistent with, and I find support for, the statement in the Newfoundland and Labrador Endangered Species Act that "all species have a right to exist." More respondents supported this idea in Saskatchewan than in the other cases, but it is difficult to know how much weight to give that finding. SARA, unlike the ESA, says Canadians value species for their "intrinsic worth," and at least one provincial law thus far supports other species' right to exist.

Perhaps these policies are picking up a uniquely Canadian attitude – one that differs from the more anthropocentric American valuation of other species. The difference also might be attributable to a variation in urban versus suburban landowners or interview versus survey methodology, among other things. So far, the finding is a new theoretical claim that needs to be tested further.

It is also important to note that numerous respondents did reject the idea of other species' right to existence. Some felt only human beings have a right to exist or that a human right to life should always come before another species' right to life. As one landowner in Utah said, "to say they (other species) have an equal right – a resounding no." Another said, "I don't think of it as a *right.*" In Indiana, a landowner felt that other species are important, but a right is "something only a human can have," such that a human right to life would always trump another species' right.

According to interview and survey respondents, it is not acceptable for human activities to result in the extinction of another species. In Indiana 50 per cent rejected extinction, in Utah 49 per cent did so, as did as many as 71 per cent of respondents in Saskatchewan. One property owner in Utah replied, "if one species is eliminated and you let it happen, then where do you draw the line? And pretty soon we are the only things living here on earth." Another adamantly felt that no "rational person wants to see a species eliminated." Some landowners did feel that extinction could be natural or unavoidable as well as sometimes justifiable for human needs. And some felt that not every single species is important. Three landowners in Saskatchewan wrote on their survey "mosquitoes?" and "virus?" suggesting that they would accept the extinction of those species. Another respondent wrote that "self-defense" would justify the extinction of another species. This mixed response suggests that landowners accept the importance of conservation, but fewer are willing to grant other species the right to exist and would view extinction as justifiable if caused by human activity.

Still, the idea that landowners have an obligation to avoid harming species found on their own property resonated with respondents: in Indiana 77 per cent and in Utah 67 per cent agreed with the proposition. In Saskatchewan – to test the kind of provincial policy respondents might support – I worded the question differently, and asked respondents if farmers and ranchers have an obligation not to harm species found on their property. Thus, for many respondents the object of the question was not themselves as landowners but other people. Nevertheless the response was similar to those in Utah and Indiana, with 74 per cent acknowledging the responsibility.

We know from the literature that farmers consider themselves to be stewards with a duty to care for the land. It appears that most urban and suburban landowners feel similarly: an Indiana landowner simply said, "I would feel that responsibility." Indiana is interesting because landowners there were the most Lockean, but 77 per cent still believed there is an obligation not to harm species on one's own property – the very centre of a Leopoldian motivation to conserve an endangered species. It is also another example of conflicting norms: landowners consider property more an intrinsic right *and* they support the stewardship of endangered species. Here the motivation is based more on ethics, as respondents interpreted conservation as consistent with their own sense of morals. This suggests that an affirmative motivation through morality might be at play (along with a myriad other motivations). In all geographical locations, across a range of non-charismatic species, and socio-economic factors, these conservative landowners generally felt that conservation is morally right, which sets the foundation for a moral commitment to comply and cooperate with the law.

In Indiana and Utah, landowners were asked a set of hypothetical questions to test their willingness to carry out certain actions to benefit the endangered bat and tortoise. The law requires none of these actions; all would be voluntary. Perhaps more important, I found that the landowners knew so little about the law that they had no idea what is required. It is true that in Utah landowners are strongly discouraged from disrupting the soil, but this action is not monitored and would not be legally enforced. A developer must have a building permit before starting any project that will disturb the soil, and the permit would state that the land has been checked and cleared of tortoises. The landowner who buys a house is not required by law to do anything for the tortoise beyond paying a 2 per cent property tax per the terms of the Habitat Conservation Plan. It is still illegal, however, for an individual landowner to kill a tortoise outright. In both cases, in effect, small landowners are allowed to alter the species' habitat without any real threat of ramifications because the law is not clear, not monitored, and not enforced.[32]

Of respondents in Indiana, 67 per cent were willing to plant more trees on their property, but only 35 per cent were willing to reduce night lighting, 27 per cent were willing to reduce pesticide use on their property, and only 25 per cent were willing to build a bat house. Such responses suggest that Indiana landowners are unwilling to steward the bat on their own property. Similarly, in Utah, 50 per cent were willing to give the USFWS access to their property to monitor the tortoise, 30 per cent would avoid disrupting the soil in their yard, and only 21 per cent would reduce pesticide use, suggesting that Utah landowners are not willing to help the tortoise on their own land.

Landowners' unwillingness to help these endangered species might signal the lack of a stewardship ethos, or it might be more closely connected to a lack of information or to more mundane reasons such as security (night lighting) or rodent control (pesticides). Since so many landowners do not know about the ESA, it is reasonable to assume they do not know much about the law or the endangered species themselves. Some landowners think they will be fined or arrested if a tortoise or bat is found in their yard. One landowner, wary of giving the USFWS access to his property, said, "What if they find one? Are they going to make my house habitat? Am I going to have to hop over a turtle fence to get into my house?" Many landowners are afraid to report tortoise sightings or do not know how to do so. Some landowners said they would consider calling the police anonymously. This is a problem for tortoise recovery since tortoises are often found dead on the roadways that go through the Red Cliff Reserve, but it could be remedied through education and outreach. Landowners could be taught the proper technique for handling tortoises on the road and be made to feel comfortable calling the USFWS to report a sighting.

All of this is to say that Leopold cannot be dismissed so easily. The intrinsic property norm that respondents in Indiana and, to a lesser extent, in Utah displayed, coupled with a general unwillingness to steward in specific ways, is mediated nonetheless by a desire to take care of the land, either through a felt obligation or a religious responsibility. This too appears to be part of the American norm of property. In Utah a landowner admitted that, "in the end we go back to my religious heritage that says it is really God's land. And we can't take it with us when we go anyway so we are really just stewards." Agreeing, another landowner said, "my basic core belief is religious. I believe it is a responsibility because it is what God has asked us to do." And in Indiana a landowner said, "we are just stewards. This land has been around for millions of years and I'm here for a short time. I have never owned a piece of property that wasn't a better piece of property when I got rid of it than when I got it." America was founded on religious freedoms and private property rights. Today these pillars remain cultural icons.

Even without a religious undertone, many landowners recognized that a wide range of responsibilities follows from owning land. It was not uncommon for a respondent to say, "Well, I think you have a responsibility to take care of land." Responsibilities in Utah and Indiana seemed to centre around three main concepts: maintaining the land (keeping it neat), not abusing the land (avoiding environmental damage), and keeping it safe. This commitment to the land also implies a stewardship ethic similar to that found by Jackson-Smith, Kreuter, and Krannich (2005) among landowners in the American West. It suggests that, even without regulation, landowners want to take care of the land. Thus, intrinsic property views are not irreconcilable with conservation: there is room for both Locke and Leopold on private property.

Although stewardship and responsibility were important to most respondents, some saw government regulation as immoral. One Indiana landowner said, "you pay for it, it is your land and you can use it within the legal system. You can do whatever you choose – build a house on it or let it grow wild, you can do whatever you want on it. It is your property." And a Utah landowner said, "if they [the government] think the species is that important, they need to compensate the landowner. People ought to be paid." Another Utah landowner unintentionally summed up such views by declaring, "I think you should be able to do whatever you want as long as it does not adversely affect someone else." These landowners' attitudes towards government regulation of private property present a challenge for policy makers.

At the same time, not all landowners who thought badly of regulation of private property felt that conservation was also wrong. One Utah landowner opposed to regulation also felt that "we are on this earth and we have dominion over the animals, but we are not supposed to abuse them. We are supposed to take care of them." Another landowner said, "everything has a right to exist," and felt that "all animals do have a purpose in the grand scheme of the way God made the earth." Another, more Lockean, landowner in Indiana said her idea of conservation is "just being good stewards and not deliberately harming [other species]."

These findings might not be as consistent or as neat as scholars and policy makers prefer, but they are evidence of affirmative motivations through legitimacy and morality on the part of landowners. Most of the respondents in these case studies interpreted conservation as consistent with their own sense of morals and as consistent with their idea of legitimacy. Such an interpretation also enabled them to hold the seemingly contradictory positions that property is more an intrinsic right and that stewardship of endangered species (on their own private property) is important. What does this mean? At the most basic level, it means stewardship is possible on private property. It will not always be easy, and landowners will not always cooperate voluntarily, but with education about specific actions they can take to benefit species and assurances that their cooperation now will not be the basis for future regulations or obligations, landowners could surprise everyone.

What does all this mean for North American conservation? It appears that Canadian and American landowners are quite similar, although evidence suggests that Saskatchewan landowners are less Lockean than their counterparts in Utah and Indiana and that Canadians might value the intrinsic worth of species, as outlined by SARA, more than Americans do. But by and large the results suggest that small, non-agricultural landowners have multidimensional views of private property and possess affirmative motivations for cooperation with conservation. It might be necessary, in policy making, to downplay the immorality of regulation that some landowners feel, while boosting the morality of stewardship that almost all landowners share. The key, in both countries, is to encourage and educate landowners to act on their affirmative motivations.

Policy Implications for Saskatchewan

When Saskatchewan creates stand-alone endangered species legislation, as it is likely to do in the next few years, what kind of policy should it implement? It seems clear that the province's urban residents think other species are important. This is a good starting place because it suggests the existence of affirmative motivations for cooperation with conservation. Most urban landowners also seem quite comfortable with the regulation of private property: only 11 per cent felt that property is an absolute right on which government should not infringe. Agricultural landowners might well feel very differently about government regulation of their land, but more research is needed on their attitudes.

What is unclear is how much people in Saskatchewan know about endangered species. Although 60 per cent of respondents had heard of the Wildlife Act, only 22 per cent had heard of SARA. Most were confused about which act applies to their land: 52 per cent incorrectly thought SARA regulates their land. When asked if they could name an endangered species in Saskatchewan, 58 per cent did so, but some misidentified a species – five respondents listed the snowy owl, which is actually thriving in the Saskatchewan wild, and another two listed the red fox, which also occurs in great abundance in the province as elsewhere in Canada and the United States. Not one respondent out of 369 correctly mentioned the endangered prairie grass. Of those who could correctly identify any endangered species (only 48 per cent), 78 per cent listed the burrowing owl, perhaps thanks to the work of the environmental organization Nature Saskatchewan, which for more than a decade has run a campaign called Operation Burrowing Owl to raise awareness of the plight of the bird in the province. Only 42 per cent of respondents were able to identify a reason that species are endangered, but of those who could, 67 per cent correctly thought it was due to habitat loss.

Overall, these results suggest that Saskatchewan landowners are largely both uninformed about policy and unaware of the endangered species around them, the case of the burrowing owl aside. It is encouraging that 60 per cent had heard of the Wildlife Act, but surprising that so few knew about SARA yet falsely believed it applies to their property. This reflects the confusion that bureaucratic overlap can create when people cannot distinguish between the responsibilities of different levels of government in Canada's federal system. In Saskatchewan one could contact a regional Wildlife office or the provincial Ministry of Environment or perhaps the provincial Department of Agriculture (if the landowner is a farmer or rancher) or the federal Environment Canada. Does lack of awareness affect affirmative motivations? If more landowners knew about the species that are in danger, more might be willing to steward and/or accept regulation on their behalf.

Given that affirmative motivations exist and that outreach might increase them, new species-at-risk legislation in Saskatchewan should regulate private property. My findings illustrate that small landowners are quite willing to accept limitations on property – in the form of, say, a temporary ban on pesticide use or on construction – for the sake of conservation. Landowners regard regulation as most legitimate and acceptable when it does not add to their financial burden. Accordingly, if regulators want to increase stewardship activities, society should be prepared to bear their cost. For example, owners of endangered species habitat in Saskatchewan should be reimbursed for the cost of using pesticides or herbicides that do not harm prairie plants. Those who find a burrowing owl on their property should be given the fencing and training necessary to care for the bird through its season in the province.

In advance of regulation, a campaign should be undertaken to inform landowners about endangered species. This would not be easy or inexpensive. Despite Nature Saskatchewan's ten-year campaign, fewer than half of the respondents could identify the burrowing owl as a species at risk in the province. Upon the law's implementation, another education campaign would be needed to inform landowners about the new regulations and ways they can help species at risk voluntarily.

Again, education is important because it can increase affirmative motivations for cooperation. In the long run, voluntary stewardship is the goal, as is clear in both SARA and the National Strategy for Species at Risk. Since Saskatchewan landowners already feel that conservation is the right thing to do – that it aligns with their sense of morals – the purpose of education would be to increase awareness about the protection of species and habitat. Also, landowners must believe that species are legitimately "at risk" if the law is to be successful. The Ontario case, in the next chapter, illustrates that, when landowners believe the government lists species as a way to regulate property, rather than to recover them, backlash and anger can ensue. If landowners understand why a species is endangered and know how to help it, they are more likely to want to steward the species on their property.

Is education an effective way to change attitudes and behaviour? Baruch-Mordo et al. (2011) point out that "little research has been conducted to evaluate whether [education] strategies are achieving their intended goal of altering behavior" among the public with regard to the environment. Their own experimental data evaluating public education and law enforcement in human and black bear conflicts in Colorado suggest that education has little impact on human behaviour. The case of the black bear is an unusual one, however, since most at-risk species pose little threat to human safety. Educating landowners about black bears might not change their attitudes because education cannot eradicate rational fears (see Olive 2011).

In contrast, Van Den Berg, Riley, and Dann (2011) argue that education can increase ecological knowledge, improve wildlife management skills, and increase volunteerism. The authors examine the Michigan Conservation Stewards Program, which includes forty hours of adult education focusing on ecology and ecosystem management. Through a before-and-after survey of participants, the authors illustrate a statistically significant positive knowledge gain after the program, as well as a positive change in attitude towards nature and certain management tools. These findings are consistent with those of similar studies based on programs in Texas and Florida (Bonneau 2003; Main 2004), which suggest that well-designed and extensive educational programs can increase knowledge and awareness as well as alter attitudes about appropriate land-management techniques. Again, education campaigns and programs are neither a fast nor an inexpensive way to reach a policy goal. The broad participation of landowners in such program likely would require the federal and/or provincial government to offer a monetary incentive. As the studies just cited show, however, the payoff from such an investment might be great in terms of future stewardship among those who participate.

In some cases compensation – beyond an incentive for stewardship – would be the only way to ensure compliance by landowners. As Hegel, Gates, and Eslinger (2009, 232) find in their study of human-wildlife conflict, landowners' "willingness to accept the burden of supporting elk as a public trust, or to tolerate the negative impacts of the elk, was very low," which leads them to conclude that "increasing the acceptance capacity of landowners will require objective economic approaches that provide financial rewards and other incentives that increase positive benefits from wildlife on public lands." Their study, however, was based not on at-risk species, but on human-wildlife conflicts – namely, between elk and farmers. Most at-risk species in Saskatchewan, such as the burrowing owl or prairie grass, do not conflict with humans.

The importance of education is highlighted by the Saskatchewan data, which reveal a link between awareness and greater affinity for stewardship. As a proxy for awareness I use the respondents who listed the burrowing owl as an endangered species in the province. The assumption is that those who so identified the owl had read or heard about it. To a certain, unknown, extent, this subset of landowners had received some level of "education" about endangered species in the province. Comparing their attitude to that of landowners who did not correctly identify the owl, one observes a statistically significant difference. As Table 6.5 illustrates, individuals who correctly identified the owl as endangered were more likely to agree that extinction of other species is not acceptable and that government should make conservation laws and enforce those laws with penalties. They were also more likely to have heard of SARA and to agree that farmers have an obligation to protect species found on their own property. The other differences in attitudes displayed in the table are notable, but not statistically significant. The burrowing owl is a SARA-listed species, so it seems reasonable to suppose that those who knew about the owl's status were

Table 6.5. Attitudes of Two Groups of Landowners towards Endangered Species, Saskatchewan

Question	Landowners Who Listed the Burrowing Owl as Endangered	Landowners Who Did Not List the Burrowing Owl as Endangered
	(per cent)	
Agree that it is important to protect other species	97	96
Agree that other species have a right to exist	80	84
Agree that extinction of other species is not okay	78	66*
Agree that it is unfair to expect landowners to bear the costs of conservation	80	76
Agree that the government should be involved in conservation	98	94
Agree that the government should make laws	94	89*
Agree that the government should punish landowners who violate laws	85	72*
Have heard of the Wildlife Act	66	56
Have heard of SARA	31	16*
Agree that farmers have an obligation to protect species	84	67*
Agree that farmers are doing a good job of stewarding the land	47	45

* Denotes significance at the .05 level in a two-tailed chi-square test

more likely to know about SARA, but the direction of the relationship is unknown: respondents might have heard about the owl when being told about SARA or they might have heard about SARA when being told about the owl. It is also not surprising that these respondents were more likely to say that farmers have an obligation to protect endangered species, since the burrowing owl is found predominately on farmland in Saskatchewan. Interestingly, however, they were also more likely to reject extinction and to accept government regulation of property for conservation.

Education is a promising approach because of its potential to increase voluntary stewardship, but this strategy will go only so far. What about other motivations for compliance and cooperation? Market mechanisms are difficult to apply in these cases. It is true that market mechanisms are a clever way to make environmentalism be in the self-interest of owners by using price signals to manipulate behaviour, but it is difficult to find a way to make biodiversity be in the immediate self-interest of landowners. That is to say, if we want people to drive less we can raise the price of gasoline; if we want people to buy fewer bottles of water we can charge more per bottle by adding a "green fee." But what do we do if we want people to conserve an owl? This is not an easy behaviour to manipulate. Analogy suggests that, if we want landowners to stop destroying habitat by building decks, putting in pools, or removing trees, we likely need to pay them to stop.

Pulling together the case studies presented here, I suggest that Saskatchewan create species-at-risk legislation with a regulatory hammer large enough to be a real threat, but small enough to be useful – the ESA's hammer is so large that penalties are rarely handed out. The ideal would be smaller, gradual sanctions, akin to speeding fines that increase as speed increases. Regardless of the size of the hammer, the leading policy approach should be outreach and a focus on increasing affirmative motivations for stewardship. The law should also have a compensation schema and an incentive strategy to entice larger landowners such as farmers, who would face a direct economic loss because of their ownership of critical habitat. The public at large would need to be educated about the importance of biodiversity to justify the allocation of taxpayers' money for compensation and incentive funds. Biodiversity is a public good; as such, the public should expect to pay for conserving it. We will depend on landowners to steward species voluntarily, and we must be willing to meet landowners halfway when their material interests are at stake.

Conclusion

The idea of conserving a public good on private lands is neither unfamiliar nor unacceptable to samples of landowners in Indiana, Utah, and Saskatchewan. Based on 22 interviews in Indiana, 35 interviews in Utah, and 369 survey responses in Saskatchewan, I conclude that there is support for three of my four expectations (see Table 6.6 for a summary of my case findings). Regarding the first two – expectations about

Table 6.6. Summary of Case Findings, Indiana, Utah, and Saskatchewan

Main Conclusion	Indiana	Utah	Saskatchewan
Respondents know about endangered species?	no	no	no
Respondents know about endangered species legislation?	no	no	no
Respondents have a Lockean view of property?	yes	yes	no
Respondents accept government involvement in conservation?	yes	yes	yes
Respondents possess affirmative motivations for cooperation with stewardship via morality?	yes	yes	yes
Respondents possess affirmative motivations for cooperation with stewardship via legitimacy?	yes	yes	yes

compliance and cooperation – I find that respondents had affirmative motivations: they interpreted conservation as consistent with both their sense of morals and their idea of legitimacy. Most thought steward-ship or regulation is moral; fewer accepted regulation as legitimate. This is not to say that all landowners act on these motivations or that other motivations are less important. The point is only to highlight the existence of such attitudes. The next step for conservation will be to design policy that elicits these motivations. If the ESA and SARA want to rely upon voluntary stewardship, steps must be put in place to foster these motivations.

Regarding the third expectation, about Lockean and Leopoldian norms, respondents did not consider property more an intrinsic than an instrumental right. Landowners in all three cases expressed some-what similar attitudes, with the greatest variation between Indiana and Saskatchewan on the property continuum. But landowners were deep-ly hesitant about regulation: they rejected the idea that landowners should bear the costs of conservation and were unsupportive of gov-ernment's fining landowners who break conservation laws. These are examples of what I would expect intellectual descendants of Locke to believe about the regulation of property. Yet, no matter how they felt about property or government, almost all respondents said they be-lieved other species are important, that government should be involved in conservation, and that all landowners have an obligation not to harm endangered species on their own land.

Thus, my final expectation is met: landowners support the steward-ship of endangered species, thus displaying a Leopoldian stewardship ethic. At the most basic level, these landowners value other species, sometimes even more so than their own property rights. This is a prom-ising finding for both scholars looking to understand citizens' willing-ness to cooperate with policy and for policy makers looking to increase compliance with the ESA and SARA. As my colleague and I conclude in an earlier study (Olive and Raymond 2010, 453), "while it would be easy to assume that a stewardship norm enhances willingness to coop-erate and an intrinsic property norm diminishes cooperation, we did not find such a straightforward relationship. The visions of Leopold and Locke are not two ends of a single normative continuum, but co-exist uneasily in the normative thinking of many landowners."

It is important not to overstate the strength of the stewardship ethic I found. Respondents, by and large, felt that landowners have an obli-gation not to harm species on their property, but they also believed it is unfair to expect landowners to bear the financial costs of conservation. A duty to steward only goes so far, as evident in the degrees of willing-ness of landowners to carry out specific voluntary actions. There is still the undeniable possibility that the Leopoldian stewardship ethos is not as prevalent or strong as policy makers had hoped when creating the ESA and SARA. And this suggests that incentives and regulation have an important role to play in conservation policy.

Lastly, one of the most surprising findings is that urban and subur-ban landowners are not familiar with endangered species laws. Only about a quarter of all respondents knew about the ESA or SARA. In Indiana, one-third of respondents did not realize they live in a conser-vation management area for the bat. In Saskatchewan, only 20 per cent had heard of the national law and fewer than half could correctly iden-tify a species at risk in the province. This presents a major policy chal-lenge in both countries. How can citizens be expected to cooperate with a law that they do not even realize exists? Ontario and Ohio, in the next chapter, are further case studies of this conundrum.

Daily (2005, 256) observes that "the future of biodiversity, and the benefits it supplies society, will be dictated largely by what happens in human-dominated, working landscapes." The landowners and resi-dents in Saskatchewan, Indiana, and Utah were not as selfish or as property-centric as the literature implies, but they also were not exactly enthusiastic about their stewardship responsibilities. Bats and tortoises are still endangered. Utah is still urbanizing. Saskatchewan is still without a policy. These are real cases, involving real landowners and residents who are living with endangered species, whether they realize it or not – real people on whom we are relying to safeguard, willingly or not, biodiversity for everyone.

7 Lake Erie Islands Case Study

The Lake Erie water snake (*Nerodia sipedon insularum*) provides an extraordinary case study of conservation policy in North America. The snake is a cross-border species that roams the islands off the Ontario and Ohio shores of Lake Erie. The law is also very similar on both sides of the border: the US Endangered Species Act (ESA) is enforced in Ohio, and in 2008 Ontario adopted an ESA-like act of its own, the Ontario Endangered Species Act (OESA). This allows us to examine the same species and virtually the same law at work in two different countries at the same time. Interestingly, the water snake was recovered in Ohio in 2011 and delisted by the US Fish and Wildlife Service; on the Canadian side, however, the snake remains endangered. Is this because ESA-like legislation works in the United States but not in Canada? If the two countries were to adopt a single policy for conservation, should it then not be based on the ESA?

Before jumping to conclusions about policy implications, however, one should examine why the snake was delisted in the United States but not yet in Canada. I argue that recovery occurred in Ohio for reasons that have little to do with the law, while in Ontario the snake's lack of recovery is the result of the way the legislation is being implemented and enforced. I conclude that greater cooperation between the two countries – specifically, in the form of data sharing and the creation of uniform standards and procedures – would be of great benefit to the protection and recovery of endangered species.

In this chapter I continue to focus on the same expectations discussed in Chapter 6 – namely, interpretations of conservation policy as moral and legitimate, and intrinsic property norms and willingness to steward. In the previous chapter, I focused primarily on morality; here,

I examine legitimacy more closely. The discussion of these themes leads to two related arguments. First, I argue that landowners generally view the endangered species law in both countries as legitimate, which fosters affirmative motivation for willingness to cooperate with the law. This sense of legitimacy is, however, vulnerable. Landowners in my Ontario sample, for instance, believed that the snake had made a full recovery and should be taken off the province's protected species list – a belief that is weakening their perception of the law's legitimacy. And the water snake's delisting in Ohio suggests that cross-collaboration might be necessary to maintain the legitimacy of conservation policy on both sides of the border. Many of my Ontario respondents saw the law as legitimate and were willing to comply, but their affirmative motivations on this basis should not be taken for granted.

Second, I argue that the relationship between regulators – the USFWS and the Ontario Ministry of Natural Resources (OMNR) – and landowners is the linchpin of the relationship between legitimacy and willingness to comply. In this regard my findings are similar to those of Winter and May (2001) and May (2004). Through interviews with different USFWS and OMNR employees, I show that the relevant governments struggle with bureaucratic overlap and a lack of outreach to landowners, which affects landowners' perceptions of procedural justice and their willingness to comply.

Ultimately this chapter is an extension of the themes of Chapter 6, but adding the more complex context of Canada-US cooperation. The comparative case is rife with lessons and missed opportunities, but successful cooperation is vital given the number of cross-border species – including the polar bear, the caribou, migratory birds, fish, and whales – that require recovery and protection. Affirmative motivations exist in both countries, even among Lockean landowners, but by not working with landowners or with each other, regulators are threatening the strength of affirmative motivations via legitimacy.

The Water Snake and the Islands

The Lake Erie water snake resides on the limestone shoreline of islands off the Ohio shore of Lake Erie near Port Clinton and off the Ontario shore near Windsor. These fifteen or so islands are the only places in the world where the snake is found, and the vast majority of its population is on the four largest US islands (Kelleys, South Bass, Middle Bass, and North Bass) and on the largest Canadian island (Pelee) (USFWS 2003, 4).

Historically the snake's range included twelve US and nine Canadian islands, but its population has declined significantly due to persecution and habitat alteration (6). In the 1700s, early French travellers to Lake Erie called the western islands "Îles aux serpentes" ("islands of snakes") because it was so common to see large groups of snakes sunning themselves on the rocky shoreline (McDermott 1947). By the time the snake was listed as threatened in the United States, its population had dwindled to an estimated two thousand or so adults (USFWS 2003, 5).

The Lake Erie water snake is fairly large, with adult females growing to 81 centimetres (32 inches) and adult males to 63.5 centimetres (25 inches). But it is neither poisonous nor aggressive. The snake swims, but remains near the shoreline where it eats small fish and amphibians. It hibernates between mid-September and late April and is quite active during the summer months. Mating season is early May to early June, and in August or September a female will give birth to an average of twenty-three young per litter (King 1986). Other than human beings, the snake's predators include herring gulls, blue herons, robins, raccoons, red fox, and blue racers (USFWS 2003, 8).

The Lake Erie islands provide an ideal habitat for the snakes because of the rocky shoreline and the limestone/dolomite shelves and ledges that provide sunning and shelter (United States 2003, 9); they also, however, provide ideal habitat for human beings. People heavily populate the four largest US islands and Canada's Pelee Island, especially in the summer months. Moreover, in addition to tourists and campers, private landowners – either year-round residents or May through September cottagers – are becoming more common on the islands. Recent development projects include shoreline and commercial construction, dock and seawall projects, marinas, roads, airports, and quarry projects (USFWS 2003, 15). The ramifications of human encroachment are substantial for the islands' biodiversity as a whole, but the water snake is especially vulnerable because of its dependence on the shoreline for its habitat, mating, and foraging. Unfortunately, lakefront property is also more desirable for cabin owners.

Almost anyone who travels to the islands on a warm summer day will agree they are an idyllic location: sunny, green, unpolluted, quiet, and peaceful. A number of landowners I interviewed used the word "paradise" to describe their island home. Perhaps it is not inappropriate, then, that serpents also inhabit this place. But neither Middle Bass Island nor Pelee Island is the Garden of Eden, or even in a state of nature. This is a story of conservation in civil society, in a now human-dominated landscape. It is a complex and multifaceted story complicated by the biblical, symbolic, and psychological factors that accompany snakes. The story likely would be different if another species, a fox or a squirrel, had been involved. But it is also in part what makes the story so interesting. At the end of the day, the Lake Erie water snake is a recovered species, and it has found a way to coexist in civil society with human beings.

Policy and Recovery in Ohio

The US ESA protects the water snake and its critical habitat in the state of Ohio. The USFWS finalized and began to implement the recovery plan for the snake in 2003. The plan outlined three conditions for the snake's recovery. First, the estimated adult US snake population would have to reach or exceed a total of 5,555 for a period of six or more consecutive years. Second, a minimum amount of habitat would have to be protected and/or managed to benefit the snake in perpetuity, to be distributed among the islands with a total protected habitat of 4.6 miles of shoreline and 126 acres of inland habitat with 226 feet of shoreline. Finally, there would have to be an overall decline in intentional persecution and accidental human-induced mortality of the snake (USFWS 2003). As of 2006 all the populations of the snake had met their recovery goals for three consecutive years, and only a small section of habitat was still needed to meet recovery goals. In 2008 the USFWS conducted public opinion surveys to assess the threat of human persecution of the snake, and by 2010 the agency was ready to begin the process of its delisting.

Besides the ESA, the Ohio Department of Natural Resources (ODNR), Division of Wildlife, also watches over the snake. The chief of the division can adopt rules to restrict the possession or taking of wildlife threatened with state-wide extirpation. The division maintains a list of endangered and threatened species, including the water snake, but since the snake is also a federally listed species the ESA takes precedent over Ohio law. The ODNR and the USFWS collaborate in numerous ways, however, on the snake's behalf. For example, the ODNR administers state parks on the islands where many of the snakes live. The state also allocates resources for outreach, and trains its officers to handle the snake and help educate the public about snakes.

As part of the federal recovery plan, the USFWS and the ODNR co-operated to engage in numerous education and outreach activities. For example, signs with "water snakes welcome here" were distributed free of charge to any island resident who requested one. A bi-annual newsletter, *LEWS News*, was mailed to island residents as well as to federal and state government agencies. Copies of the newsletter could also be found at island parks and businesses. The newsletter provided basic information about the snake and kept landowners abreast of rules and regulations as well as recovery updates. Outreach activities also included USFWS and ODNR participation in workshops, camps, and festivals on the islands. There is also a permanent display about the snake at the Lake Erie Islands Historical Society Museum on South Bass Island (USFWS 2003).

Key to the outreach and education campaign for the water snake was the unwavering dedication of a PhD student from Northern Illinois University. Kristen Stanford, lovingly referred to as the "Snake Lady" on the Ohio islands, was researching the snake for her dissertation (Stanford 2012). During her fieldwork she became enamoured with the islands and found funding from the USFWS (as well as other organiza-tions) for outreach activities. During the water snake's recovery pro-cess, Stanford was the face of the snake on all the Ohio islands. She personally conducted workshops and ran summer camps for children to educate people about snakes. She often wrote a column in the *LEWS News* and made herself available to assist landowners who found a snake on their property. For her own research she monitored the snake popu-lation on the islands, a task in which she was joined by the USFWS.

In the end, through no intervention by the USFWS, the snake came upon an important new food source – an invasive fish species called the round goby (*Neogobius melanostromus*) – that helped its population re-bound quickly. It is believed the fish came to the Great Lakes in the 1980s from eastern European ships that were dumping ballast in the St Clair River. Although potentially devastating to the other species in the Great Lakes, the goby was a stroke of luck for the water snake.

During the recovery process, the USFWS also regulated private prop-erty. From the time the snake came under ESA protection, landowners required building permits for new structures as well as additions to their property. It became illegal for shoreline property owners to alter the lakefront. Thus, no landowners now have a dock or bring their boats onshore outside island marinas. It was also illegal to kill the snake even when they got into cabins, as they often do during the winter months. So, for a short period of time on the Ohio Lake Erie Islands, landowners' behaviour and property were regulated on behalf of the water snake. The regulations were lifted when the snake was deemed to have recovered.

Policy and Recovery in Ontario

In Ontario SARA extends only to federal Crown lands, none of which are the water snake's habitat. Accordingly, the snake's critical habitat in the province, which is predominately found on private property, is governed by provincial legislation. The province manages three provincial parks and nature reserves on Pelee Island that house snake habitat. The island also has some large landowners in the form of The Nature Conservancy and the Black Swamp Conservancy. Both organizations privately manage large tracks of land for the purpose of biodiversity conservation. The rest of the land is privately owned and used mainly for cabins. There are a few businesses on the island; the largest is likely the island winery, but there is also a bakery, a bike shop, a grocery store, a couple of restaurants, a museum, and a marina.

Ontario has the most biodiversity at risk and, in OESA, arguably the strongest species-at-risk law of any province. The law, which came into effect on 30 June 2008 after a year of debate in the Ontario Legislative Assembly, prohibits the killing or harming of threatened or endangered species or the destruction of their habitat. The law applies to private property, and it prevents landowners from being able to use their own land in certain contexts if a threatened or endangered species co-habits the property. In many ways the OESA takes the same "stewardship first" approach as SARA, but in its regulation of private property when necessary it more closely reflects the type of law that SARA was originally intended to be when first introduced in the House of Commons by environment minister David Anderson. The act also shares some aspects with the US ESA, which is exactly what the federal government tried to avoid with SARA.

Similar to the debate at the federal level, the issue of private property was integral from the outset in Ontario, whose lawmakers tended to focus on stewardship instead of regulation. Upon introducing the bill, natural resources minister David Ramsay said "many of our province's species that need protection are found on private land. This makes voluntary stewardship activities essential and the primary approach to achieving any kind of success in reversing the rate of species decline that is now happening in Ontario. Stewardship is not just a responsibility for government" (Ramsay 2007). Other Members of the Provincial Parliament echo this theme as they discussed the bill's subtler nuances. For example, Norman Sterling told the Legislative Assembly that "you have to strike a balance that is acceptable to the people" such that property, development, and conservation are all respected in the process (Sterling 2007). MPP Toby Barrett said that conservation in his riding, "depends on the commitment of both public and private interests. Again, much of the land is private land ... hence it's so important to work with private landowners and to be proactive; certainly not to be punitive" (Barrett 2007). The overall tone of the debate in the Assembly was the need to regulate property but to proceed with carrots instead of sticks. In this vein, the OESA established the Species at Risk in Ontario Stewardship Program, with C$18 million of funding over four years. Similar to the federal program, this program is intended to foster individual or group stewardship across a variety of parcel types, including large and small private properties.

When the bill passed in 2008, the Legislative Assembly believed it was passing "the strongest law in North America" for conservation (Mussell, Schmidt, and Seguin 2010, 2). The provincial government claimed the law was fair to landowners, given the stewardship programs and the existence of take permits,[33] but also fair to endangered species that live on diverse land parcels and need protection everywhere. Given the law's short history thus far, few studies have examined it in action. Save Ontario Species, an umbrella group representing the David Suzuki Foundation, Ecojustice, Environmental Defence, Forest Ethics, and Ontario Nature, was actively involved in the passage of the law and has provided critical assessments of it for the past three years. A major point of contention is the temporary exemption of the forest industry, which affects 45 per cent of the province's land area, from the provisions of the act just a few weeks before the law went into force. This was a slap in the face of environmentalists, many of whom questioned the ability of the law to make a difference to biodiversity in the province.

In 2009 Save Ontario Species created a "report card" grading OESA implementation. It handed the province a B– for the law's description of habitat and a C– for types of protected habitat, charging that the law focuses too heavily upon where species are found, not their entire ranges. The umbrella group gave no specific grade for the province's progress with respect to the Lake Erie water snake, but awarded it an F for the caribou, another F for the American badger, a D for the barn owl, a C+ for the peregrine falcon, and its only A for the few-flowered club-rush, a plant whose habitat had been fully identified and protected by the law (Save Ontario's Species 2009). There is consensus among conservation groups that the OESA is not living up to its potential. Like Kristen Stanford in Ohio, a graduate student named Ben Porchuk wrote his master's thesis about the water snake and became involved in outreach on Pelee Island. Unfortunately for Porchuk, the political climate on the island was hostile to government regulation at the time and Porchuk became associated, through no fault of his own, with the OMNR and with heavy-handed property regulation. He was unable to foster the same type of relationship with Pelee as Stanford had done in Ohio.

Despite criticism, Ontario is doing more than any other province save perhaps for Quebec to protect its species at risk. Ontario might be struggling to implement its law, but it is head and shoulders above provinces such as Alberta and Saskatchewan in this effort. The water snake is also listed in the federal SARA, but Ottawa has undertaken no initiative for the species. A recovery team was assembled in the early 2000s but no recovery or action plan was ever created, and little if any outreach has been attempted. Since Pelee Island shares the same environment and food sources as the US islands in Lake Erie, those factors do not play a role in the water snake's status in Ontario; the snake's fate thus hinges on Ontario's ability to implement a recovery plan.

Since the water snake is a listed species in Ontario and the OESA regulates private property, landowners in the province, as in Ohio, need a permit to build on their land or add additions to existing structures. Docks are prohibited, and boats must stay in the marina while their owners are on Pelee Island. Shoreline habitat cannot be altered or harmed, and killing snakes is illegal regardless of where they are found on the island.

The story of the water snake in Ontario is surprisingly similar to that in Ohio. The biggest difference, however, is institutional capacity. In both Ohio and Ontario overlapping jurisdictions exist. In Ohio the ESA takes precedent automatically, but both the state and the USFWS manage snake habitat and assist in outreach and enforcement. Ultimately the USFWS is responsible for implementing a recovery plan and deciding at what point the species is considered recovered. In Ontario, in contrast, SARA does not take precedent automatically and can be applied only to non-federal lands through the federal government's invoking the safety net provision that enables it to act within a province that fails to protect an at-risk species, which has not been tried for the water snake. Instead, the provincial law takes precedent on all non-federal lands and the OMNR must implement a recovery plan and decide when the species is recovered. In part, the separate stories of Canadian Pelee and US Middle Bass provide important lessons about collaboration and leadership.

On Middle Bass Island, I interviewed forty-four landowners;[34] on Pelee Island I interviewed eighteen.[35] On both islands I conducted the same semi-structured interviews that I used in the Indiana and Utah case studies. These lasted between thirty and sixty minutes, and were recorded digitally for transcription purposes. I probed landowners on a number of issues, including the importance of conservation, the role of government in species protection, their attitudes about private property, and their knowledge of local endangered species. As well, in Ohio, I interviewed four bureaucrats: a USFWS biologist who is familiar with the water snake case and has interacted with Middle Bass Island landowners regarding conservation and recovery; a USFWS enforcement officer for Ohio and Michigan regarding the agency's approach to ESA enforcement and landowners; a USFWS field director for the Partners for Fish and Wildlife program in Ohio; and, finally, Northern Illinois University PhD student Kristen Stanford, who does not work officially for the USFWS, but whose grant money associated with her studies came partly from the Service and from the Ohio Department of Natural Resources. These four additional interviews helped me understand the relationship between landowners and the bureaucracy as it relates to landowners' perceived legitimacy of the law.

Results and Discussion

After transcribing the interviews, I coded and quantified the responses, which are presented in Tables 7.1 through 7.6. I should emphasize, however, that the eighteen interviewees on Pelee Island are an extraordinarily small sample and not a simple random one. Moreover, the simple conversion to percentages can be misleading, and reminds us that, although numbers and statistics help us to understand the world, we should not place undue emphasis on them. I thus also draw upon the qualitative findings and rely upon quotations from the interviews themselves. Similar to the last chapter, the focus is on Locke and private property and on Leopold and stewardship.

Pelee and Middle Bass are very small islands – akin to experimental test tubes – which made research in these cases different than in Indiana and Utah. Almost all landowners and visitors arrive on a ferry, save for the few who fly their own planes. Closed off from the rest of world, everyone is aware of everyone else. There are no hiding places on small islands. If the USFWS or the OMNR were on the island, landowners likely would know or hear about it within a day.

Gossip is prevalent; even my own presence was noted by many landowners. Although my research presents data only from those landowners who willingly participated and signed consent forms, I spoke to hundreds of others people on the islands during my trips. In 2007, when I arrived on Middle Bass, my car had Saskatchewan licence plates, and everyone would ask me about this – some would even knock on the door of my cabin to ask me where I was from. People were disappointed that they were not in my sample because they really wanted to talk about the snakes or about the island. In 2010, when I arrived on Pelee, my car had a Saskatchewan plate in the front and a Michigan plate in the back. This pleased everyone because the island itself is home to many Canadians and some Americans. The Canadians felt that I understood them because I was one of them, while the Americans did so because I was living in their country. Although I made it clear that my research was not affiliated with any government, some landowners were suspicious given past experiences; very few on Pelee Island were willing to sign the consent form, and thus could not be included in the data I present here.

Landowners and the Law

Overall, landowners on both islands were unfamiliar with endangered species legislation and had little knowledge of, or contact with, regulators. As reported in Table 7.1, almost no landowners in Ohio – only 9 per cent (four out of forty-four people in total) – were familiar with the law; in Ontario 11 per cent (two out of eighteen) claimed to be familiar with the OESA. In both cases all landowners in the sample owned land that has been declared critical habitat for the water snake, and they were aware of at least some of the regulations and rules pertaining to wildlife on the islands. For example, landowners not familiar with the ESA might still know it was illegal to kill an endangered species and that regulations forbade their building a dock or bringing a boat up to

Table 7.1. Landowners' Attitudes towards Endangered Species Legislation
and Enforcement, Ohio and Ontario

		Yes	No	Don't Know
Question	Location		(per cent)	
Are you familiar with	Ohio	1	99	0
the Endangered Species	Ontario	12	88	0
Act/Ontario Endangered				
Species Act?				
Have you had any contact	Ohio	10	90	0
with a USFWS or OMNR officer	Ontario	53	47	0
in any capacity?				
Have you come into contact	Ohio	0	100	0
with regulators from	Ontario	18	82	0
the USFWS or OMNR?				

the shore. There is thus a disjoint between the regulations governments try to enforce on the islands and what the federal and provincial laws actually mandate. Indeed, landowners often did not realize that such laws were in place.

Only one in ten Ohio landowners reported having any contact with wildlife enforcement officers, while about half of those interviewed in Ontario did so. But these numbers can be misleading. It was common for an Ohio landowner to ask, "are the [USFWS] guys in the [state park] by the docks?" The answer was no because the "guys in the park" were actually with the Ohio Department of Natural Resources. Some landowners believed Kristen Stanford, the Snake Lady, worked for the USFWS, which she did not; for example, when asked if they had contact with the USFWS, it was typical for a landowner to reply, "I have called the Snake Lady," or "I talked to the students when they are here." The situation was similar on Pelee Island, where landowners would confuse the OMNR with Essex County surveyors and Environment Canada field officers. This suggests a lack of understanding about bureaucratic structure; landowners, regardless of country, lumped the different levels and branches of "government" together, and no one seemed the least bit interested in such distinctions.

It is somewhat surprising that more Ontario landowners were not familiar with SARA or the OESA. One "in-the-know" landowner said there is "no difference between pre- and post- [Ontario] ESA" because implementation and regulation have not changed on the island. There is no OMNR or Environment Canada field station on Pelee Island, and it appears that visits by regulators are infrequent. So the following data should be understood in the context of landowners who know they are being regulated, but do not fully understand why or by whom.

Locke and Private Property

Ohio landowners on the Lake Erie islands were less Lockean than Indiana landowners and more like landowners in Utah; the attitudes of Ontario landowners were somewhat similar to those in Saskatchewan. In Ohio, 41 per cent agreed with the instrumental notion of property and 52 per cent agreed with the more Lockean notion (Table 7.2). When asked to place themselves on a continuum from intrinsic to instrumental, a majority (54 per cent) were Lockean with 25 per cent in the middle and 22 per cent siding towards the instrumental notion (Figure 7.1). One Ohio landowner captured the Lockean conception when he claimed that "I think this country was founded on – when I studied history a lot of people said it was religious freedoms, but the real key was private property rights." On the other side, similar to those in Utah and Indiana, some Ohio landowners connected religion and property in their expression of the more instrumental view. One said, "because of my Christian beliefs and those fall under God's law, God's direction. And that is simply respecting the rights of others to co-habit the planet." A fellow Ohio owner felt that "we borrow [the land]. We don't own it. We borrow it from someone a lot more superior than us."

Almost half of the landowners in my US cases came closer to the Lockean conception of property than to the more social/government-created conception. As one landowner said, "I truly believe that in all circumstances, the bond between man and land is supreme. The quickest way to put a dispute between two civil people is to put up a fence and have a boundary dispute. It brings out ugliness in people because man's land is supreme." In Ontario, in contrast, 65 per cent agreed with the instrumental notion and only 35 per cent with the Lockean. On the continuum, only 29 per cent were at the intrinsic end while 47 per cent sided with the instrumental notion. This is reminiscent of the Saskatchewan case, where 54 per cent of landowners placed themselves at the instrumental end, 35 per cent in the middle, and just 11 per cent felt closer to the Lockean view. Expressing the Lockean view, one Ontario landowner felt strongly that land is such a deeply entrenched value that "the emotional math" of stewardship would never add up,

Table 7.2. Landowners' Attitudes towards Private Property, Ohio and Ontario

Question	Location	Agree	Disagree	Don't Know
		(per cent)		
Some people think of private property as a right created by government that can be changed over time according to the changing needs to society. What do you think of this view?	Ohio Ontario	41 66	36 28	23 6
Some people think of private property as an absolute or "God-given" right that must be respected by a legitimate government. What do you think of this view?	Ohio Ontario	52 32	30 62	18 6
Do you think it is unfair to expect landowners to bear the cost of protecting endangered species on their property?	Ohio Ontario	57 59	23 41	20 0
Do you think it would be appropriate for the government to place some limitations on your private property rights for the sake of conservation?	Ohio Ontario	41 78	14 16	45 6
Do you trust the government to protect your private property rights?	Ohio Ontario	38 46	60 42	2 12

so incentives would always be necessary. Essentially, she felt an emotional connection to her property that the government cannot regulate. By and large, though, most Ontario landowners did not feel this way, but instead accepted the changing and social nature of property.

My data suggest a difference in the way Canadian and American landowners think about private property. Canadians appear more willing than Americans to accept the idea that owning property is a government-created right that can change over time. The reason for the difference is not clear. The influence of the Founding Fathers, particularly Thomas Jefferson, on American attitudes might explain the difference to a certain extent, while the existence of a larger welfare state in Canada might make Canadians more accepting of government involvement in their everyday lives. But it is important to keep in mind that the

Figure 7.1. Landowners' Attitudes towards Private Property on a Continuum from an Intrinsic to an Instrumental Right, Ohio and Ontario

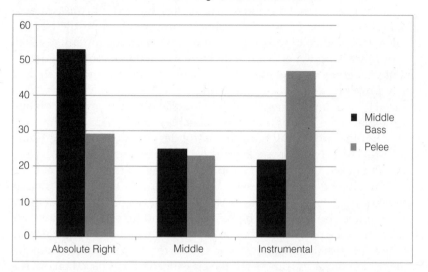

difference is not sharp, and could be more regional in nature – consider that attitudes of respondents in Saskatchewan and Utah were similar, as were those in Indiana and Ohio.

There is little difference in US and Canadian landowners' attitudes towards government, regulation, or biodiversity conservation. The implication is that individual attitudes towards private property might be overemphasized in the politics of conservation. Certainly, the way landowners think about property will affect the way they think about government and regulation, but it also seems evident that those with a Lockean conception of property are as equally as open to stewardship as are other landowners, a point I take up again in Chapter 9.

The same percentage of landowners, a near supermajority, in both Ohio and Ontario agreed that it is unfair for society to expect landowners to bear the costs of conservation on private property. In other words they did not want to shoulder the financial burden associated with conservation, such as paying more taxes or paying to improve snake habitat on their property. Still, a strong majority in Ontario (78 per cent) and almost half in Ohio (41 per cent) were willing to accept limitations on their rights – such as regulating construction, prohibiting docks, and imposing other non-financial burdens – for the purposes of conservation.

Finally, islanders distrusted government's ability to protect their property rights, with only 46 per cent of Ontarians and 38 per cent of Ohioans agreeing that it could be trusted to do so. In Ohio this response was related to the issue of shoreline property deeds on the islands, which was politically salient at the time I was conducting my research there. Many landowners were extremely worried that the Ohio government was going to take away their exclusive right to the shoreline of their property and declare all shoreline to be public property. This caused a lot of landowners to feel insecure about their property rights.

In Ontario the lack of trust was palatable. Landowners felt that conservation law was being used to control development on Pelee Island and prevent privatization. Trust was also problematic because landowners in both Ontario and Ohio felt that the water snake was not a legitimately endangered species. Indeed, this was the unquestionable theme of my island experiences. Although it was not an official question or otherwise part of the interview, time and time again landowners raised the issue of whether the snake was really in danger of extinction. Some felt the snake's listing was an excuse for the government to regulate private property; others felt the classification was based on old scientific findings. Most landowners – I estimate about 85 per cent – had encountered a water snake. To their minds the snakes were everywhere and could not possibly be in danger of extinction. What most did not know – because they have never been told – is that the status of a species is more than just population numbers.

With regard to regulation of property, landowners felt strongly – 68 per cent in Ohio and 94 per cent in Ontario – that government should be involved in the protection of endangered species (see Table 7.3). Almost the same proportion agreed that government should create such laws. One Ontario landowner said, "we believe that people will drive reasonably, but we still want to have laws just in case." An Ohio landowner felt that "I don't think it could be protected any other way. I think if the government wasn't involved you would have a few self-conscious people doing their best efforts, but you would have a large amount of people who wouldn't do it." This strikes at the very heart of the collective action problem that endangered species conservation presents. One landowner who was aware of this problem pointed out that "our government is way too big and they have their hands in way too many things. On the other hand, if you didn't have one central government that was doing things like that then it probably wouldn't get done. So there is a give and take." This suggests that landowners think

Table 7.3. Landowners' Attitudes towards Government Regulation of Private Property, Ohio and Ontario

Question	Location	Yes/Agree	No/Disagree	Don't Know
		(*per cent*)		
Do you think that the government should be involved in protecting endangered species?	Ohio	68	18	14
	Ontario	94	6	0
Do you think the government should make laws to protect endangered species?	Ohio	68	16	16
	Ontario	88	12	0
Do you think the government should fine landowners who harm endangered species on their own property?	Ohio	61	16	23
	Ontario	70	18	12

that conservation of endangered species on private property by the federal government is legitimate.

But fewer agreed with government's fining landowners for harming endangered species found on their property. This mimics the results from Utah and Saskatchewan. It is not surprising that sanctions are unpopular among landowners. Moreover, it suggests that hammering harder would be a politically unfavourable strategy. Landowners might be willing to steward other species, but creating policy with stiff penalties might create backlash and foster resentment. In Ontario, the two or three respondents who were aware that regulations already existed felt strongly, for example, that "the government should not be involved in anything" because "people are sick of government" and regulation actually causes people to do more harm than they otherwise would have on their land.

Leopold and Stewardship

Given the somewhat Lockean attitudes towards regulation of property that prevail on the islands, to what extent does an ethic of stewardship also exist there? As Table 7.4 reports, 77 per cent of Ohio landowners and 82 per cent of Ontario landowners in my sample believed it is important for human beings to protect other species. An Ohio property owner said, "I think that is how God made us. I think that ... everyone has a purpose on this earth – every creature." A Middle Bass landowner

Table 7.4. Landowners' Attitudes towards Leopoldian Conceptions of Species, Ohio and Ontario

Question	Location	Agree/ Important	Disagree/ Not Important	Don't Know
		(per cent)		
How important would you say it is for human beings to protect endangered species?	Ohio	77	5	18
	Ontario	82	18	0
Some people argue that all species have a right to exist. What do you think of this idea?	Ohio	70	9	21
	Ontario	70	18	12
Some people argue that sometimes it is okay for human activities to result in the extinction of a species. What do you think of this idea?	Ohio	32	52	16
	Ontario	29	65	6
Some people say that private landowners have an obligation not to harm endangered species found on their property. Do you agree?	Ohio	73	14	13
	Ontario	82	12	6
Do you personally care about the LEWS?	Ohio	48	46	6
	Ontario	53	41	6

with a fresh snake bite on his leg felt it was important to protect all creatures because we are all part of the same ecosystem. The balance of nature seemed to be a prevalent theme on the islands, perhaps because balance is more visible on a small island.

Most landowners in Ohio and Ontario (77 per cent and 82 per cent, respectively) also agreed that other species have a right to exist. One Ohio landowner said, "anything that has a foothold on earth has a right to exist." Likewise in Ontario a landowner felt that, "if they are here, that must mean something. We shouldn't have … they have just as much right as anything." This willingness to extend a right to existence to other species is somewhat surprising. Again, it suggests support for Newfoundland and Labrador's assertion in its Endangered Species Act that "other species have a right to exist." The minority of landowners who did not believe in that right, however, had strong attitudes about the water snake. One Pelee Island landowner said that if he ever saw a snake on his land he would "blow that sucker up," and spoke openly about the "shoot, shovel, and shut-up" approach that he and some other landowners used on the island. This landowner even admitted that the snakes had never affected him personally. What explains such an attitude? In this case, it was his anger towards the government. To take another example, a different Pelee Island landowner told me that he liked wildlife, donated money to such causes, and considered himself a real steward, but had killed a snake "as a symbol" [of rejection of the law] instead of writing letters to politicians. Obviously such an attitude is not as simple as the denial of a right to existence of other species, although clearly this landowner would deny the snake that right. For other landowners, a right was just not something that a non-human could possess.

By and large, however, these landowners rejected the idea that it was acceptable for humans to cause the extinction of other species. In Ohio, numerous landowners said they did not know how they felt, but only 32 per cent agreed that it was sometimes acceptable; in Ontario only 29 per cent thought so. One landowner said, "as far as it comes to population being in danger of total extinction, it is never okay"; another responded, almost in surprise, "Oh glory no. It is not for us to say." Some landowners did feel that extinction could be natural or unavoidable as well as sometimes justifiable for human needs. And some felt that not every single species is important. As one landowner, in a frank tone, said, "I think if you took a survey, 95 per cent of the people who would come in contact with the snake don't care whether it is here or not. And yet it is on the endangered species list. I see no reason why it should be protected. And if it were to go away, I don't think anyone would miss it and I don't think it would hurt anything." Like the landowners in Indiana, Utah, and Saskatchewan, however, most of those in Ohio and Ontario (73 per cent and 82 per cent, respectively) felt an obligation not to harm endangered species found on their own property. One said, "I think in general there is a moral reason why a person should try to protect a species." An Ohio islander took the position that "I don't like snakes, but I shouldn't harm them. If they don't bother you, you shouldn't bother them."

Moving from general attitudes to willingness to take action, the results are more mixed (see Table 7.5). None of the voluntary actions I asked respondents if they would take is required by law. The possible exception is the need to avoid springtime construction in Ohio – "possible," because the ESA is rather ambiguous when it comes to small landowners, particularly those involved in a larger HCP. I know from

Table 7.5. Landowners' Willingness to Steward, Ohio and Ontario

Action	Yes	No	Don't Know
		(per cent)	
Ohio			
Give the USFWS access to property?	71	14	15
Refrain from pesticides?	52	21	27
Put up a sign?	48	41	11
Ontario			
Give the OMNR access to property?	69	19	12
Refrain from pesticides?	41	41	18

talking to USFWS representatives that no one is monitoring springtime construction on Middle Bass Island and, therefore, no one is enforcing any type of regulation. I also know from reading the water snake's recovery plan, however, that springtime construction along the shoreline requires a special permit. Unlike those in the Indiana and Utah case studies, landowners on these Lake Erie islands were generally willing to help steward an endangered species: a surprising 71 per cent of landowners in Ohio and 65 per cent in Ontario were willing to give government access to their private property to monitor the water snake. The motivation for this action is somewhat ironic. For a number of landowners, willingness is motivated by a desire to prove that the snake has recovered and no longer needs to protected by a law that regulates landowner behaviour (as opposed to genuine concern for the snake). While Ohio landowners felt positively towards endangered species in general, only 48 per cent personally cared about the snake. The fact that landowners were willing to do anything at all for the snake suggests they felt the law is legitimate and conservation ethically appropriate. The story is complicated, however, because there are so many snakes that landowners want the species delisted – this, in fact, was their primary motive for allowing the USFWS on their property.

Almost half of Ohio interviewees were willing to put a USFWS "Lake Erie Snakes Welcome Here" sign on their property. These signs are intended to bolster outreach, increase awareness, and encourage landowners' involvement in snake recovery. Since one of the main reasons the snake is endangered is human persecution, spreading awareness and improving landowners' feelings about the creature is an important aspect of its recovery. One landowner said "snakes cannot read," and refused to participate; others said they used to be more willing to put up signs but no longer feel they are necessary. Again, the fact that many landowners felt the water snake is not really endangered affected their willingness to cooperate. The link between perceived legitimacy and willingness to cooperate is relatively clear here.

Finally, half of Ohio landowners and 41 per cent of those in Ontario were willing to reduce pesticide use on their property for the sake of the snake. Many admitted they had made no connection between pesticides/herbicides and the snakes – it had never occurred to them that their lawn-care habits might affect the creature. Some landowners, roughly a dozen in each case, felt government should provide alternatives if they were prohibited from using pesticides on their property. Again, part of their unwillingness to steward stems from their disbelief that the snake is endangered. Some 30 per cent of landowners did not know the snake is listed at all, and closer to 50 per cent felt that, regardless of its official status, the snake is not endangered and, therefore, were unwilling to help steward it. One Ontario islander said the snake and other endangered species are a "conspiracy" by which "the government is trying to get people off the island." If islanders truly feel that way, it is not surprising that their stewardship ethic is weak and their motivation through legitimacy is lacking.

Essentially, landowners noted that there are now snakes all over the islands, including in the water, in boats, in cabins, and along the shoreline. Landowners said they were willing to respect the snake when it was first listed. One Ohio landowner told me: "when they passed this thing people responded and were very respectful of the snakes. People were very protective. You don't hurt the snakes – everyone had that mindset. People did, obviously – I mean they recovered." But as time wore on and the snake population increased without changes in the law, landowners had grown frustrated and angry, and less willing to comply or cooperate. For example, some landowners had been willing to put up a snake sign on their property five years previously, but had since taken the signs down. And it was evident that landowners were frustrated with the ESA as they watched it play out in practice. Essentially, more were beginning to feel that the law is no longer legitimate because the snake is not "truly" endangered. In almost every interview landowners told me it was time to "get the snake off the list."

Lessons and Opportunities

The Lake Erie water snake recovered in Ohio, but without any help from landowners. This could imply that the cooperation of landowners is not necessary for species recovery. Or it could be that the state missed

the opportunity to engage landowners and foster the type of stewardship ethos on which the ESA depends in the long run. In talking to
landowners it was evident to me that most believed that other species,
even snakes, are important and that they were willing to help steward
the snake on their land. The problem for many was lack of awareness:
by and large, landowners knew almost nothing about the ESA or how
it is enforced or by whom, and many did not know anything substantive about the water snake or what its stewardship might involve.

In Ohio, bureaucratic overlap between the state's Department of
Natural Resources and the USFWS is so profound that almost no landowner made a distinction between the two agencies during the interviews. Since the water snake is listed as threatened under both the state
and the federal ESA, both agencies have a claim to be involved. But, in
the case of Middle Bass Island, it appears as though ODNR has the run
of the place. The state bought a huge section of land on the island in the
spring of 2001 for a state park and a number of employees and rangers
now regularly work there. The USFWS, in contrast, is spread so thin in
terms of funding and staffing that it makes only irregular appearances
on the island. In my 2007 interview with her, Kristen Stanford said,
with regard to the USFWS, that, "as far as [their] being a direct presence
on the island [is concerned], they are not." And the lead USFWS biologist noted that she had not been to the islands in the previous two years.
So it is not surprising that landowners had little idea what the USFWS
is, what it does, or what the ESA requires of private property owners.
The problem becomes a breakdown in procedural justice since landowners did not even know the process of endangered species protection in the United States. As Stanford also noted, "a lot of people are not
100 per cent clear on the boundaries between state and federal government. They just don't understand it. So, to understand the ESA on a
federal level – landowners are not ready to understand it." Thus, there
is an indication that bureaucratic overlap is somewhat problematic for
landowners.

The positive lesson that Ontario can draw from Ohio is that landowners are willing to steward, but they also need education and outreach. The problem, it seems, comes down to money, as so many
political problems do. An OMNR ecologist said there is no money for
recovery plans in Ontario or resources to monitor the snakes on Pelee.
There is technically a two-year timeline for writing a recovery plan after a species has been listed under the OESA, but since it applies only to
species listed after the creation of the law, plans for newer-listed species

tend to get priority. Currently, recovery plans for forty-seven of one hundred and ninety listed species have been finalized by the ministry (Ontario 2012). Thus, because the Lake Erie water snake was originally listed as endangered in Ontario in 1973, there is, ironically, no legal pressure to write a recovery plan for it quickly. Both Ontario and Ohio are missing opportunities to capitalize on affirmative motivations while they still exist.

Other Missed Opportunities

During the early 2000s, both Canada and the United States worked to recover the Lake Erie water snake, but they did so in virtual isolation from each other. Megan Seymour, the lead biologist for the water snake at the USFWS, reported that, in the late 1990s, she went over to the Canadian side to meet with Ontario and Canadian officials regarding the water snake. For a brief time, a "cross-border species" initiative evolved, and plans were made for ongoing communication. But Seymour admits that no one kept up with the project, mostly because of turnover at the institutional level on both sides of the border. Seymour went to Ontario just that one time and admitted that she knew very little about how policy and recovery works in Canada. Similarly, the fieldworkers I spoke with in Ontario from Environment Canada and the OMNR also admitted they knew very little about what Ohio was doing regarding the snake. An endangered species existing on islands less than five miles apart is managed by two separate countries with virtually no communication between them regarding habitat, population, landowners, or the law.

Canada and the United States have a history of collaboration on cross-border environmental issues such as water, migratory birds, and caribou. For endangered species there is the Canada-US-Mexico Trilateral Committee for Wildlife and Ecosystem Conservation and Management, the 1997 US-Canada Framework for Cooperation, and the Commission for Environmental Cooperation. But there is nothing to ensure that communication takes place in the case of cross-border species. Sometimes the relationship develops naturally and both sides collaborate to draft recovery plans – such as with the woodland caribou in the North and the Karner blue butterfly in Ontario and Wisconsin – but most species do not enjoy this luxury. In 2000, Canada, the United States, and Mexico jointly created a working draft of a document on Species of Common Conservation Concern in North America, outlining the potential for collaboration on the recovery of fifteen shared species. Nothing further resulted, however, and there is no shared norm of collaboration among them during the recovery process of a shared endangered species.

The Lake Erie water snake is an example of a species that has slipped through the cracks. The USFWS recovered the Ohio population of the snake by writing and implementing a recovery plan. This could have – and should have – been a joint effort with Canada, and a policy should have been in place to ensure cross-border communication. The snake is no longer in danger of extinction, yet resources will continue to be used and landowners will continue to be regulated in Canada because of institutional lag. This could prove problematic for landowners' relations with government. One Ontario landowner felt that the snake should be delisted "as a reward for good behaviour" and a signal to landowners that the government cares about them. From his perspective, the snake has recovered in Ohio, which means it is no longer in danger of going extinct in the wild, so Ontario should delist it and stop regulating Pelee Island. Since no one is even monitoring the snake population on the island, it seemed unfair to keep it listed as endangered.

There is an interesting tension on the islands between those who live there (the landowners) and the government. Most islanders, like western farmers, consider themselves to be good stewards of their land. The problem is when outsiders try to implement regulations without input from the community. As one Pelee Islander said, "there is no substitute for local input." The landowners on Pelee and Middle Bass were similar to landowners in my other cases and in the literature, with multidimensional views of property and a general acknowledgment of the importance of conservation. Some, however, were really angry, which prevented them from willingly stewarding their land. They did not know how to steward the snake, and they distrusted government so much that they were not interested in learning, an attitude that was more apparent in Ontario than in Ohio. This speaks to a breakdown in communication and the central weakness of the "hammer harder" approach, both of which detract from affirmative motivations to cooperate via legitimacy.

These attitudes also suggest a possible opportunity for environmental non-governmental organizations (eNGOs) to become more involved in encouraging the affirmative motivations that exist among landowners. Wilkins (2011, 74) argues that the ESA should be revised to allow eNGOs, or other qualified third parties, to work with landowners in the development of recovery actions connected with conservation incentives. He says "landowners are more likely to trust non-government organizations with site-specific information and property access." North American eNGOs have a proven track record of working with landowners on stewardship. The largest, such as Ducks Unlimited, The Nature Conservancy, and Sierra Club, have a presence in all fifty US states and many Canadian provinces. Smaller, local organizations such as the Prairie Conservation Action Plan in Saskatchewan are also working actively with landowners.

In Ontario, The Nature Conservancy has been acquiring land on Pelee Island, much to the chagrin of local landowners who are worried about the local tax base on a small island. A better arrangement might be for The Nature Conservancy to work with individual landowners to steward snake habitat. As the case makes evident, landowners on Pelee are as sceptical of the OMNR as their Ohio counterparts on Middle Bass are of the USFWS; perhaps The Nature Conservancy could take on the tasks of property monitoring and leading landowner projects in the place of these government agencies. Wherever legitimacy is in question because of the action (or inaction) of government, there is space for eNGOs to step in and maintain, and even enhance, affirmative motivations through morality and legitimacy.

Conclusions

Echoing the Indiana, Utah, and Saskatchewan cases, my studies of landowners in Ohio and Ontario also support my expectations (see Table 7.6). Landowners in my samples believed conservation is the right thing to do, but some no longer thought the law is legitimate. The existence of affirmative motivations, therefore, was more limited here than in the previous cases. Nevertheless, landowners did support stewardship and genuinely wanted to take care of their island paradise. Moreover, as in the previous cases, they were not all as Lockean as I had expected.

Today the Lake Erie water snake is considered endangered in Ontario but not in any part of the United States. Two similar islands in two similar countries with the same species of snake – how could the end result be so different? The landowners on the Lake Erie islands are similar in their beliefs and attitudes towards government regulation and water snakes. Both the USFWS and the OMNR are working with similar people on nearly identical islands with the same ecological characteristics. The reason the water snake was delisted in Ohio is that the USFWS was able to write and implement a recovery strategy for it; in Ontario the ministry lacks the institutional capacity to write a recovery plan, let alone implement one.

Table 7.6. Summary of Case Findings, Ohio and Ontario

Conclusion	Ohio	Ontario
Respondents knew about endangered species?	no	no
Respondents knew about endangered species legislation?	no	no
Respondents had a Lockean view of property?	yes	yes
Respondents accepted government involvement in conservation?	yes	yes
Respondents possessed affirmative motivations for cooperation with stewardship via morality?	yes	yes
Respondents possessed affirmative motivations for cooperation with stewardship via legitimacy?	yes	yes

This case study speaks to the importance of recovery plans, but it also tells a greater story about working with, instead of regulating, landowners. As did those in the previous case studies, landowners in Ohio and Ontario interpreted conservation as consistent with their own sense of morality; they also supported the stewardship of endangered species. What is different is that the island landowners were less inclined to consider conservation consistent with their idea of legitimacy, since, in their view, the water snake is not a legitimately endangered species and thus not in need of conservation or stewardship. That the relevant government agencies rarely visit to monitor or count snakes also suggested to landowners that this is not a serious case of a species about to go extinct. It is true that the lack of legitimacy did not prevent the snake from being recovered in Ohio, but it likely slowed recovery and could make it difficult to recover other species (including other snakes) in the area in the future. And if landowners in Ontario catch wind that the species was delisted in Ohio, they may become even less willing to steward the snakes. This does not bode well for conservation efforts on the islands.

A big part of the problem is the lack of communication between the bureaucracy and the landowners. In general individuals seemed quite open to conservation and willing to steward. But ignorance abounds. As Coombs (1980) outlines, knowledge of the law and its requirements is a precondition for compliance. As I discussed in Chapter 4, citizens might fail to comply because of ignorance – being either completely unaware of the law or confused and unsure about its requirements. However, since I am not measuring actual compliance with the ESA, knowledge of the law and its exact details becomes somewhat less important. I did ask landowners details about the law, but knowledge of the law is not a key motivation in my model of willingness to comply. Knowledge is important in cases where it builds understanding of the rationale for rules, which in turn fosters a stronger sense of obligation to comply (May 2004). In my survey, knowledge is an indicator of communication between the USFWS and landowners. To the extent that landowners lack basic information about the law, a species, or habitat, it can be assumed that there is a failure of communication and outreach. This is ultimately reflective of landowners' relationship with the USFWS and, perhaps, predictive of their perceptions of the legitimacy of the law and its enforcement.

Similarly, Mussell, Schmidt, and Seguin (2010) point out that the OESA is "somewhat remarkable in terms of its implicit assumptions regarding compliance." This is not because landowners must self-comply in most circumstances (due to lack of enforcement) but because the act assumes landowners know the list of species at risk, can identify and monitor those species, and are aware of the penalties for non-compliance. Pelee Island is a good example of the problem with these assumptions, as its landowners have never been given this information officially but have been left to figure it out for themselves.

According to the theory of affirmative motivations, if the USFWS or OMNR were interested in securing compliance with the ESA or OESA, they would establish and maintain conditions that led the public to accept their decisions and policies. Normally, regulation is thought of as enforced directives, with compliance compelled by enforcement practices and sanctions for violation (May 2004). The existence of affirmative motivations, however, creates a different way of thinking about regulation. A commitment through legitimacy sets up the possibility of a social contract in which compliance is based on a shared commitment to carry out the provisions of the contract (Goldberg 1976; May 2004). For such a social contract to be established, the relevant government agencies need to have repeated (positive) interactions with landowners and provide open lines of communication so that landowners understand how recovery works and what it entails beyond just population statistics.

In Ontario, where the Lake Erie water snake is still considered endangered, hammering harder seems like an unlikely strategy for success because landowners do not know about the law or the snake. Land acquisition has already been tried on Pelee Island, but it frustrates landowners – when non-profit organizations such as The Nature

Conservancy buy land, they remove that land from the tax base. More-over, there will always be holdouts – government and environmental groups cannot buy all the lakeshore habitat, so they have to find a way to conserve the snake on private land. Incentives might be necessary – the OMNR might have to purchase landowner cooperation to meet recovery goals – but first, cooperative management needs to be tested. Both landowners and government seem interested. An OMNR field officer said, "OMNR needs to demonstrate a willingness to work with landowners and educate landowners – find a middle ground between snakes and property." The snake population is already rebounding be-cause of its new food source, the round gopy fish; with a little help from landowners the OMNR could have a major success story on its hands and begin to foster the type of stewardship that is necessary to recover other endangered reptiles on Pelee Island, such as the blue racer snake and the eastern fox snake.

Since the Lake Erie water snake is not in danger of extinction in the wild, it would be best for Canada to create a recovery plan and imple-ment it quickly, or perhaps just to acknowledge that the snake is recov-ered in its ecosystem. This would lead to the snake's delisting, which would be good public relations for SARA and the OESA and a source of pride for Pelee Islanders. Canada and the United States have so many species in dire need of resources that they must find ways to work to-gether to recover them. And each country needs to stop focusing on species with thriving populations in the other country. There are too many species and too little time.

8 Indigenous Peoples and a Nunavut Case Study

In 1993 Canada ratified the UN Convention on Biological Diversity (UNCBD) at the Rio Summit,[36] committing it to Article 8(j) of that convention:

> Subject to its national legislation, respect, preserve and maintain knowledge, innovations and practices of indigenous and local communities embodying traditional lifestyles relevant for the conservation and sustainable use of biological diversity and promote their wider application with the approval and involvement of the holders of such knowledge, innovation and practices, and encourage the equitable sharing of the benefits arising from the utilization of such knowledge, innovations and practices.

Canada was partly responsible for the article's inclusion in the UNCBD; throughout the negotiation process Canada "led the way in putting the concerns of Native peoples on the agenda and promoting measures that would protect traditional knowledge" (Le Prestre and Stoett 2001, 208). Together with Peru and Sweden, Canada formulated the idea of "equitable sharing of benefits" arising from the exploitation of genetic material. Recognizing that biological resources have cultural and intrinsic worth but can also be exploited for economic gain "lies at the core of Native peoples' perspective" (208). By 2010, however, Canada had reversed its position on this issue and has recently taken a more neutral, or perhaps even adverse, approach to indigenous inclusion.

Aboriginal peoples play a large role in the Canadian Biodiversity Strategy, which sets Canada's approach to conservation apart from that of the United States. The 1996 Accord for the Protection of Species at Risk involves the participation of the territories, which are populated largely by Aboriginal peoples, and Canada's Species at Risk Act (SARA) carves out a large role for Aboriginal participation, specifically aboriginal traditional knowledge. In this chapter I focus on Aboriginal involvement in conservation policy and present as a case study the territory of Nunavut, which manages wildlife in a way unlike most other places in North America. This complex area of study is both under-researched and not well understood in Canada.

In looking at environmental justice – a type of social justice concerned with equity and fairness in environmental management (Fletcher 2003, 12) – I step away from the focus on Locke and Leopold, but continue to examine notions of legitimacy and morality, especially as they relate to procedural justice and willingness to steward. There is virtually no private property in Nunavut,[37] so here landowners cannot be the right level of analysis and theories that apply to other cases I have examined do not apply. Moreover, Canada's indigenous peoples have a different historical relationship to the land than do other Canadians. Private ownership of land parcels is not a traditional concept of Aboriginal peoples, and never part of the nomadic lifestyle of the Inuit who make up the great majority of Nunavut's indigenous population (see Henderson 2007). The central argument is that Nunavut's collaborative management schema suffers numerous drawbacks and challenges, but the approach brings the Inuit closer to achieving environmental justice through wildlife management.

More broadly, in this chapter I hope not only to show the importance of understanding not only procedural justice, but also to piece together the crucial differences between Canadian and US approaches to conservation. I begin with a discussion of the role of Aboriginal peoples, including Inuit, Métis, and First Nations, in the Canadian Biodiversity Strategy through a discussion of Parliament's review of SARA's first five years. Aboriginal leaders across Canada are disappointed in the implementation of SARA, and have called for significant and immediate changes to policy. Although we commonly think of endangered species policy as an issue of (in)justice for other species, this chapter demonstrates that such policies must also acknowledge the human dimension, only this time it is not about fairness for landowners, but about procedural justice for Aboriginals across North America.

Aboriginals and the Canadian Biodiversity Strategy

Canada's commitment under the UNCBD not only required the inclusion of Aboriginal peoples in conservation policy decision making, but also included a pledge to "maintain the socio-cultural diversity of indigenous and local communities" (UNEP 2010). Part of maintaining such diversity is the safeguarding of indigenous languages, since that is means by which knowledge and practices concerning the natural environment are communicated. As the UNCBD notes, "[l]inguists and anthropologists have suggested that the diversity of ideas carried by different languages and sustained by different cultures is one aspect required to maintain and transmit ecosystem specific knowledge. The extinction of each language results in the irrecoverable loss of unique cultural, historical, and ecological knowledge" (UNEP 2010).

In explaining the goal of "maintaining the socio-cultural diversity of indigenous and local communities," Canada's fourth report to the UNCBD (Canada 2009a, 27–8) acknowledges that Aboriginal languages are critical to the sharing of traditional knowledge between generations, since such knowledge contains terminology that affects ecological interpretations and long-term trends in biodiversity. Canada's First Nations, Métis, and Inuit peoples speak more than sixty different languages. Among First Nations people, however, only 29 per cent speak an Aboriginal language, and only 4 per cent of Métis do so, but, critical for the Nunavut case, 69 per cent of Inuit speak an indigenous language, due largely to their isolation (Canada 2009a, 27–8). Canada monitors language use among its Aboriginal peoples, albeit in a somewhat limited way as it groups languages together, thereby sweeping over dialects that are likely to be lost in the twenty-first century. To foster Aboriginal languages, Canada is committed to increasing control over territorial lands through land claims agreements, increasing collaboration among government, businesses, and Aboriginal peoples, and using Aboriginal traditional knowledge in species assessment and ecosystem planning (Canada 2009b, 132).

Beyond the crucial role of language and the preservation of traditional knowledge, Canada has tried to include Aboriginal peoples in all stages of conservation. In the following three sections, I present the role ascribed to Aboriginals in the Accord, the Habitat Stewardship Program, and SARA. This leads to a review of the comments by Aboriginal leaders and spokespeople during the parliamentary review of SARA, whose testimonies tell a story that differs from the appearance on paper of a large and important role for Aboriginals in almost every aspect of biodiversity conservation.

Aboriginals and the Accord

As discussed in Chapter 3, the 1996 Accord for the Protection of Species at Risk is a non-binding agreement among the federal, provincial, and

territorial governments (except Nunavut) to protect species at risk collaboratively across jurisdictions. There is no specific agreement, however, between governments and Aboriginal peoples when it comes to
species at risk. Instead, Aboriginal peoples provide input for federal,
provincial, and territorial legislation. The federal government oversees reserve lands (or "reservations" as Americans refer to them), so
laws and agreements pertaining to federal lands apply also to reserves
(unless otherwise specified). Thus, reserves are exempt from provincial
endangered species legislation, falling instead under the federal SARA.
Although Aboriginal peoples have been open and willing to participate in the process of conservation under SARA, the intergovernmental Accord does not leave much room for the active involvement of
Aboriginal peoples.

Aboriginals and the HSP

In 2004 the Aboriginal Fund for Species at Risk was created under the
Habitat Stewardship Program, part of Canada's Strategy for the Protection of Species at Risk. Two specific types of funding are available under the fund: the Aboriginal Capacity Building Fund, which assists
communities in building the capacity to enable their participation in
conservation efforts, and the Aboriginal Critical Habitat Protection
Fund, which assists communities in protecting and recovering critical
habitat on Aboriginal lands. Both funds are co-managed by Environment
Canada, Parks Canada, and Fisheries and Oceans Canada, and are available for any Aboriginal organization, including tribal councils, reserve
school authorities, cultural education centres, and Aboriginal land
managers. Together the Aboriginal funds entail C$3.3 million per year,
and between 2004 and 2010 $13 million was provided in support of
422 diverse projects involving 90 communities and 270 listed species
(Canada 2012). For example, in fiscal year 2009/10 the Federation of
Saskatchewan First Nations received $40,000 for a population and
habitat mapping project for lake sturgeon, while the Lesser Slave Lake
Indian Council in Alberta received the same amount for a project to
assess critical habit for the woodland caribou and a water bird, the yel-
low rail. In the Northwest Territories, the Yellowknife Dene First Nations
were awarded $35,000 to collect traditional knowledge of a fish, the
shortjaw cisco, in Great Slave Lake.

Despite such funding, however, these programs are in jeopardy.
Although money is still put aside for these programs under the current

Conservative government of Stephen Harper, awards often are not granted until July, making it difficult for projects to complete their main objectives within the budget cycle.[38] This delay means that researchers begin to look for summer students to hire only in mid-July, and that not all the allocated funds are used in the shorter research project timeline, which makes it appear as though the funds were not needed and which thus decreases the amount of funds awarded in the following year.

Aboriginals and SARA

The preamble to SARA makes clear that "the roles of aboriginal peoples of Canada and of wildlife management boards established under land claims agreements in the conservation of wildlife in this country are essential" and, therefore, "the traditional knowledge of the aboriginals [sic] peoples of Canada should be considered in the assessment of which species may be at risk and in developing and implementing recovery measures." Under SARA Environment Canada has established the National Aboriginal Council on Species at Risk (NACOSAR), consisting of six representatives of Aboriginal peoples selected by the minister of the environment based upon recommendations from Aboriginal organizations. The role of the council is to advise the minister on the administration of the act and to provide advice and recommendations to the Canadian Endangered Species Conservation Council. NACOSAR meets once a year with the minister to report on recovery, stewardship, enforcement, or other areas of concern to Aboriginal peoples.[39]

In addition to NACOSAR, the law also states that a Committee on the Status of Endangered Wildlife in Canada (COSEWIC) "must carry out its functions on the basis of the best available information on the biological status of a species, including scientific knowledge, community knowledge and aboriginal traditional knowledge." To accomplish this, COSEWIC has established a subcommittee of at least nine members who are appointed by the minister on the recommendation of Aboriginal organizations and who specialize in Aboriginal traditional knowledge to ensure that COSEWIC is incorporating such knowledge in its assessments and reports to the minister. In 2010 COSEWIC developed guidelines that describe Aboriginal traditional knowledge as based on "knowledge of the relationships between humans, wildlife, spirituality, environmental conditions, and land forms in a defined locality and, frequently, over lengthy time periods" (Canada 2010b). As I discuss further below, however, neither the express language of SARA nor its subsequent interpretations offer adequate guidance on how aboriginal traditional knowledge is to be collected or used for conservation purposes.

With respect to action plans and management plans SARA also says that, "to the extent possible, the recovery strategy [for a species at risk] must be prepared in cooperation with … every aboriginal organization that the competent Minister considers will be directly affected by the strategy"; importantly, however, the inclusion of Aboriginals is discretionary, and it is up to the minister to judge who is likely to be directly affected. Overall, SARA clearly carves out a large role for Aboriginal peoples, and if the law were followed as written, NACOSAR and the subcommittee on Aboriginal traditional knowledge would be meaningfully involved in almost every step of conservation. The law does not work that way in practice, however, which creates a problem of environmental justice for Canada's Aboriginals.

Aboriginals and Environmental Justice

Environmental justice and its sister concept, ecological justice, often defy strict definition, like the concept on which they both depend: justice. Very broadly speaking, environmental justice addresses "risks within human communities," while ecological justice is "focused on the relationship between those human communities and the rest of the natural world" (Schlosberg 2007, 3). In the remainder of this chapter I examine environmental justice, first as a concept and then as a principle in action in Nunavut, and I also consider ecological justice using the polar bear as a case study. My main goal is to show that collaborative ecosystem management in Nunavut is bringing environmental justice, in the sense of capabilities, to the Inuit, but that ecological justice for species at risk is not only missing, but sometimes in direct conflict with environmental justice.

The environmental justice movement is often considered to be a US phenomenon, as its central ideas developed in the context of race and environmental risk in the 1980s. It was through a 1990 conference on Race and the Incidence of Environmental Hazards at the University of Michigan that the US Environmental Protection Agency (EPA) became interested in the concept. In 1992 the EPA created an Office of Environmental Justice and officially defined environmental justice as "the fair treatment and meaningful involvement of all people regardless of race, color, national origin, or income with respect to the development, implementation, and enforcement of environmental laws, regulations, and policies" (United States 1992). This uniquely American concept is largely considered an offshoot of the civil rights movement (Fletcher 2003, 12) and not part of the Canadian cultural fabric, although it is recognized that "distributive and procedural equity concerns are often central to environmental disputes" (69) in Canada. Agyeman et al. (2009, 3) argue that Canada's environmental justice movement has been "contextualized within the purview of social justice and human rights advocacy movements," and they point out that Aboriginal peoples have cared about environmental justice since time immemorial.

Numerous scholars have illustrated, however, that environmental justice is about more than just claims of equity (see, for example, Bryant 1995; Nussbaum and Sen 1992; Schlosberg 2007; Schlosberg and Carruthers 2010). For example, environmental justice has been said to "refer to those cultural norms and values, rules, regulations, behaviors, policies and decisions to support sustainable communities, where people can interact with confidence that their environment is safe" (Bryant 1995, 6). Even looking to the 1991 First National People of Colour Environmental Leadership Summit's "Principles of Environmental Justice," one can see a call for environmental policy based on mutual respect, equal participation, authentic inclusion, self-determination, ethical and sustainable land-use, and socio-environmental education (EJRC 1991). Thus, while justice is a tricky term, so too is environmental justice.

At its core, environmental justice is about obtaining the "various capabilities necessary for individuals and communities to be free, equal, and functioning" (Schlosberg and Carruthers 2010, 15; see also Schlosberg 2007). Capability theory focuses on the basic functioning of those components necessary for a self-sustaining life; this might include procedural justice, as discussed in Chapter 4, but also decent-paying and safe jobs, quality schools and housing, and access to health care (Bryant 1995). Moreover, a capabilities approach to environmental justice focuses not only on individuals' ability to be and do things, but also on the community's ability to flourish, sustain, and renew itself (Schlosberg and Carruthers 2010). Do Canada's Aboriginals experience this type of environmental justice under SARA, as the UNCBD intended?

Ecological justice is a separate idea and less accepted by mainstream scholars, let alone the general public. Theory and practice take seriously the idea of justice for and towards other species, both animals and plants. Nussbaum (2000, 2006a, 2006b) suggests that relations between humans and non-humans should be regulated by a conception of justice, as "the fact that humans act in ways that deny animals a dignified existence appears to be an issue of justice" (2006a, 326). Other justice scholars avoid this debate by denying non-humans agency and placing them in the category of "subjects," thereby denying the rights afforded to agents (human beings). "Green" democracy is a response to this view, and is in part a movement to achieve status for non-human nature and give it a voice in the democratic process. Similarly, capability theory can "treat nonhuman animals as ends, and do this by focusing on the things that limit the flourishing of animal existence" (Schlosberg 2007, 144). The radical nature of this view makes the findings in Chapters 6 and 7 even more astounding: landowners overwhelmingly agreed that other species have a right to exist and that it is not acceptable for species to go extinct because of human activities.

Most of this discussion lies outside the scope of this book, but it is important to note that the Inuit consider animals, including the polar bear, to be agents – active participants in their own lives. As I illustrate below, ecological justice has always been an important concept for the Inuit and is part of the territory of Nunavut's Wildlife Act, although it is not referred to there as such. But a capabilities approach for the Inuit is becoming impossible to achieve without violating the principles of ecological justice. Thus, environmental justice is a paradox for the Inuit. To flourish as a community the Inuit need to preserve their cultural values and practices, such as hunting, but they also cannot hunt species at risk of extinction. I explore this paradox in greater depth below.

From April 2009 to May 2010 the House of Commons Standing Committee on Environment and Sustainable Development conducted a review of SARA's first five years. During the review the Committee heard testimonies from representatives of seven different Aboriginal groups, including the Assembly of First Nations (AFN), the Maritime Aboriginal Peoples Council, the Congress of Aboriginal Peoples, the Elders Council, and the Athabasca Chipewyan and Walpole Island First Nations. The Committee also heard testimony from a representative of the Nunavut Wildlife Management Board, an institution of public governance that I describe below. These testimonies are the best summation of Aboriginal attitudes towards SARA, particularly as it relates to calls for environmental justice (see also Olive 2012c). Based on these testimonies, one may conclude that Canada's Aboriginal peoples feel the country has yet to achieve any sort of environmental justice when it comes to the conservation of species at risk.

On 13 April 2010 the Committee heard from Shawn Atleo, National Chief of the AFN, the national organization of First Nations in Canada. There are more than six hundred First Nations communities across Canada, each with its own chief and each is a member of the AFN. Chiefs meet annually to set national policy in a collaborative manner, while also convening throughout the year at the "Confederacy of Nations" to communicate and set ongoing direction. Every three years a national chief is elected to a three-year term (see the AFN Web site at http://www.afn.ca/index.php/en/about-afn/description-of-the-afn).

At the Committee meeting Chief Atleo began by pointing out that his peoples had "not helped to shape in a real way how the legislation is drafted, delivered, executed or implemented," and there was no equal participation in the process or outcome of conservation (Atleo 2010). Atleo presented six major points that the AFN wanted to see addressed by Parliament and that it considered as a starting place for improving SARA legislation. First, "First Nations must be included in the administration of the Act"; specifically, Atleo argued that the listing of species is an infringement on First Nations' treaty rights because it directly imposes limitations on their habitat. Thus, "mutual recognition and respect," according to Atleo, should be the cornerstone of procedural matters related to SARA, whereby First Nations actively take part in the process of listing species and regulating habitat.

Atleo's second recommendation was for NACOSAR to recognize the three distinct peoples of Canada's Constitution (First Nations, Métis, and Inuit) and to go directly to the appropriate representatives of those peoples when electing members and carrying out its main tasks. Third, Atleo thought that more needed to be done to ensure that Aboriginal tradition knowledge is protected from theft and misuse, since SARA places that knowledge in the public domain. In this regard, he believed that a First Nations-specific advisory body should be created to ensure the protection and proper use of such knowledge.

Fourth, Atleo argued that stewardship plans be crafted in a way that respects First Nations' treaties and the federal government's duty to consult First Nations. This is especially important because the regulation of reserve land for the purposes of conservation must be undertaken with careful consideration and a deep understanding of Aboriginal rights, Canadian history, and the lifestyles of the peoples who live on-reserve, and for stewardship plans to be created in full consultation and collaboration with Aboriginal peoples.

Related, Atleo's fifth recommendation was that SARA be amended to provide for a different compensation schema, since regulation affects Aboriginal peoples differently than other landowners. Reserves differ from private property: individual First Nations or Inuit people do not own parcels of reserve land over which they have control or on which they pay property tax. Instead, title to reserve lands is vested in the Crown, and reserves are managed by the First Nations. Aboriginal peoples, some of whom have lived in the same geographical area for thousands of years, have a historical claim to their land through treaties signed with the Crown in right of the federal government. Thus, when a private landowner loses part of his land, it is different than when a First Nation loses part of its treaty land or traditional homeland.

Finally, Chief Atleo called for the full involvement of First Nations communities not only in SARA's enforcement but in all its stages, particularly as they relate to Aboriginal lands (Atleo 2010). These suggestions were nothing short of a call for environmental justice, particularly legitimacy and procedural justice, in the implementation of the act.

On that same day, Elder Pat Marcel from the Athabasca Chipewyan First Nation in Alberta spoke to the Committee about the woodland caribou and bison, stressing the need for consultations and meaningful inclusion in SARA. The Athabasca Chipewyan First Nation recently has been thrust into the spotlight in conflicts over Alberta's oil sands. Marcel did not present key recommendations, but spoke at length about the need for improved consultation and communication between Environment Canada and Aboriginal peoples. Moreover, he opposed Canada's often top-down consultation approach whereby Ottawa informs Aboriginal peoples rather than actually "consulting" with them; as he noted, "consultation is between two nations with equal representation, working with trust and belief in each other" (Marcel 2010). Yet, such consultation was desperately lacking, and the Chipewyan were growing increasingly frustrated watching ancient caribou and bison herds go extinct for reasons beyond their control.

The last speaker on 13 April was Joshua McNeely, from the Maritime Aboriginal Peoples Council (MAPC), which deals with regional issues affecting Aboriginal peoples in the Maritime provinces, including 25,000 who continue to live on traditional ancestral lands as opposed to reserves (McNeely 2010). MAPC meets regularly and makes recommendations directly to the Council of Maritime Premiers (see the Web site at http://www.mapcorp.ca). McNeely reminded the House Committee that Aboriginal peoples had lobbied Parliament for the passage of SARA from the beginning and had long supported Canada's commitment to the UNCBD. He specifically drew attention to the words used in the Convention: "We understand those terms: 'precautionary approach', 'sustainable development'; that's in our language. In Mi'kmaq we have a word called *netukulinmk*. In English it quite often gets translated into 'harvest' but it's a lot more than that. It's harvesting for what you need today, leaving for tomorrow, leaving for future generations" (McNeely 2010). For MAPC, SARA is a good first step towards fulfilling Canada's commitment under Article 8 of the UNCBD, but the organization wants immediate improvement of SARA's implementation, particularly by focusing on biodiversity and conservation at the national and international levels. In this vein, McNeely spoke to the need for Canada to adopt the UN Declaration of the Rights of Indigenous Peoples,[40] as well as to approve a national policy on sustainable development. McNeely also felt that it is time for an open discussion of the benefits and sharing of biological diversity in Canada and around the globe. This could be achieved, McNeely suggested, through the creation of local, regional, and national discussion forums on biodiversity, as well as by supporting a full Aboriginal review of the Convention on Biological Diversity. Finally, McNeely recommend that the federal government embrace and actively encourage Aboriginal participation in SARA. Again, this was a call for equal participation and authentic inclusion, the backbone of environmental justice.

Two weeks later, on 27 April 2010, the Committee heard from Alastair McPhee, a policy advisor for the Congress of Aboriginal Peoples (CAP), which had been founded in 1971 as the Native Council of Canada. The umbrella organization represents non-status Indians and Métis, who are a very large segment of Canada's Aboriginal population and a segment that traditionally has gone unrecognized and excluded from federal responsibility (see the Web site http://www.abo-peoples.org). Although McPhee acknowledged that SARA is "well written and includes many sections that reference Aboriginal peoples," he also argued that, "in the development of recovery strategies, the Aboriginal voice is lost" (McPhee 2010). He strongly encouraged the Committee to strengthen the role of Aboriginal traditional knowledge in recovery strategies, action, and management plans. He also stated that "the non-derogation clause in section 3 of SARA is something we don't support ... We don't accept it because it's not in the language of the Constitution,"[41] and he called for the clause to be amended by including appropriate language (as determined by the federal Interpretations

Act) to protect the rights of Aboriginal peoples. Lastly, McPhee argued that the duty to consult is of central importance because "critical habitat designation is equal to a land grab if done without First Nations consent. Critical habitat orders on reserve lands under section 58 should require First Nations consent" (McPhee 2010). Similar to Atleo, McPhee was concerned that SARA authorizes government agencies to regulate Aboriginal treaty lands without the consent of Aboriginal peoples. The way the law is written, if land is declared to be "critical habitat" for an endangered species, the species and the land it requires for recovery is protected by the law and all individuals are restricted from using that land without proper permits. For CAP, therefore, it is imperative that SARA recognize a duty to consult with Aboriginal peoples about all matters pertaining to their lands.

Speaking on the same day as McPhee was Councillor Kennon Johnson of the Walpole Island First Nation, located on an island in the St Clair River between Ontario and Michigan. Geographically the island is environmentally blessed with almost seven thousand hectares of wetlands. It is also home to some very rare flora and fauna (see the Walpole Island First Nation Web site at http://www.iisd.org/50comm/commdb/desc/d09.htm). Johnson testified that the single species approach taken by SARA is something that his peoples feel will fail. He recommended the federal government adopt a more holistic and ecosystem-based approach when implementing SARA. In 1995 an International Advisory Committee selected fifty communities in the world that illustrate successful citizen initiatives in areas of listed importance to the United Nations.[42] Walpole Island was selected in the category of Environment and Sustainability, with the award recognizing that, as its Web site notes, it had always viewed life in a "spiritual, holistic and dynamic way."

Similar to representatives of other Aboriginal organizations, Johnson had strong feelings about the federal government's duty to consult First Nations people. He argued, "[t]okenism on the part of SARA-responsible authorities when consulting First Nations must end. In what is supposed to be a time of reconciliation between Canada and Aboriginal peoples, the inequitable burden that SARA has placed on Aboriginal communities has undermined that spirit at almost every turn" (Johnson 2010). Echoing what other Aboriginal organizations had already told the House Committee, Johnson spoke about the need for sincere and equitable consultation from the outset throughout the process of SARA. He also encouraged the Committee to strengthen the role of Aboriginal traditional knowledge in all aspects of SARA, from listing to recovery. The government has a responsibility, he said, to consult Aboriginal peoples and to use traditional knowledge gained through consultation and through the committee process.

A week later, on 6 May 2010, the Committee heard from Michael d'Eca, legal counsel for the Nunavut Wildlife Management Board (NWMB), which oversees the protection of wildlife and habitat for sustainable Inuit living in an area that is almost one-fifth of Canada's total territory. The NWMB works in direct collaboration with the federal government and is headed by Inuit so as to include them in all decisions related to the future development of their land (see the NWMB's Web site at http://www.nwmb.com). D'Eca began his testimony with three recommendations, each a component of environmental justice. His first was to "add a new section to SARA, section 27, which states: The Minister and the Governor in Council must take into account any applicable provisions of treaty and land claims agreements when carrying out their functions" (d'Eca 2010). This recommendation stemmed from the fact that SARA does not recognize the jurisdiction of the NWMB with respect to the Nunavut Land Claims Agreement of 1993. NWMB is a creation of a constitutionally protected land claim, so, by definition, SARA must give way to it. But, of course, since "most of Ottawa doesn't have a clue about land claims," it would be helpful, according to d'Eca, to have additional language.

D'Eca's second recommendation, echoing the concern of the Congress of Aboriginal Peoples, was to "remove the ineffective non-derogation clause currently in section 3 of SARA and replace it with an effective non-derogation provision" (d'Eca 2010). Specifically, he wanted the new clause to be placed inside the federal Interpretation Act, the most recent and clearest legal precedent for language relating to Aboriginal rights that stem from the Constitution. His concern speaks to a larger issue not specified by SARA: the historical inconsistencies in Canada's legal code when it comes to references and clauses regarding the rights of Aboriginal peoples. The Interpretation Act was updated most recently in 2009, and d'Eca wanted SARA to be amended to reflect the most recent non-derogation provision. This language protects Aboriginal rights, and it is important that Canadian laws be consistent and precise in all language relating to Aboriginal peoples. This is a call for equity and human rights for Aboriginals, not just in the environmental realm, but in all social matters.

Finally, d'Eca recommended an effort to "improve the language of SARA concerning the inclusion of [Aboriginal traditional knowledge] in management, protection, and recovery measures undertaken pursuant to the act, and consider the establishment of an aboriginal traditional knowledge institute" (d'Eca 2010). This was a particularly important recommendation: the Inuit, who live far removed from most other Canadians, have a lot of traditional knowledge and use it to monitor and protect wildlife. In 1995, for example, the NWMB undertook a massive and extraordinary study of the bowhead whale. It conducted (and transcribed and analysed) more than 250 interviews, and held numerous workshops to collect data about the "behaviour and ecology, and the cultural and traditional importance of the bowhead whale to Inuit" (NWMB 2000). At the time no study of this magnitude or import documenting Aboriginal traditional knowledge existed, and it underscores the need for an institute to gather and house such knowledge.

Given the diversity of Aboriginal peoples across Canada, it is no surprise that the individuals and organizations testifying before the House Committee did not speak with a unified voice. Common themes of environmental (in)justice, however, were readily apparent: transparency and communication need to be at the forefront of SARA implementation, the law needs to both acknowledge and respect treaties and land (settled and disputed) claims, and Aboriginal traditional knowledge must be protected while also being used to its full potential. Canada's Aboriginal people desire equal participation, mutual respect, self-determination, authentic inclusion, and sustainable land use. In the realm of species conservation, SARA is falling short of delivering these components of Aboriginal community well-being.

Environmental Justice in Nunavut

I come now to the location of my final case study, Nunavut, a territory created in 1999 through an agreement between the federal government, the government of the Northwest Territories, and Nunavut Tunngavik Incorporated (NTI), an Inuit organization. As a result of the agreement, Nunavut gained status as a territory independent of the Northwest Territories. As part of the 1993 Land Claims Agreement, the Inuit had given up title to their traditional lands in return for fee simple ownership of about 15 per cent of those lands and jurisdiction over wildlife management, a substantial responsibility given the territory's 1.9 million square kilometres in size (see Figure 8.1).

Figure 8.1. Map of Nunavut

Source: © Map of Canada courtesy of Environment Canada.

Wildlife is the economic foundation of traditional Inuit life. Nowhere else in Canada do citizens live the way Inuit do. Grant (2010, 9) notes that, "because of the uniqueness of their culture and remoteness of the Arctic, Inuit in Canada have retained their separate identity in an increasingly multicultural nation." Hunting is an essential part of the Inuit's modern mixed system of subsistence living and a wage-based economy (see Aarluk Consulting 2008, 4). Wildlife plays a critical role in the economy, diet, and culture of Nunavummiut (people who live in Nunavut, including non-Inuit). They depend on marine life and caribou for food and for tourism and economic trade. But the hunting-based economy has come under increasing pressure in recent years because of the rising cost of harvesting (oil, gasoline, ammunition, snowmobiles, and boats), fluctuating prices for fur, meat, and fish, rising transportation costs, wage employment, and a gradual reduction in land skills among Inuit youth (Aarluk Consulting 2008, 4). Environmental and economic shifts are jeopardizing the sustainability of the Inuit way of life. And although Arctic Canada is not urbanized, it is still a human-dominated landscape because of the effects people have on the environment, most notably climate change.

Nunavut does not have stand-alone species-at-risk legislation, but the territory's 2008 Wildlife Act does make provisions for endangered species. Nunavut is not part of the 1996 intergovernmental Accord because the territory did not then exist, but its extensive tracts of Crown land are under the jurisdiction of the federal government and SARA, and the territory is a designated voting member of the Committee on the Status of Endangered Wildlife in Canada (COSEWIC). At the same time, however, although Nunavut is part of the overall National Strategy for Species at Risk, the territory is not fully immersed in the process because of the large amount of Inuit-owned land. As d'Eca pointed in his testimony to the House Committee, the Nunavut Wildlife Management Board has territory-wide jurisdiction that SARA should respect.

It is in this sense that Nunavut offers a case study of the possibilities for environmental justice for Aboriginals. Their approach to wildlife management is a form of collaborative, community-based ecosystem management. Wildlife management in Nunavut is complex and dates back to the First World War era, when the federal government started legislating hunting in the region. Most of the game ordinances before that time exempted Aboriginals, but in 1917 new legislation regulated Aboriginal hunting and protected the musk ox (Kulchyski and Tester 2007, 31–3). The law remained unchanged until 1949, but it was not well enforced due to the size of the territory and the numerous responsibilities of the Royal Canadian Mounted Police. Another issue was the status of the Inuit: who was really responsible for them? Through the 1920s the federal government debated strategies for the Northern peoples and tried to work out a balancing act between assimilation and preventing dependence on the state (Kulchyski and Tester 2010). In 1939 the Supreme Court of Canada ruled that, for administrative purposes, "Inuit were Indians," and thus a federal responsibility. And only in 1999 was Nunavut was finally created and the governance structure for the Inuit changed. Since 1999, and under the Nunavut Land Claims Agreement (NLCA), responsibility for wildlife and conservation in the territory has been shared among the federal government, the NTI, the government of Nunavut, the NWMB, hunter and trapper organizations, and regional wildlife organizations.

Nunavut Tunngavik Incorporated is the organization recognized under the land claim agreement as the body responsible for representing Inuit interests with respect to claim implementation and other issues; its president and other senior officials are elected by all Nunavut Inuit. The NTI's mandate is to ensure that the federal and territorial governments are implementing their respective responsibilities in the area of wildlife management, to advocate on behalf of Inuit, and to initiate projects and support programs (see the NTI Web site at http://www.tunngavik.com/about). This body is central to the overall administration and oversight of wildlife policy in the territory.

The NWMB is an appointed body of public governance, meaning it is open to Inuit and non-Inuit (who may or may not reside in the territory). The Board was established under the NLCA and is "the main instrument of wildlife management in the Nunavut Settlement Area" (NLCA 5.2.33). Its role is to bring together the knowledge and perspective of the Inuit and government to provide for wildlife conservation and the exercise of Inuit harvesting rights (Aarluk Consulting 2008, 8). Its responsibilities include preparing an annual budget for hunter and trapper organizations (as well as provide some funding to these organizations), participate in research, conduct harvest studies, promote wildlife education, encourage training of Inuit in the fields of wildlife research and management, and promote the employment of Inuit in research and technical positions made available through the government or the private sector (NLCA 1993, s. 5). The NWMB plays a role in the assessment of Nunavut species and, as specified in the NLCA, must "approve designation of rare, threatened and endangered species" (s. 5.2.34 f), which, as I discuss below, in part is why SARA does not list the polar bear as endangered.

The territorial government is also an institution of public governance, open to Inuit and non-Inuit residents, and it must cooperate with NTI, the NWMB, and the federal government. The legislative assembly has nineteen elected officials, one from each district, who then elect a premier and a cabinet. The assembly functions on a consensus basis, however – an unusual form of government that does not exist in many other places in North America. The territory has had three premiers since 1999, all Inuit.

Hunter and trapper organizations represent "the frontline of grassroots wildlife management in Nunavut," as they administer NTI's harvester support programs, sponsor local educational activities, and deliver community training related to hunting, survival, and wildlife management (Aarluk Consulting 2008, 10). Regional wildlife organizations provide a forum for coordinating Inuit harvesting interests at a regional level. Their responsibilities include overseeing the exercise of harvesting rights by Inuit in each region, regulating harvesting practices and techniques of hunter and trapper organizations, and sponsoring economic projects designed to benefit Inuit.

Hunter and trapper organizations and regional wildlife organizations are important because of the remoteness of each of Nunavut's twenty-six settled communities. There are no roads in the territory, and often the only way to travel is via snowmobile, boat, or aircraft, making it difficult and expensive to travel from one community to another. All these communities are situated on coastal waters and are self-reliant for traditional foods. "Southern" cargo finds its way into these communities largely by aircraft. The individuals, largely men, who make up the hunter and trapper organizations are responsible for controlling the supply of local food sources – they lead hunts and maintain the cultural rituals surrounding the hunt and the distribution and consumption of the harvest. Thus, any wildlife management policy would have to filter through these individuals to be implemented successfully in the territory.

The role of the federal government is to enforce SARA and other federal legislation on public lands and to co-manage (with the Inuit) National Parks in the territory. Iqaluit, the capital of Nunavut, houses most government offices, including those of Environment Canada. As part of SARA, Environment Canada consults with Inuit communities about species protection and recovery, and is responsible for writing recovery and action plans for endangered species and ensuring their implementation. Currently, only seven SARA-listed species are found in the territory: the beluga whale, the Peary caribou, a moss called Porsild's bryum, and four birds (the Eskimo curlew, the ivory gull, the red knot rufa subspecies, and Ross's gull).

Collaborative Wildlife Management

Nunavut has chosen a path of collaborative wildlife management. Together with Environment Canada and the federal Department of Fisheries and Oceans, the territory's government must work with NTI, NWMB, hunter and trapper organizations, and regional wildlife organizations to manage species. The central concern is whether this is an effective system of management and for whom: the people of Nunavut or the species of Nunavut? This is an entirely "Southern" question, since the Inuit likely would make no such distinction between themselves and their environment, but it is becoming an increasingly important consideration. The Inuit are sometimes put in the situation of having to protect a species on which they have traditionally relied for food and other resources. One such species is the polar bear, which the Inuit have decided against listing as a species of concern under SARA, invoking international controversy. The short histories of both Nunavut and SARA make it difficult to gauge impact and success regarding the health of ecosystems in the territory, but from an analytical approach one can readily see the strengths and weaknesses of collaborative management for the Inuit in Nunavut as well as for species such as the polar bear.

The most important strength of the Inuit approach to wildlife management can be couched in terms of environmental justice. As noted the Inuit are full participants in the government of Nunavut and the NWMB, and are the only participants in the NTI and in hunter and trapper and regional wildlife organizations. This gives them some degree of self-determination, and creates space for respect and authentic inclusion, allowing them to obtain information about ethical and sustainable land use as well as social and environmental education. As one example, in Iqaluit the Nunavut Research Institute provides physical space for researchers and Inuit to interact and share knowledge, and holds numerous workshops regarding the environment and public health. While I was in Iqaluit in June 2008, public officials from the federal Department of Health were holding workshops on healthy food systems in the North, particularly as they relate to a new program for subsidized healthy options in the territory. Moreover, the NWMB filters all decisions pertaining to wildlife, which ensures Inuit participation, and provides some control and something more akin to a "capabilities approach" (Schlosberg 2007). Before determining hunting quotas for any given community, for example, the NWMB consults with local hunter and trapper and regional wildlife organizations as well as with Environment Canada. At each step there is input from Inuit, which is used as the basis for decision making, unlike the case of First Nations or Métis in Canada's provinces.

The Nunavut system of wildlife management also allows for *Inuit qaujimajatuqangit* (IQ), Inuit traditional knowledge, to be included meaningfully in decision making. Indeed, IQ is the basis for management decisions; it is "not merely observations of the environment; it is a paradigm for viewing the world and the place of humans in it" (Dowsley and Wenzel 2008, 178). Tester and Irniq (2008, 49) argue that IQ is more than a decision tool; it is a "social, political and economic worldview" that needs to be understood in the proper context. This aligns with the views of Bell (2002, 3), who defines IQ as "the Inuit way of doing things, and includes the past, present and future knowledge of Inuit society." IQ is the cornerstone of the lives of Inuit, which is why the NWMB's Michael d'Eca spoke at the House of Commons Committee hearings about the importance of an institute of traditional knowledge, which has not yet been realized. The Inuit are very active in collecting this knowledge and in applying it to species at risk such as the bowhead whale, the caribou, and the polar bear. When SARA was created, with the provision that COSEWIC would use Western science and Aboriginal traditional knowledge in its listing decisions, the law provided no specific means for how that should happen. In Nunavut, the Inuit have found a way to do this through institutions such as the NTI and NWMB.

Another strength of wildlife management in Nunavut is that, with so many layers of institutions involved, it is unlikely the system will overlook something or make too hasty a decision. The hunter and trapper and regional wildlife organizations are on-the-ground institutions – hunters dependent on the land and keenly attuned to subtle changes in the environment. They are in ongoing communication with the NWMB and with the territorial government, both of which are responsible for their funding and oversight. From hunter and trapper organizations, information moves up to regional wildlife organizations and then to the NWMB, with information assessed at each level of governance. At the same time the complexity of this process could also constitute a significant weakness. With so many institutions involved, the management process can be very slow. To make a decision about wildlife, the NWMB must consult with hunter and trapper and regional wildlife organizations, Inuit elders (for IQ), the Nunavut government, affected communities, and, depending on the situation, Environment Canada. These consultations take time – and time is precious when it comes to endangered species. Environmental groups such as Ecojustice fear that species will "wink out" because consultation drags on too long (Pinkus 2010). This criticism is more germane to consultations outside Nunavut because SARA offers few guidelines on Aboriginal traditional knowledge and consultations, which is what Ecojustice wants defined and streamlined. But even in Nunavut hunter and trapper organizations need a few hunting seasons to track environmental changes before beginning the consultation process with distant institutions in Iqaluit.

There is the added complexity and challenge of integrating the long historical outlook of IQ with the more recent and changing, as well as more data-driven, outlook of Western science. The challenge is primarily to governance structures, but also to the coordination and collaboration of societies with different worldviews where one society (non-native Canada) is politically more powerful than the other (Inuit and First Nations). Numerous studies have examined the conflict between Western science and IQ (see Table 8.1 for a comparison of Western science and IQ).[43] Western science is often portrayed as dualist (culture: nature), objective, and data driven (Berkes 1990), and based on a strict worldview of foundationalism that lends itself to calculation and rational decision-making models. Science tends to favour concepts such as "validity" and "reliability," as well as "generalizability" and "precision" (King, Keohane, and Verba 1994). IQ naturally conflicts with science because it is often placed in a "significant moral and ethical context," and emphasizes a holistic view encompassing culture and nature. IQ values oral knowledge, spiritual meaning, and community wisdom, and tends to be local rather than universal (Peters 2003).

In a number of understated and important ways Nunavut's Wildlife Act already integrates both IQ and Western science and takes seriously each way of knowing. The legislation refers to the precautionary principle and scientific data as well as to Inuit principles (Tester and Irniq 2008). The subsection of the act addressing species at risk makes clear that "the guiding principles and concepts of [IQ] are important to the management of wildlife and habitat and should be described and made an integral part of this act" (129 (1)(f)). Thus, the Inuit principle of *avatimik kamattiarniq* is "the treatment of nature with respect, recognizing that what is done to something has implications for something else and that actions can have good and bad consequences" (Tester and Irniq 2008, 51). The Inuit believe that hunters and prey are connected in a cycle of exchange in which hunters depend on the animal for survival and the animal is brought to life again and again by the rules of respect in Inuit culture (Laugrand and Oosten 2010, 120). This principle is intended to guide individual action in Nunavut for the purposes of wildlife management.

The principle of *illiijaaqaqtallniq* means "prohibiting treating animals with disrespect" (Tester and Irniq 2008, 51). Respect for prey and the overall hunt is considered a core value in modern Inuit society (Laugrand and Oosten 2010, 103). Inuit make a connection between "maintaining proper relationships with animals through respectful

Table 8.1. A Comparison of *Inuit Qaujimajatuqangit* (Inuit Traditional Knowledge) and Western Science

Characteristics of Inuit Traditional Knowledge	Characteristics of Western Science
Local	Universal
Communal	Individual
Holistic	Dualist
Moral/spiritual	Objective
Oral	Data driven

hunting" and the perpetuation of the system, including the availability of animals and the flow of food (Schmidt and Dowsley 2010, 380). It is not surprising, therefore, that the Wildlife Act acknowledges the holistic and cyclical human-prey relationship: "wildlife and habitat should be managed comprehensively since humans, animals and plants in Nunavut are all inter-connected" (129 (1)(a)). It is through such principles that the law strives to protect and respect not only the animals, but also their habitat.

Finally, the principle of *papattniq* is "the idea that nature is not a commodity" (Tester and Irniq 2008, 51). As the Wildlife Act states, "all wildlife and habitat should be recognized as intrinsically valuable and worth more than just the benefits derived from harvesting and commercial activities" (129). Similar to other Canadians, the Inuit acknowledge and value the "intrinsic worth" of other species. Moreover, it should be acknowledged that Inuit principles recognize ecological justice and see other species as "agents" worthy of respect, compassion, and the type of dignity afforded to human beings.

Also, in line with non-Inuit, or *Qallunaat*, values, the Wildlife Act says that, "to be comprehensive, the management of wildlife and habitat should include research, analysis, education, harvesting, regulation, conservation, protection, restoration and revitalization" (129 (1)(b)). There is thus a place for Western science and research in Nunavut, as well as the recognition of the need for "regulation," as the Wildlife Act draws from non-indigenous Canadian concepts and language. The precautionary principle is also a guiding value of the act: "the precautionary principle should govern decision making under this Act" (129 (1)(e)). Moreover, NWA acknowledges the importance of socio-political decision making, and requires that the minister of environment "evaluate the socio-economic costs of the recovery policy and the benefits to be derived from its implementation, and the costs of not proceeding with the policy" (129 (1)). Cost-benefit analysis is not historically an Inuit practice, but the Wildlife Act is a pragmatic piece of legislation that attempts to deal with a twenty-first-century problem: wildlife management and the recovery of at-risk species.

In many respects, Nunavut's Wildlife Act is potentially the right balance between IQ and Western science, but two problems remain: implementation and authority. Studies of co-management in the North have documented the challenge of "the lack of effective integration of the perspectives and ecological data of resource harvesters" (Dowsley 2009). Suluk and Blakney (2008, 67) report that "members [of hunter and trapper organizations] often feel that their advice, when given, is not taken seriously, and that the Southern researchers lack the ability to understand IQ." Considerable research demonstrates frustration between Inuit and non-Inuit when it comes to using IQ. Existing institutions – the Nunavut government, the NWMB, and hunter and trapper and regional wildlife organizations – have a framework in which to address this frustration, but it is slow to evolve, in part because of the tension between IQ governance and Western bureaucracy.

It is in this sense that properly designated authority could be problematic, as non-indigenous Canadians value individualism, hierarchy, and clear chains of command, whereas IQ is more community focused. Usher, Duhaime, and Searles (2003) point to a strong "ethos of communalism" within Inuit society, where collective beliefs are pursued at the expense of individual benefits (see also Angell and Parkins 2011). Henderson (2007, 198) comments on "IQ notions of power and the way power was traditionally linked to skill and practice, suggesting that IQ is the opposite of 'rigid hierarchy and credentialism,' both of which are hallmarks of Westminster-inspired systems of government." Similarly, White (2006, 409) suggests that characteristics of bureaucracy are not consistent with Inuit culture, and even though IQ is considered in decision making, "the conceptual framework within which the [NWMB] operates significantly limits the influence of IQ." As he notes, IQ cannot work when it is forced into a system of rational evaluation, merit, hierarchy, division of labour, and adversarial decision-making procedures. What is needed is a straightforward discussion about communication and power. Inuit and non-Inuit in Canada have ideological differences, including entrenched notions of individualism and civil society. The institutions that exist in Canada are based on majority rule with a recognized hierarchy and structure that do not necessarily translate to other cultures. The implication is that wildlife management in the North might require Canadians to rethink notions of governance in the region.

It must also be acknowledged that, despite a rather progressive Wildlife Act and the appearance of a capabilities approach, the Inuit still face enormous social and economic challenges that can be linked to ongoing colonialism (Hicks 2007). In this respect they are not unlike their southern counterparts: First Nations, Métis, and Native Americans. Unemployment, alcoholism, and teenage pregnancy rates in Nunavut are higher than the national average (Hicks 2007; Kirmayer et al. 2007). Housing and food costs remain problematic for most families (Hicks 2007). To this end, Ford et al. (2007) explore "adaption policy," whereby IQ is central to creating the policy required to reduce or moderate the negative effects of climate change, including social problems linked to changes in the environment. Specifically, they examine the recent erosion of IQ among Inuit youth, who have become dependent on wage-based employment and are spending less time with elders and on the land. They conclude that adaption requires a renewed commitment to IQ as cultural preservation as well as a sound method of wildlife management.

Related, "cultural ecology" is an emerging area of study that concerns how technology is used in new social and environmental settings, with close attention to cultural adaptation (Wenzel 2001). Research in this area has examined how the Inuit use traditional knowledge to navigate in an era of rapid resources development (Angell and Parkins 2011; Champagne 2007; Usher, Duhaime, and Searles 2003). Although the Inuit stand at the crossroads of economic dependence and economic development, and although they are making strides with respect to justice in wildlife management, other types of social justices and human rights are still problematic, which spills over into the environmental realm. Without addressing the larger socio-economic context of Nunavut, environmental justice in wildlife management is a losing battle. A true "capabilities approach" would see the Inuit rise to a socio-economic standard whereby they did not have to make desperate choices between employment and wildlife protection. The case of the polar bear is illustrative of the problem with wildlife management in Nunavut.

The Polar Bear in Nunavut

What happens when environmental justice for the Inuit clashes with environmental justice for species at risk? What happens when Western science and IQ disagree? This is the conundrum facing the listing of the polar bear as an at-risk species in Canada. In May 2010 the Nunavut minister of environment announced that the territorial government would not support Environment Canada's proposal to list the polar bear as a species of Special Concern under SARA. The reasons for Nunavut's decision include lack of scientific evidence, since hunter and trapper organizations have observed a thriving polar bear population in the region. Inuit knowledge suggests that the polar bear can and will adapt to changing climate conditions (Nunavut 2010).

The International Union for the Conservation of Nature (IUCN) immediately came out against Nunavut's decision. IUCN is the world's oldest and largest global environmental network – with more than 1,000 government and non-governmental member organizations and almost 11,000 volunteer scientists in more than 160 countries (see the IUCN's Web site at http://www.iucn.org/about/). The Polar Bear Specialist Group within the IUCN believes Nunavut's position is "contrary to all available evidence and will not lead to the best possible consideration of the species" (IUCN 2011). The polar bear was listed in the United States as "threatened throughout its range" under the Endangered Species Act, a decision "based on extensive reviews of the scientific evidence suggesting a significant loss of sea habitat projected or observed over a period of three generations" (IUCN 2011). The polar bear has also been listed in Manitoba, Newfoundland and Labrador, and Ontario as threatened or vulnerable. Greenland has also listed some populations of polar bears as vulnerable.

Is this a case of Western science is "right" and IQ is "wrong" in Nunavut? Not necessarily. Western science has been wrong before, such as when scientists determined that the bowhead whale was near extinction only to find thousands more in existence; the federal government made a similar error in 1980 when it declared the Beverly caribou to be extinct (CBC 2008). Indeed, in April 2012 the federal government released a report based on aerial surveillance of Nunavut indicating that polar bear populations might be larger than originally thought (NTI 2012).

The disjuncture between Western science and IQ is important because collaborative wildlife management requires both. Dowsley (2009, 45) points out that "Nunavut's polar bear management system is at the forefront in terms of developing mechanisms for incorporating traditional ecological knowledge as an information source, and has been developing the governance role of communities, at least in part because of the importance of this species at all levels of the social scale, incorporating economic, cultural, existence and symbolic values." She examines how the Inuit have been able to use IQ not only to manage the polar bear adequately, but also to create new relationships and systems of governance. The Nunavut government and co-management partners such as the NWMB collected both traditional knowledge and scientific data on each of Nunavut's twelve polar bear populations before making a decision about quotas (Meek et al. 2011). This is emblematic of possibilities for endangered species protection and recovery in Nunavut.

Dowsley and Wenzel (2008) explore a concrete example of the tension between IQ and science in the polar bear management schema. In 2004 IQ from Baffin Bay and western Hudson Bay indicated an increase in polar bears, so the NWMB raised the harvest limit, which was then approved by Nunavut's minister of environment. International groups, especially the Polar Bear Specialist Group of the IUCN, heavily criticized the Inuit for not using Western science. The international community has relied on radio collars, aircraft, and remote data collection as well as long-term weather pattern data to determine the status of the polar bear, on the basis of which the United States, Greenland, and Russia have taken legislative action to protect the bear. Nevertheless, in 2005 and 2006 the Inuit decided not to reduce quotas because IQ did not deem it necessary (Dowsley and Wenzel 2008).

The Inuit face an impossible situation. If they choose to list the polar bear as endangered and stop harvesting it, such a move would be a major cultural and economic blow to already-suffering communities. Polar bear hunting expeditions are a good source of income for Inuit hunters – a single expedition can cost upward of $50,000, and a polar bear pelt, if the client does not keep it,[44] is worth $15,000 on Asian and Russian markets (Kohler 2012). Moreover, to decrease the quota, limit an economic resource, and infringe upon a cultural tradition would be to accept punishment for a crime they did not commit: overharvesting or habitat destruction by the Inuit is not the main reason the international community thinks the polar bear is on the decline. Thus, it seems unfair – from an environmental justice standpoint – that the Inuit should have to carry the burden of conservation almost exclusively, any more than landowners in my Southern cases should be expected to bear the financial costs associated with conservation. In short, environmental justice for the Inuit is at odds with ecological justice for the polar bear. This should not have to be an either-or situation, but with such immense climate pressure from the South and the lack of economic resources in the North, the Inuit are caught in a difficult situation. The solution is unclear, but will require all stakeholders at the table to make decisions about the North. Canadians already have agreed to preserve Aboriginal traditional knowledge and to respect indigenous ways of life while preserving biodiversity. If they are to take these commitments seriously, they must put the necessary resources into collaborative wildlife management.

Despite equal participation and authentic inclusion, environmental justice remains somewhat elusive for the Inuit, while ecological justice for species at risk, something the Inuit have long practised, is also problematic. The design of their institutions is a tremendous step towards the goal of ethical and sustainable living for the Inuit, but a true capabilities approach requires more than what Nunavut currently provides. To be "free, equal, and functioning" (Schlosberg and Carruthers 2010), the Inuit need to overcome a history of active colonialism. They, perhaps more so than other Canadians, understand stewardship of the environment, and their way of life predisposes them to cooperation with SARA. As individuals, Inuit reject private property and their relationship with nature provides a model that differs from those of Muir and Leopold or Sifton and Pinchot. These Canadians have their own traditions and their own history. Their cultural norms are different than those of most other Canadians and Americans. Like all citizens, however, it matters to them whether or not the law is legitimate and reflective of their personal ethics. The Inuit have made it clear that they do not want to follow regulations that do not respect the hunter-prey relationship. And they also want to be included in the process of making endangered species law in the territory – real inclusion of the sort environmental justice demands.

Conclusion: Aboriginals and Conservation

In 1993 Canada committed itself to including Aboriginal peoples in conservation efforts across the country. Article 8(j) of the UNCBD cements the importance of Aboriginal traditional knowledge as well as the meaningful participation of Aboriginals in the process of conservation. Through the National Strategy for Species at Risk, Canada has mapped out this relationship. The languages of Canada's three distinct peoples are purportedly monitored and supported by the federal government. The 1996 federal-provincial-territorial Accord for the Protection of Species at Risk opens up dialogue among the various levels of government and Aboriginal groups to facilitate conservation. The Habitat Stewardship Program provides funding for Aboriginal projects, both on- and off-reserve. Finally, SARA carves out a large role for Aboriginal peoples in each step of listing, protecting, and recovering species at risk. Yet, although Aboriginal spokespeople acknowledged during the parliamentary hearings on the act's five-year review that SARA is a good first step, they largely felt that the policy falls short of environmental justice. Improvements in the implementation of the law are required, especially concerning consultation, since the process should enhance authentic participation and mutual respect. First Nations, Métis, and Inuit want meaningful involvement in the process of conservation in Canada.

Standing at the "geographic, demographic and economic periphery of Canada" (Trainor et al. 2009, 144), the Inuit have found a path towards environmental justice in the management of wildlife. Through collaborative ecosystem management, they are experiencing something more akin to a capabilities approach, but can institutions lead to environmental justice? Only time will tell. The Inuit are building upon a capabilities approach to environmental justice in the hope that it enhances the community's ability to "flourish, sustain and renew itself" (Schlosberg and Carruthers 2010). The Inuit have lived in balance with nature for as long as they have resided in the North. Their ability to flourish as hunters and to renew their language and traditions depends on the survival of the polar bear, the caribou, whales, and other northern life. Their fates are entangled.

The case of the polar bear highlights the complexity and challenges of conservation in Canada. The country is committed to the principles of the UNCBD, which places a high premium not just on the diversity of non-human species, but on all biological, genetic, and cultural diversity. Canada is committed to preserving the cultural and linguistic diversity of its peoples. Canada is also committed to Article 8(j) of the Convention and the principles of environmental justice. There must be a way to reconcile the needs of the Inuit with those of the polar bear. It could be argued that the people of Nunavut have a greater degree of moral motivation to cooperate with conservation efforts. Their worldview and historical balance with nature prioritizes the spiritual and cultural value of wildlife. Of course they also practise hunting and rely on wildlife for anthropocentric reasons such as food and medicine. But one could say they are culturally predisposed to respecting other species through sustainable harvesting and other principles. This is not to claim that Inuit have only affirmative motivations through morality to cooperate with conservation, but only to point out that there is a real basis for cooperation because of their desire and need to live in balance with other species.

The legitimacy of federal laws is a significant problem. Through the federal system, as made evident in the five-year review of SARA, Canada's indigenous peoples are struggling for meaningful inclusion in the creation and implementation of policy. There is too little focus on procedural justice for Aboriginals in environmental planning, which damages not only the prospects of environmental justice and a true capabilities approach, but also the relationship between regulator and regulated that the Ohio and Ontario case studies highlighted. In one sense, there has been tremendous integration of IQ and Western science in relation to questions of authority. For example, the establishment of a Western bureaucratic structure of government in Nunavut is itself an example of the Inuit meeting Canada more than halfway in the integration of IQ and Western science. When Nunavut was created, institutions had to grapple with design issues sensitive to Canadian and Inuit governance. This is how the territory fostered management boards and the legislative assembly, but also how institutions rely on IQ and consensus decision making. Moreover, the degree to which institutions like the NWMB have been willing to take written minutes in meetings and produce annual reports (White 2006) illustrates how adaptive the Inuit can be to new forms of governance. Unfortunately, it seems that other Canadians have been less willing to adapt and meet the Inuit halfway. This could be in part because of the emphasis continually placed upon the values of science and economics as opposed to values such as precaution, spirituality, recreation, and justice.

In the coming years both Canada and the United States will have to confront environmental justice for northern and other Aboriginal communities in the two countries. The US Supreme Court has never decided whether the ESA applies to Native American tribes or what would happen in the event of a direct conflict between the ESA and treaty rights (Spohr and Fowler 2009). This is also true in Canada, where there has yet to be a conflict between the powers of SARA and the rights of Aboriginal peoples as outlined through treaties and the common law. So far there has been informal negotiation and collaboration with indigenous peoples on both sides of the border. We have seen this in the case of the polar bear in Nunavut, but also famous is the Cheyenne River Sioux reservation, where half the tribal land is in trust status for the purpose of creating a grasslands "prairie reserve" (Torbit and McNaught 2001).

One famous exception to the collaborative approach is that of the White Mountain Apaches, who declared in 1994 that "critical habitat without tribal consent is a violation of American Indian tribal rights, tribal Sovereignty and Federal Indian law principles" (Rodgers Jr 2006, 173). This is similar to the objections Chief Shawn Atleo raised regarding SARA and Aboriginal lands in Canada. The Apache moved to evict USFWS employees from their reservation, for which they received media attention. Even in this case, however, "the crisis yielded hasty negotiations" whereby the USFWS agreed to recognize tribal sovereignty and the Apache agreed to cooperate in the creation of an ecosystem management plan for the Apache trout (Rodgers Jr 2006). In response to this incident and other similar confrontations, in 1997 Secretary of the Interior Bruce Babbitt and Secretary of Commerce William Daley jointly issued an order entitled *American Indian Tribal Rights, Federal-Tribal Trust Responsibilities, and the Endangered Species Act*. The order sets out a general policy that the departments and their agencies should carry out their responsibilities "in a manner that ... strives to ensure that Indian tribes do not bear a disproportionate burden for the conservation of listed species, so as to avoid or minimize the potential for conflict and confrontation" (see Sanders 2007).

Since Native Americans and Canadian Aboriginals have a unique relationship to the land, the legitimacy of US and Canadian laws as they relate to wildlife, habitat, and traditional homelands is of the utmost importance to indigenous peoples. Canada committed to include Aboriginal peoples meaningfully in endangered species initiatives, but SARA fails to fulfil this ambition. The United States has yet to make a similar commitment with respect to the ESA. Both countries are forgoing an opportunity to create affirmative motivation through legitimacy among important land managers on the continent. There is good reason to believe that indigenous people have a motivation through morality to steward wildlife. One hopes this motivation is strong enough to overcome the shortcomings of the ESA and SARA.

9 The Future of Conservation in Canada and the United States

Canada and the United States have taken different paths to the conservation of biodiversity. The Canadian approach, inspired by the UN Convention on Biological Diversity and by negative lessons learned from its southern neighbour, is anchored by the Species at Risk Act (SARA) and buttressed by provincial and territorial legislation as well as by federal habitat stewardship funds. The US approach is anchored by the Endangered Species Act (ESA), but complemented by state initiatives. Are these strategies working to protect and recover species at risk? This question is difficult to answer, and in the case of SARA it is too soon to tell. A different question would be: what would be the status of biodiversity in North America without the ESA and SARA? There seems to be consensus that, as faulty as these policies appear, things could be worse. If nothing else, more people and more levels of government know more and think more about biodiversity. As the famous ESA legal scholar Holly Doremus reminds us, "it is not disputed that the ESA has done far more to protect American biota than any other law" (2006, 196).

Perhaps a more important question is: could we make better biodiversity policy in Canada and the United States? The answer has to be yes. Policy should be able to prevent, protect, and recover ecosystems, and to meet the criteria for environmental justice – not just for Aboriginal peoples, but for landowners and other citizens as well. In this concluding chapter I examines changes that could improve conservation. As different as the ESA and SARA appear to be on paper, both rely heavily on voluntary stewardship by citizens, especially landowners. In both countries farmers and ranchers as well as smaller, more urban landowners must educate themselves about species at risk and actively steward them if large-scale recovery is to be feasible. In this important way, necessary policy changes in the two countries are virtually identical.

A degree of convergence in policy approaches is already taking place. In the past three decades the ESA has been slowly transformed: more incentives are being created for landowners and more cooperative management strategies are being attempted. The ESA is beginning to look more like a "stewardship first" policy than a command-and-control policy, and is backed by incentives such as tax credits, Habitat Conservation Plans, Safe Harbor Agreements, and other landowner programs. In Canada regulatory provincial legislation is popping up across the country to support SARA. The Ontario Endangered Species Act (OESA), in its present form, looks like an ESA-SARA hybrid, as it includes a regulatory hammer for private land but also uses incentives and stewardship funds to entice landowners into conservation. Thus, in both countries there is a greater degree of regulation and stewardship mixing across all land parcels. How could each country improve this relationship?

Domestic Policy

Ultimately, my argument favours cooperative management of biodiversity based on the full model of compliance I presented in Chapter 4. Extensive research indicates that individuals are motivated by negative motivations (punishment and incentives); I have presented research that suggests landowners are also motivated by affirmative motivations. What is needed, therefore, in both Canadian and US domestic strategies, is a larger policy toolkit that, while it contains a regulatory hammer, begins with other tools. In the case of the ESA the regulatory hammer is too large to be useful; in the case of SARA the hammer is virtually invisible. Moreover, in both cases, other tools are not used adequately due to breakdowns in communications, a lack of education, and the misuse of, or over-reliance on, incentives. My research contains a number of key findings that should give policy makers much to consider.

Again, it is important to stress that my case studies involved a small set of landowners and urban residents: in total, I spoke with 101 US landowners and 18 Canadian landowners, and obtained 369 survey responses from urban residents in Canada. Thus, I cannot generalize my findings to all landowners or urban residents in the two countries. But the findings of my case studies are nonetheless significant. The almost five hundred individuals who participated represent a unique and understudied segment of the population. Private property – the right to control access and make land-management decisions – is perhaps the quintessential American right. Yet many species live on private land, so that conservation and private property have always been in tension. Numerous studies and media reports have documented the negative attitudes of farmers and ranchers who have been forced to take conservation actions at their own cost. These studies and reports have created the misperception, however, that all landowners oppose the ESA and that all landowners believe private property rights precede, and are superior to, conservation law. Although it is true that some landowners feel this way, empirical support is lacking to conclude that all or even most landowners oppose the ESA. I therefore suggest that political discourse needs to engage small private landowners as well as farmers and ranchers.[45]

An appropriate place to start is to understand different landowners' willingness to cooperate with conservation policy. In Chapter 4 I explored models of compliance and non-compliance with public policy, with a particular eye to affirmative motivations. Relying on the work of Levi (1997), May (2004), and Tyler (1990) in the field of citizen compliance, I posed two main theoretical expectations: *landowners will interpret conservation policy as consistent with their own sense of morals* and *landowners will interpret conservation policy as consistent with their idea of legitimacy*. In Chapter 5 I provided an overview of commonly accepted norms in Canada and the United States, including a Lockean norm of property and a Leopoldian norm of stewardship. This led to two further expectations: *landowners will consider private property to be more of an intrinsic right than an instrumental right* and *landowners will support the stewardship of endangered species*.

Overall, as the summary of my findings in Table 9.1 makes clear, my case studies suggest that affirmative motivations through morality and legitimacy do exist. In all six cases, respondents felt that conservation of endangered species is morally appropriate. These feelings were stronger in Canada than in the United States. In all cases with the exception of Nunavut, respondents acknowledged the legitimacy of conservation law and agreed that government should create laws for endangered species. Landowners on Pelee Island were becoming increasingly frustrated with the enforcement of SARA and the OESA,

Table 9.1. Summary of Case Findings

Main Conclusion	Indiana	Utah	Ohio	Ontario	Saskatchewan	Nunavut
Respondents know about endangered species?	no	no	no	no	no	n/a
Respondents know about endangered species legislation?	yes	yes	yes	yes	yes	n/a
Respondents have a Lockean view of property?	yes	yes	yes	no	no	no
Respondents accept government involvement in conservation?	yes	yes	yes	yes	yes	no
Respondents possess affirmative motivations for cooperation with stewardship via morality?	yes	yes	yes	yes	yes	yes
Respondents possess affirmative motivations for cooperation with stewardship via legitimacy?	yes	yes	yes	yes	yes	no

suggesting that the legitimacy of these laws might be in crisis soon. I formally interviewed no individuals in Nunavut, but testimony by Aboriginal spokespeople before the House of Commons Standing Committee on Environment and Sustainable Development suggests that the implementation of SARA falls short of the expectations of procedural justice.

Not all respondents agreed with the Lockean conception of property. Although a majority of American landowners did agree, it was always a slim majority, and those respondents remained fairly open to the idea of limits on property rights for the purposes of conservation. Canadian respondents were more likely to reject the Lockean notion of property, but not overwhelmingly so. Despite property attitudes, respondents in all cases accepted government involvement in conservation, and the stewardship of endangered species was important to the vast majority of participants.

Implications and Lessons

Beyond these rather basic findings, one can draw a number of important lessons. First, it should be acknowledged that property norms do not provide a simple answer to problems of conservation or conservation policy compliance and cooperation. It would be easy to say that a stewardship norm enhances cooperation and an intrinsic property norm diminishes cooperation, but I did not find such a straightforward equation. Instead, I found evidence of overlapping and potentially conflicting norms among landowners. Many small non-agricultural landowners share the value of land stewardship, but different pathways lead to this norm: some landowners have developed it through religious faith; others have arrived at it through science or a notion of civic responsibility. Regardless of the pathway, I found that this widely shared value could coexist with either an instrumental or an intrinsic view of property. Thus, Leopold and Locke are not at two ends of a continuum, but can coexist on the same land parcel. For example, many landowners who were hesitant about government involvement and desired an absolute right to property (the intrinsic view) still possessed a keen sense of responsibility to their land and harboured a desire to improve their property for future generations. Similarly, landowners who were more willing to accept government regulation of property (the instrumental view) also possessed a sense of obligation to the land and future generations. Thus, I conclude that the relationship between property norms, including this complementary norm of stewardship, and landowner decisions about endangered species habitat is not simple. One cannot assume that all Lockeans require incentives or that all Leopoldians accept regulation.

Related to this, it is possible to say that small urban landowners by and large expressed similar attitudes. They varied in where they placed themselves on the continuum from intrinsic to instrumental, but an examination of the other regulation-related questions reveals more similarity than difference. This suggests either that landowners' anti-regulation attitudes have been overstated in the literature or that there is a real difference between farmers and ranchers on the one hand and small landowners on the other. Perhaps both are true. Although even the former have a multidimensional view of property, agricultural landowners, particularly in the West, feel that property is an absolute right and reject its regulation. My results do not indicate that non-agricultural landowners feel the same. Speculating on why that would be the case, the literature suggests that individuals who are not tied to the land to make a living feel less strongly about regulation and rules (Kreuter et al. 2006). This is perhaps good news for endangered species that increasingly are found on non-agricultural land whose owners are more willing to accept property as instrumental and regulation for the social good as morally appropriate.

Despite the similarities in attitudes towards regulation it is worth noting that Canadians appear to be less Lockean than Americans – at least on the basis of my small samples. Liberal individualism is the root of both US and Canadian political culture, but my data suggest a difference in willingness to accept government regulation. This could be explained in a number of ways. First, perhaps Canadians simply value conservation more than Americans do and are more willing to accept the costs of conservation. SARA does say that Canadians value the intrinsic worth of other species, whereas the ESA focuses almost solely on anthropocentric reasons for conservation. My landowner data support this claim. It could also be that Canadians are more accustomed to government regulation because Canada is a large welfare state with higher taxes and more publicly provided services than the United States – in Saskatchewan, for example, the government also provides phone services, car insurance, and power. It is reasonable, therefore, to expect these individuals to accept more readily the idea of property as instrumental. Even in Ontario one landowner said, "you don't buy land in Canada – you just lease it from the government." More research, with a much larger sample size, is needed to explore the differences in attitudes on these issues between Canadians and Americans. Ideally, such research would examine the values of Canadian farmers as well to see if they are less Lockean than their US counterparts.

Perhaps more important, the existence of these shared beliefs matter for at least three reasons. First, these beliefs influence landowners' willingness to cooperate with government. I found evidence to suggest that beliefs, particularly regarding the morality and legitimacy of policy, influence willingness to cooperate to help achieve policy goals. In the case of the ESA, this meant landowners were willing to take certain actions on their own property (sometimes at their own expense) to help conserve endangered or threatened species. Second, with regard to the ESA and SARA, the existence and influence of these beliefs create the foundation for cooperative management as a policy strategy. The US Fish and Wildlife Service and Environment Canada can build upon landowners' already-existing desire to cooperate with conservation efforts. With more outreach (communication) and education, there is serious potential to boost compliance with the ESA and SARA.

Third, the existence and influence of shared beliefs in the morality and legitimacy of the ESA and Canadian conservation laws is an encouraging finding for authors such as Tyler, upon whose work I have drawn heavily, who are trying to illustrate the significance of affirmation motivations in theories of compliance. I am able to add empirical support to his claim that legitimacy, or procedural justice, is an influential motivation for willingness to cooperate and comply on the part of landowners. For example, in Ohio landowners who felt the Lake Erie water snake is no longer a legitimate endangered species expressed dissatisfaction with the ESA, and some claimed to be less willing to cooperate or even comply with the law. In Nunavut the Inuit feel displaced by the dominance of Western science in SARA and are less likely to accept the law as legitimate and worthy of compliance. My work also signifies the need for more attention to morality as a motivation. A norm surfaced among these landowners and residents regarding the moral importance of other species and their right to exist; such a norm rests heavily upon moral attitudes.

Beyond the importance of these shared beliefs, my empirical case studies also make evident that no "one policy fits all" for reform of the ESA or SARA. I found that landowners possessed numerous motivations for cooperation, including affirmative motivations driven by morality and legitimacy. Both the ESA and SARA are based upon moral principles, and policy makers assumed that individuals would be willing to steward endangered species. To a certain extent, their assumption is true, but landowners are still also motivated by punishment and incentives. Thus, enhancing compliance and cooperation will require a variety of strategies, some of which will not work in conjunction with others and some of which will work only under certain conditions.

I recognize that incentives are sometimes the only way to encourage compliance or cooperation. This is because voluntary compliance quickly reaches rope's end in at least two types of situations: first, where private landowners' economic interests are high and, second, where stewardship norms are non-existent. With regard to the first, literature on farmers and ranchers shows that often the only way to appease landowners is through incentive programs. A similar finding might result from studies of commercial landowners whose primary income is tied to the land. And where the concept of stewardship is foreign to landowners, incentives and punishment will be needed to support conservation efforts.

Similarly, other literature suggests that different strategies are necessary where property norms vary. Jackson-Smith, Kreuter, and Krannich (2005) conclude that strategies aimed at encouraging environmentally sound land-management practices might use different approaches for landowners with stronger stewardship values (perhaps using an educational message that celebrates and reinforces these values and encourages voluntary self-regulation) than for landowners who believe private property rights are defined mainly through individualistic values. I found that small landowners were more likely to possess stewardship norms than were agricultural landowners, who appeared to have more utilitarian notions of property. This implies that small landowners might be motivated more easily through education and outreach, whereas agricultural landowners might require more incentive-based motivations.

In terms of a purely regulatory approach, it is important to realize that government actually could extinguish affirmative motivations by simply demanding compliance. In the case of the Indiana bat, for instance, if regulators required landowners to build bat houses and place them in trees throughout their properties, this could decrease willingness to cooperate, because so many of Indiana landowners hold a Lockean norm of property. If regulators educated landowners about bat habitat and asked them to build bat houses – perhaps cost sharing with the landowners – and place them on trees of their choice, it is possible that such a strategy would increase willingness to cooperate. Regulating habitat and attempting to increase compliance and cooperation is a complex task. Incentives are not always the answer, and neither is education or punishment. This is why it is important for regulators to have a better understanding of landowners' shared values and motivations before trying to implement any strategy or combination of strategies.

It is readily apparent that listing a species as endangered is not enough to invoke stewardship. An important theme emerging from the case studies is that landowners are not aware of species-at-risk laws and lack even basic information about the species they are supposedly stewarding on their property. Regulators and policy makers must abandon the idea that landowners will steward a species simply because it is listed. In Indiana 32 per cent of landowners had never heard of the Conservation Management Area for the bat, even though their property is inside the area; in Ohio only 23 per cent of landowners could correctly identify Lake Erie water snake habitat, even though the entire island they live on is habitat for the snake. This evidence suggests that studies dealing with compliance (through methods such as monitoring behaviour and land-management decisions of landowners) might run up against the problem of non-compliance due to ignorance – as opposed to non-compliance because of more substantive issues such as disagreement with policy goals or problems of legitimacy. More important, it suggests that education must precede incentives or regulation for such strategies to be optimal.

It is difficult to enforce a law that people do not know anything about. Although 80 per cent of US landowners in my surveys believed there were fines for violating the ESA, no one knew what the fines were or had ever heard of anyone's being fined. In Utah one landowner said, "I don't even know. There should be a fine at least"; another believed "the fines are stiff – like 25,000, 75,000, 50,000 depending on what [the violation] was." And not one landowner in any of the three states or in Ontario knew with any degree of certainty the consequences of a violation. This too casts doubt upon the degree to which landowners are motivated to comply with the law for deterrence reasons. Moreover, information gaps are also evident in landowners' knowledge of their role in the law. In Ohio and Utah, 67 per cent of landowners did not know for certain if the law even applies to their property, and in Saskatchewan 55 per cent wrongly assumed that SARA regulates their property. Since the ESA is a federal law that applies to all citizens and all government agencies (save for the military in most cases), I expected landowners who live close to an endangered species to be aware that the law exists and has implications for their actions and behaviour. Instead, even those who landowners cohabit with endangered species have very little knowledge or understanding of the ESA.

Related to the above discussion, more communication between landowners and government is necessary for cooperation to take root. One problem with a social contract notion of ESA enforcement is that "an implicit social contract results from the shared expectations that evolve from repeated interactions over time between regulatory authorities and regulatees" (May 2004, 43). Figure 9.1 illustrates the results of a similar aspect of my study where I asked landowners about their desire for communication. Essentially, my data show that there is very little interaction between landowners and regulators and virtually none on a repeated or consistent basis. This lack of outreach might signal to landowners that the government does not value the law or, perhaps worse,

Figure 9.1. How Government Can Best Help Landowners: Responses from Indiana, Utah, and Ohio

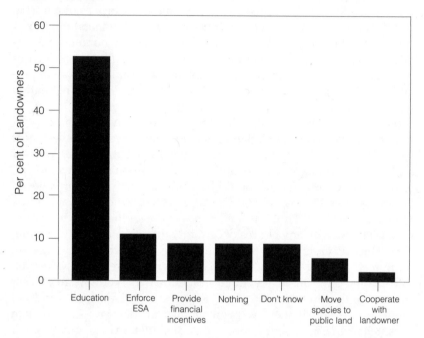

does not value cooperation with landowners. It is not unreasonable to expect that every landowner with a critical endangered species on their land to meet (individually or in a group) with wildlife officers who can explain the importance of the species and cost-free ways to enhance habitat. Stewarding an endangered species should be a task associated with pride, not with punishment. Landowners must be applauded for their efforts.

At the end of every interview in Utah and Ohio, I asked landowners what they thought was the best way government could help conserve endangered species on private property. This was an open-ended question, and landowners were not given options or categories. As Figure 9.1 shows, 53 per cent felt that education would be the best way, while only 11 per cent mentioned incentives and another 11 per cent mentioned enforcement. One Utah landowner told me, "I think education always works better than enforcement. I would not hesitate to take any of my grandkids to be educated about the tortoise." Education is central because in all geographical locations landowners reported feeling helpless, as they did not understand how their actions could help or harm the bat, snake, or tortoise. For example, Lake Erie island landowners seemed to have no idea of the effect of lawn fertilizers on the water snake, and some thought a cement sea wall would help the snake, although such a structure is greatly harmful. One landowner replied, "I guess [it would be better] if we were more educated on the snake because we don't know what the snake needs. We don't know the ins and outs." In Indiana, a landowner who had recently relocated from Wisconsin felt that, "in Wisconsin you know who to call and [the USFWS] are in your face more, and here they are laid back. It would be nice if they would publicize what [landowners] could do [to help the species]." In Utah, landowners had no idea how their land-management decisions could help or harm the desert tortoise. An Indiana landowner summed up the lack of awareness by saying, "the bat never enters my mind."

Some landowners did not understand how helping an endangered species could help the ecosystem or even their own land. During one interview in Ohio a landowner asked me, "what do [water snakes] even eat?" After the interview I informed him that one of their major food sources is gobies, a menacing foreign fish recently brought to Lake Erie by cargo ships. Shocked, he replied: "that information could go a long way on this island in terms of protecting that snake," since the only thing these landowners hated more than snakes and mosquitoes seemed to be gobies. Such basic information was often lacking on the Lake Erie islands, and the landowner's remark illustrates that making a connection between conservation and personal benefit is one way outreach could improve willingness to cooperate.

Surprisingly, USFWS employees seemed well aware of the lack of outreach and its consequences. The Ohio enforcement officer, for example, said, "the USFWS is absent. There are great opportunities lost. I think we suffer from a lack of interaction with the public." Likewise, Kristen Stanford, who has had the most contact with landowners on the islands, said in my interview with her that "[m]ost people want to do the right thing and if the law says 'I am not supposed to do this' then people want to obey it. The harder part [for landowners] is understanding why this is the law. If they don't understand why then they have a harder time wanting to comply." Thus, the USFWS needs outreach to help explain the "why" behind conservation. Essentially, by influencing knowledge and values – and potentially reducing the need to change behaviour through lengthy and costly regulatory processes – education might be one of the cheapest long-term strategies for biodiversity protection (Yaffee 2006).

Beyond creating a knowledge base, outreach and education could also establish an enforcement style based on cooperative management and help the USFWS and Environment Canada understand landowners. The regulator's enforcement style should matter for compliance, but very little regulation is occurring in these locations, so it is difficult to assess the relationship. Winter and May (2001) and May (2004) find that regulators who engage in facilitation foster affirmative motivations, while those whose approach is based on formalism detract from such motivations. If so, in devising a regulatory style the USFWS and Environment Canada have a great opportunity to build on affirmative motivations – which we now know exist – through facilitation. Outreach could help create a relationship whereby landowners are willing to cooperate with government simply because they have been asked.

One should not overestimate the power of information, however. Scott Findlay, Canadian SARA expert and professor at the University of Ottawa, has told me that "lack of education or information is a shield that too many people hide behind." He feels it is not a case of citizens' ignorance, but of their *wilful* ignorance: most people simply are not interested in knowing. He thus advocates for changes in the tax code to reward stewardship, and I agree this might be necessary in some cases. Educating the population about endangered species, however, is neither straightforward nor easy. It is not simply a matter of sending letters or flyers featuring a picture of the species. Making landowners understand the gravity of at-risk species and their stewardship responsibility might require door-to-door visits by wildlife officers. Publicity in other media – newspaper articles, a larger presence on Facebook and Twitter, even a reality TV show – is another approach to explore. Educating citizens about biodiversity, in fact, should be a national priority in both Canada and the United States.

To that end education could also involve the primary and secondary school system. "Ecoliteracy" is the term used to describe ecology studies for young citizens. Similar to Scott Findlay's view, David Suzuki (2011) cynically argues that governments have only two feasible tools to alter human behaviour: regulation and taxation. He suggests that "we have a vast experience to know that voluntary compliance does not work" and that "regulation does work" (252). As examples, he points to alcohol, cigarette, and garbage taxes. Instead of advocating for a larger hammer in the SARA tool belt, however, Suzuki proposes the development and implementation of an eco-literacy K-12 program, because "children can be a powerful force for change" (252). That is to say, regulatory and incentive-based stewardship backed by an awareness and education campaign might change the behaviour of landowners today, while a focus on ecoliteracy in public education might create better landowners tomorrow.

Lastly, my research suggests that Aboriginal peoples have been absent from the implementation of conservation policy in Canada, and other research suggests this is true in the United States as well (see, for example, Rodgers Jr 2003; Sanders 2007). Aboriginal reserves in Canada and Indian reservations in the United States are managed by the respective federal governments and thus fall under the jurisdiction of SARA and the ESA. Unfortunately, environmental justice has not been at the forefront of this effort. Designating critical habitat is essential for endangered species recovery, but it is important to recognize cases where that habitat – whether tribal land or farmland – is also critical for the survival of people. Broadly speaking, like farmers, indigenous peoples have shown enormous stewardship potential and a genuine willingness to cooperate, but more often than not they have been left out of decisions that affect their land. A duty to consult should be written into both the ESA and SARA, and a more prominent role should be given to traditional knowledge – and local knowledge, in the case of farmers – in implementing these laws, particularly in writing recovery plans. Traditional knowledge is a vast resource system that should not only be respected, but used in conservation policy, and the broader public should be made more aware of the importance of traditional knowledge to conversation.

The Key Lesson: Cooperative Management

Pulling together the main findings of my research leads me to advocate a cooperative management approach at the domestic level in both countries. The ESA and SARA are different – both on paper and in practice – but ultimately stewardship will require cooperative governance. Landowners, Lockean or not, are willing to steward biodiversity under certain circumstances or in certain contexts. This is crucial information. But more is required from government (and taxpayers) if this strategy is going to work. Simply put, cooperative management based on the full model of compliance requires a regulatory hammer as well as a realistic expectation of stewardship and the proper and reasonable use of incentives (that is to say, taxpayers' money). This strategy hinges completely on procedural justice and increased communication and education.

Both the ESA and SARA contain a regulatory hammer. It is probably fair to say that the ESA's is more akin to a sledgehammer, whereas SARA's is similar to a butter knife. In both cases, however, the hammer is necessary: the threat of punishment is important in models of compliance, as discussed in Chapter 4. SARA suffers, however, because the threat is illusory: the "safety net" provision that enables Ottawa to act if a province fails to protect an at-risk species has been used only once (for the greater sage grouse) in eleven years, and environmentalists who have tried to invoke it have lost every time. Thus, there is nothing to scare (or manipulate or force) provinces into creating stand-alone policy, and little to deter industry, such as the oil sands development, from carrying on with "business as usual." The ESA also suffers, but because its hammer is so large – stiff fines or imprisonment – that penalties are never handed out. As I discussed in Chapters 2 and 4, large deterrents are difficult to enforce as well as unpopular. This is likely why no small landowner has ever been sanctioned under the ESA. Both countries should adopt a more uniform approach, with sanctions ranging from warnings and small fines to large fines and possible imprisonment for repeat violations – and enforced. Sanctions should not be the backbone of conservation; rather, compliance and cooperation should be secured through affirmative motivations. But the full model of compliance adequately captures the need for deterrence, as some people are motivated only in this way.

The existence of affirmative motivations suggests that we can expect landowners to steward endangered species. By and large, property owners value species and do not want them to go extinct. In democratic societies citizens generally accept and obey the law, which means we can expect most landowners not to kill endangered or threatened species intentionally when they know the species' status; it also means that we can expect landowners to undertake some stewardship activity. For example, in Ohio and Ontario we can expect landowners to avoid activities – springtime construction or mowing their lawn during certain times of the day – that might harm the water snake, but we cannot expect them to build and pay for snake habitat on their own land without some form of compensation. In Indiana we can expect landowners to plant more trees if asked, but not to construct and install bat houses at their own expense on their own land.

The practical implications of these expectations are quite complex. First, to encourage stewardship activities that they otherwise cannot be expected to undertake, landowners need to be offered incentives – ideally in the form of cost-sharing programs or tax-based credits. Governments are beginning to move in this direction, but they need to go farther. Leopold himself acknowledged that conservation policy would involve "rewarding the private landowner who conserves the public interest" (quoted in Bean 1998, 10701). After examining six different reward systems, including impact fees and easements, Parkhurst and Shogren (2003, 258) can conclude only that no "single mechanism is preferable in all situations." They argue, as I do, that money should be spent to determine the conditions under which incentives are necessary, and there will always be such cases. As a starting place, there needs to be greater awareness of the link between biodiversity and the public interest. It is doubtful most taxpayers even realize that landowners provide a public service by stewarding biodiversity. Once that is made clear, it should be easier (although never easy) to use tax dollars for such programs.

Second, the crux is to draw the line between what can be expected and what must be incentivized. Exactly where to draw it might be difficult to determine, but the starting point should not be "nothing is expected, everything is compensated." As is often forgotten in the social sciences, it is the citizens – more specifically, the voters – who ultimately make the law. At the very least, we can expect landowners, and all other citizens, to comply with the law free of cost. That is why we do not pay people to wear motorcycle helmets or users to quit taking drugs. After that we can expect that, if a species is legitimately in danger, and if landowners know that and also know what they can do to help – in the form of actions that cost little if any money – then landowners will steward. This approach will not cost taxpayers anything. But we need to read that sentence again. Landowners must know the species is endangered. That will take some work on behalf of the USFWS – or, in the case of marine species, the National Marine Fisheries Service – and Environment Canada and the Department of Fisheries and Oceans. Landowners must also *believe* the species is in real danger of extinction. This will take more work. Landowners also must be made aware of actions they can take to steward. Again, more work.

Others have argued that what is needed is a new "land ethic" that places the Leopoldian biotic community, of which man is part, at the centre of our social lives. Eric Freyfogle is one of the louder advocates for such an approach. He claims that "local people simply must find ways to rise above the radical individualism of our day. They have to gain the sense that living where they do, they necessarily form and participate in the land community ... once this first, hard step is taken, then comes the need to get people to care more about the health of the community" (2003, 3). Normatively I do not disagree with Freyfogle – it would be a better world if individuals cared about their community in the ways Leopold and Freyfogle want. From a policy standpoint, however, I do not think that norms of property – which are widely shared beliefs – are going to shift. The good news is that they do not have to. Stewardship of the kind that Leopold envisioned can happen in an individualistic, property-oriented society. It will not be easy, but it is possible. It will require cooperation, regulation, outreach, and sometimes incentives. These are the things we can do today.

Is all this work actually cheaper than an incentives-only approach? Perhaps not in the short run, because a massive and extensive education campaign would require innumerable resources if done correctly. In the long run, however, this strategy likely would pay for itself over and over again. Suzuki uses the example of spitting in public places in Japan. When he was a child the Japanese government used advertising and signs to discourage the practice; today, very few people spit in public, and the government spends nothing on education or enforcement, but to get from A to B, for a short period of time it cost Japan a lot of money to regulate (Suzuki 2011). Similarly, Parkhurst and Shogren (2003, 258) argue that "expending resources to understand these factors for different cases will be costly, but worth it." Therefore, Canada and the United States should front the money now to fund education and then test the willingness to steward. This would save resources spent on conflict further down the road.

All the lessons I have presented here can be implemented in both countries in the coming decade. As I argued in Chapters 2 and 3, the political obstacles to such changes cannot be overlooked or downplayed – many are reasons nothing has happened with the ESA since its expiration in 1992. These obstacles must be combatted with a large policy toolkit that includes regulation, outreach, and carefully planned incentives. Other barriers to conservation – in particular, the exploitation of the Alberta oil sands, increasing development in the Arctic, and, in Canada, the lack of leadership on conservation issues by the governing Conservative Party – also pose unique challenges to conservation in North America and warrant a brief discussion.

THE ALBERTA OIL SANDS

Alberta's oil sands pose a particular challenge to conservation for a number of reasons, including disagreements over the proposed Keystone XL pipeline and the lack of concern for species such as the caribou and migratory birds. The pipeline, as planned by TransCanada Corporation, is intended to take oil from the Athabasca oil sands in Alberta down to Texas, where it can be refined for commercial purposes. The multibillion-dollar project would further integrate US and Canadian energy production and security. President Barack Obama has thus far rejected the pipeline, however, citing insufficient time to assess its environmental impact.

The pipeline project is a problem for biodiversity not just because it commits the two countries to continuing oil dependency for the coming years, but also because it would have a direct effect on biodiversity, natural habitats, and water aquifers across the two countries. The proposed pipeline would extend through four distinct bioregions and cause significant disruption in each during the construction phase. If the pipeline is finished and becomes fully functional, the major problems would be pollution and economic power: a resource such as oil that is important for the economy and for the immediate self-interest of political actors and voters usually takes precedence over long-term environmental concerns if history is any indication.

Of course many pipelines already carry oil and natural gas from Alberta to other parts of Canada and the United States. The key difference with the Keystone XL project is public salience and consent: never have any of those pipelines been in the public eye or under much public scrutiny. For the first time the American and Canadian publics are having the debate over trade-offs. With a slow US economy and jobs hanging in the balance, there is little chance that the Obama administration ultimately will reject Keystone. Public consent of Keystone XL could set a precedent that will have negative long-term effects, as it would be more difficult to reject similar projects in the future. Conservative governments, especially Alberta's and Canada's, might see public support for Keystone as its support also for the repealing or undermining of conservation laws. This would be a mistake.

Furthermore, balancing habitat and oil sands development will continue to be a challenge. The Athabasca watershed is under immense pressure because the oil sands require so much water for extraction purposes and also because the tailing ponds, where oil sands waste is deposited, are quickly leaching into the ground and the river system, wreaking havoc on the habitat of many fish and harming other animals, such as birds, deer, and caribou, that drink the water. The project is also so large that it has destroyed a boreal forest the size of Florida, land that home to thousands of different species, from insects to birds to mammals (Nikiforuk 2010). Although some of it is reclaimable, it will never return to its natural state. It is not exactly like "putting lipstick on a corpse" as Nikiforuk claims (111), but it will mean replanting different trees that are hardier and can survive in saltier soil.

There is really no way around it: oil is bad for biodiversity, but important for North Americans (especially their economy). Thus, Americans and Canadians who both benefit from the oil sands must compensate biodiversity either by footing the environmental bill for protection and the cleanup necessary to mitigate the damage or by forcing industry to foot the bill. It would not have to mean an increase in oil prices, but it might mean changing the oil royalty scheme in Alberta so the province receives more oil revenues. Or the province could offer environmental protection by resuscitating the Alberta Heritage Fund – although such a move is unlikely since the fund has not been added to since the late 1980s and is politically unpopular. Whatever Alberta decides, Canada and the United States should ensure jointly that biodiversity conservation is at the forefront.

ARCTIC DEVELOPMENT

The Arctic region is becoming the most important shared interest in US-Canadian relations. And it might be the Arctic that finally forces the two countries to work together on issues of environmental security, although it might not be to the benefit of endangered species or biodiversity more generally. The Arctic is thought to contain at least 13 per cent of the world's oil and 30 per cent of its natural gas (US Geological Survey 2008). It will be hard for ice-worms or ivory gulls to compete with these immediately recognizable "precious resources." Moreover, the Arctic has been a zone of interest to the US military since the Second World War, when a string of radio and weather stations was built from Alaska through Canada and into Greenland (Grant 2010). The Arctic was also on the front line during the Cold War. Given the increasing militarization of the Arctic and the increasing importance of oil and gas discoveries in the region, how will policy unfold?

In 1996 an intergovernmental forum called the Arctic Council was formed in Ottawa, but not through a binding treaty as Canada had wanted, since the United States would have refused to join in that event. Accordingly the Council is a voluntary body with limited powers (Huebert 2011). The eight Arctic member nations make joint, consensus-based decisions on Arctic matters. One of the Council's guiding principles is environmental stewardship, but it cannot settle territorial disputes nor has it signalled its intention to address climate change. Instead, it is likely that Canada and the United States will devise bilateral agreements in these areas. For example, whether the Northwest Passage is an international strait (as the United States claims) or Canadian territory (as Canada claims) probably will be settled through an agreement that gives Canada sovereignty but allows the United States passage through the waters. In any event, it is not the Arctic Council that will make the decision; Canada and the United States will be forced to cooperate and negotiate.

Rob Huebert, a Canadian expert on Arctic security issues, claims that, "ultimately, the two states must find ways to cooperate in the Arctic, since it is in their mutual interest to do so. Both states need to ensure that the new activities in the Arctic are controlled in such a manner that environmental protection remains a core requirement" (2011, 63). One can hardly disagree, but with so much attention given to security and economic development, how can conservation remain a focal point? Even Huebert's colleague Whitney Lackenbauer (2011, 93) argues for a "basic 3-D approach – one that integrates defence, diplomacy, and development" to all things Arctic in North America. He puts a lot of emphasis on diplomacy and coordination, especially in the areas of defence and economic development, but where is the environment? It is almost completely missing from his strategy, although often raised as an issue or a concern – more an afterthought than a core requirement. Safeguarding biodiversity in the Arctic is a significant challenge.

The Arctic differs from other regions in that most land there is not privately owned. In Alaska non-Native private land amounts to less than 1 per cent of the total. In the Canadian territories most of the land is either Inuit-owned (as is 350,000 square kilometres of Nunavut), or Crown land. This means conservation issues are entirely different in the Arctic than in the rest of Canada and the United States. Arctic biodiversity does not rest in the hands of private landowners, but with government (either federal or tribal), and stewardship will have to come from the top down. Moreover, few threats to Arctic biodiversity originate in the sparsely populated region – the biggest threat, climate change, emanates from the south. Effective governance thus will have to steward Arctic biodiversity not just in the Arctic but across the continent.

Canada and the United States likely will collaborate in the Arctic in ways one cannot predict. But important questions remain: will cooperation include the people who reside on the land? Will this cooperation include biodiversity conservation at all? Canada is chairing the Arctic Council from 2013 until 2015, when the United States will assume the chair to 2017. If the two countries worked together, they could oversee the Council for the next four years, giving them an opportunity to take command of environmental stewardship in the region. Given US hesitation to sign international treaties such as the UN Convention on Biological Diversity, it is, as Grant (2011) says, "time for Americans to find their moral compass and show real leadership" in the North. The Arctic could be the best thing to happen to the conservation movement in North America.

FEDERAL CONSERVATIVE PARTY LEADERSHIP

SARA's passage through Parliament occurred during a Liberal government in Ottawa. Since 2006, however, first as a minority government and after June 2011 as a majority, the Conservative Party of Canada under the leadership of Prime Minister Stephen Harper has not been pro-environment. The Harper government has used its majority in the House of Commons to limit environmental regulation across the country either through a lack of appropriate policy or through lax funding. For example, the Conservatives have attempted to weaken government oversight of the clean-up of contaminated sites by requiring fewer assessments and by handing power to provinces, in part because they want to "streamline the environmental assessment process so that it does not delay legitimate economic activity" (Environment Commissioner Scott Vaughn, quoted in Scoffield 2012). As another example, and related to both Arctic development and the Keystone XL pipeline project, the 2012 federal budget includes provisions to transfer the environmental assessment of pipeline projects to the National Energy Board from the Canadian Environment Assessment Agency (Scoffield 2012).

Thus far the governing Conservatives have made no attempt to repeal or amend SARA, but as they will be in power at least until 2015, changes in the way the act works are possible. Under the 2012 federal budget, for example, reviews of fish habitat are no longer required for all projects as the Fisheries Act states; instead, reviews will be completed only on projects that impact economically important species (McCarthy 2012), a process could result in endangered species getting carried out with the tide. What the environmental political sphere will look like in

2015 is hard to imagine, but if the 2012 budget is any indication Canada can expect deregulation and a prioritization of the economy over the environment. This will certainly prove challenging for conservation.

Indeed, over the next several years, both Canada and the United States can expect more attention to be paid to the economy than to the environment. A Conservative government in Canada and a gridlocked Congress in the United States assure that aggressive endangered species legislation will not make it into law any time soon. This means that affirmative motivations are more important than ever. Landowners and land managers across the continent need to take the initiative to act on their moral and judicial conscience to steward species across varied landscapes.

Why We Must Remain Hopeful

The good news is that none of the challenges I have described is likely to decrease affirmative motivations for cooperation with conservation. My findings show that, assumptions to the contrary, private landowners are not a barrier to conservation – in fact, under the right conditions, they might foster conservation. Whether in Utah or Ontario, landowners I surveyed possessed affirmative motivations for cooperation with the ESA, SARA, and state and provincial legislation. Democratic societies make laws with the expectation that citizens will obey them. Thus, Americans and Canadian obey the ESA and SARA because they believe conservation is morally appropriate and because they believe in the legitimacy of government's involvement in conservation, even on private lands.

At the end of *Collapse: How Societies Choose to Fail or Succeed*, Jared Diamond reminds us that "we are not beset by insoluble problems" (2006, 521). This is true of biodiversity conservation in North America. Although it is a perplexing and challenging problem, we will be able to address many of the challenges, such as the lack of stewardship across varied landscapes. Diamond also points out that, "because we are the cause of our environmental problems, we are the ones in control of them and we can choose or not choose to stop causing them and start solving them" (521). This would also be true of biodiversity conservation in North America. And, luckily, we have already started to solve the problem. The ESA and SARA are credible commitments to endangered species protection and recovery. The laws are not perfect, but they are solid starting places.

Thus, we must remain hopeful, not just because the alternative is too bleak, but also because the United States and Canada have all the tools necessary for cooperative governance. Recently, while driving from Regina to Swift Current to interview farmers in the southwestern part of Saskatchewan, I brought my vehicle to a stop on the Trans-Canada Highway to watch a small herd of deer tear across the rolling prairie. The lead deer, a large male, slowed and briefly hesitated once he reached the pavement of the highway. After looking in both directions he quickly gained speed, leading his dozen or so mates across the road, through the ditch on the other side, over train tracks, and bounding over a fence. These deer traversed every human boundary placed in their way without looking back. I watched them move from private land to provincial highway to federal railway and back on to private land. It occurred to me that we might hesitate when we reach a political boundary or official border, but, like the deer, we too must quickly move forward. Stewardship across boundaries is possible. The United States and Canada are different countries with different people. Yet they share a continent, countless ecoregions, many cross-border species, and, most important, the belief that it is important for human beings to take care of other species.

Appendix

Interview Instrument (Indiana)[46]

Introduction

As you know from the introductory letter, I am doing some research on the attitudes of private landowners towards property rights and environmental conservation. My goal is to learn in greater detail how people who own land think about some of these important issues, and how they make choices about managing their properties. It is very important to stress two things at the outset:

1) I am not working for any official agency, including FWS, and your responses will be totally anonymous in any report or publication I produce from this research.

    That said, my hope is that policy makers might read the results of our work, and use that information to make better policies in working with landowners on certain conservation issues. Which brings us to the second point:

2) I have no specific ideas about right or wrong answers to any of these questions – my interest is in LEARNING more about what you think on these issues. Only in this way can I hope to make a useful contribution to those studying and making policy affecting private landowners.

Any questions, then, before we start?

I. Basic and Demographic and Land-Management Information
   1. How long have you lived at your property?

2. Describe your motivations for buying land in this area. What attracted you to the property?
3. What do you mainly use your land for?
4. What kinds of landscaping or maintenance actions do you regularly take on your land?
5. Have you undertaken any larger, one-time changes to your property (construction, clearing trees, brush, letting areas go fallow, etc)? When and what type?
6. Have you planted or cleared any trees on your property over time?
7. Do you use pesticides or herbicides on your land? How regularly?
8. What kind of outdoor lighting do you have?

II. Endangered Species Norms/Values

9. Are you familiar with the Endangered Species Act? What is your understanding of how the law works?
10. [Skip if don't know law under 9]. Do you support the Endangered Species Act as it is implemented right now? Why or why not?
11. How important would you say it is for humans to protect other endangered species?
11b. Can you explain a little why you think it is important or not important in the way you just described?
12. Some people argue that all species have a right to exist. What do you think of this idea?
13. Some people argue that it is sometimes OK for human activities to result in the extinction of a species. What do you think of this idea? (When and why?)
14. Do you think the reasons for protecting endangered species vary by *species*? If so, how?

III. Property Rights (Norms)

15. Let's talk very generally about property rights for a moment. What kinds of rights and responsibilities do you think come with being an owner of land?
16. Some people think of private property as a right created by governments that can be changed over time according to changing needs for society. Thus, landowners might have specific powers (such as tiling and draining their land, or building a subdivision) in one era but not in another, as society's views and goals change. What do you think of this view?

17. Others view property in a different manner. They see private ownership as an absolute or God-given right that must be respected by any legitimate government. This view generally sees ownership as including specific powers that don't change over time. What do you think of this view?
18. Of those two perspectives, which do you see as closer to you own personal views? Can you explain why a little bit?
19. Based on the preceding discussion, what do you think about the status of private property rights in this country today? Are they too strong, not strong enough, or about right?

IV. Assessment of Knowledge: Project and Endangered Species

20. Do you know of any endangered species that live on or near your property?
21. Have you heard of the Indiana bat? If so, what do you know about it and where did you get the info?
22. Have you ever heard of the Conservation Management Area for the Indiana bat? If so, what do you know about it and how did you find out? [if they don't volunteer that they are in it, then probe: Do you know if your parcel is part of the CMA or not?]
23. In your experience how does living in the CMA affect you? Does it affect your choices about managing your land in any way? How?
24. Have you ever taken part in a meeting about the CMA or the Indiana bat?
25. Are you aware of the airport's program to buy property in this area? If so, from what source? Have you ever considered selling your land under this program?
26. How much contact do you have with employees of the airport? Any other conservation officials or government employees? Describe your relationship with these persons? regular or infrequent, positive or difficult?
27. Do you feel like you have been provided with enough information about the CMA and the Indiana bat? What additional information would you like, if any?

V. Bat and Land-Management Decisions

28. Has wildlife, including the bat, ever caused problems for you in the past? How did you deal with it?
29. Have you ever taken any specific actions on your property because of the bat or being in the CMA? What were they and why?

30. Have you ever NOT taken any specific actions on your property because of the bat or being in the CMA? What were they and why?
31. Under what circumstances would you consider the taking the following actions (listed below) in order to help bat recovery efforts:

    – lowering herbicide/pesticide use?
    – reducing night lighting?
    – planting trees/creating more forested habitat for roosting?

32. Have you and a neighbour ever discussed the CMA? The Indiana bat? In what context?
33. To what degree do you think your fellow landowners in the bat conservation area take or refrain from similar actions affecting the bat?
34. Would you take any action if you knew or suspected that your neighbour was harming the bat in some way? What action would you take?

VI. Trade-offs between Property Rights and the ESA
35. Some people think it is unfair to expect private landowners to bear the cost of protecting endangered species on their property. Do you agree?
36. Some people say that private landowners have an obligation to not harm endangered species found on their property. Do you agree?
37. What limits on private property rights, if any, do you think are appropriate for protecting endangered species? Why?
38. As a private landowner, what do you think are the best ways the government could help protect endangered species on private lands like yours?
39. Are you familiar with the following terms?

    – HCP
    – No Surprises Policy
    – Safe Harbor Policy

39b. [If they are, ask]: What is your view of such policies. Positive or negative? Why?
40. Any final thoughts or comments you would like to add?

Survey Instrument (Saskatchewan)

Urban Residents' Survey Questions

Please remember that your participation is voluntary and *your answers are anonymous*. Please read each question carefully and answer honestly. If you do not know or are unsure, please select "don't know." If you do not feel comfortable answering a specific question, please leave it blank. These surveys will help assess the attitudes and beliefs of urban residents in Saskatchewan.

1. Does your home have a yard with grass and/or trees?
   a. yes;   b. no
2. How many years have you lived in your current home? _____
3. How many years have you lived in Saskatchewan? _____
4. How important would you say it is for humans to protect endangered species? a. very important; b. important; c. not very important; d. not important at all
5. Some people argue that all species, human and otherwise, have a right to exist. Do you agree?
   a. yes;   b. no;   c. don't know
6. Do you agree that it is sometimes OK for human activities to cause the extinction of a species?
   a. yes;   b. no;   c. don't know
7. Have you heard of the Saskatchewan Ministry of Environment?
   a. yes;   b. no;   c. don't know
8. Do you agree that it is unfair to expect private landowners to bear the cost of protecting endangered species on their property?
   a. agree;   b. disagree;   c. don't know
9. Do you think it is good idea for the government to protect endangered species?
   a. yes;   b no;   c. don't know
10. Do you think it is okay for the government to create laws to protect species?
    a. yes;   b. no;   c. don't know
11. Do you think it is okay for the government to fine landowners for harming endangered species on their own property?
    a. yes;   b. no;   c. don't know
12. Have you heard of Nature Saskatchewan?
    a. yes;   b. no;   c. don't know

13. Would you like to learn more about how you can help protect endangered species?
    a. yes;   b. maybe;   c. no;   d. don't know

14. Are you aware of the Wildlife Act in Saskatchewan?
    a. yes;   b. no;   c. not sure

15. Are you aware of Canada's Species at Risk Act?
    a. yes;   b. no;   c. not sure

16. Can you name an endangered or threatened species in Saskatchewan? (If so, please list here.)

17. Can you indicate why it is considered to be endangered or threatened?

18. Some people think of private property as a right created by governments that can be changed over time according to changing needs for society. Thus, landowners might have specific powers (such as draining their land or building a subdivision) in one era but not in another, as society's views and goals change. What do you think of this view?
    a. strongly agree;   b. agree;   c. disagree;
    d. strongly disagree;   e. don't know

19. Others view property in a different manner. They see private ownership as an absolute or "God-given" right that must be respected by any legitimate government. This view generally sees ownership as including specific powers that don't change over time. What do you think of this view?
    a. strongly agree;   b. agree;   c. disagree;
    d. strongly disagree;   e. don't know

20. Of those two perspectives, which do you see as closer to you own personal views?
    a. the viewpoint in 18;   b. the viewpoint in 19;
    c. I am in between the two;   d. not sure

21. Do you recycle in your home?
    a. always;   b. sometimes;   c. never

22. Do you think farmers and ranchers have an obligation to protect endangered species found on their property?
    a. yes;   b. no;   c. not sure

23. Do you think farmers/ranchers do a good job of stewarding land for the people of Saskatchewan?
    a. yes;   b. no;   c. not sure

24. Would you be interested joining an environmental organization, such as Nature Saskatchewan?

a. yes, I am already a member;   b. yes;   c. no;

d. no, I am a member of another environmental organization;

e. maybe;   f. not sure

25. In which city do you live?

Regina;   Swift Current;   Moose Jaw;   Saskatoon

Demographic Survey (Saskatchewan/Indiana)

Demographics: Please remember that all your answers are confidential so be as honest as possible.

Gender: male; female

Age: 18–30; 31–40; 41–50; 51–60; 61–70; 71 and older

Income: <$25,000; 25,000–50,000; 50,000–100,000; >100, 000

Highest education achieved: elementary school; high school; college; post-graduate; professional degree; technical diploma

How important of role does religion play in your life?

a. very important;   b. important;   c. not very important;

d. not important

Which religion do you identify with most:

a. Protestant;   b. Catholic;   c. Mormon;   d. Christian, non-denominational;   e. Jewish;   f. Other, specify _____

Which political party do you identify with most:

a. Republican/Conservative;   b. Democrat/Liberal;   c. NDP;

d. Green;   e. Other, specify _____

On a political spectrum, please indicate where your views fit best:

Liberal _____Conservative

         1   2   3   4   5   6   7

Do you consider yourself to be an environmentalist?

a. yes;   b. no

Are you member of any environmental groups?

a. yes;   b. no

The Saskatchewan Wildlife Act applies to your residence?

a. true;   b. false

The Species at Risk Act includes fines for violations?

a. true;   b. false

How much do you trust the government to protect your rights as a property owner?

a. very much;   b. somewhat;   c. not very much;   d. not at all

Notes

1 There is a vast literature to document Canada-US relations. For recent examples see Bow (2009); Clarkson and Mildenberger (2011); and Gagnon (2011).
2 See LePreste and Stoett (2001) for a summary of international initiatives.
3 It should be noted that even though the United States has not ratified the UNCBD, it does play a large role in the United Nations, including financial contributions to the Global Environmental Fund for research and policy development in conservation across the world.
4 Roughly 90 per cent of Canada's land is technically "Crown" land, and thereby owned by either the province or the federal government. Often, however, this land is leased to private landowners and placed under private management. This is important because private individuals make everyday decisions about that land that can greatly affect wildlife. For example, a farmer in Saskatchewan who has leased Crown land can choose to use pesticides on the land without asking permission from the Crown.
5 Land trusts are so popular in the United States that an organization called American Friends of Canadian Land Trusts allows Americans to trust their Canadian property holdings without being "thwarted by tax barriers created by American and Canadian governments" (see the Web site of American Friends at http://afoclt.org). The US Internal Revenue Service recognized American Friends as a 501(c)(3) charity in 2006, allowing it to accept tax-deductible contributions from Americans. It took until 2010 – and required nationwide pressure and support from Canadian land trusts and other conservation partners – for American Friends to secure the necessary Prescribed Donee designation in Canada to make cross-border conservation possible. In 2011, American Friends completed its first three land transactions: Ingersoll Island, gift of fee title, partnership with Georgian

Bay Land Trust; Little Annapolis Lake, gift of a conservation easement, partnership with Nova Scotia Nature Trust; and Delta Eaton Lodge, gift of fee title, partnership with Ducks Unlimited Canada.

6 Ted Turner owns roughly two million acres of land in the United States and manages the Turner Endangered Species Fund. On numerous property holdings, he oversees conservation projects. For examples, see http://www.vermejoparkranch.com/conservation_projects.php.

7 These provisions are outlined in the Constitution Act, 1867 (U.K.), 30 & 31 Victoria, c. 3; see Harrison (1996) and Wojciechowski et al. (2011) for a discussion of this division of power.

8 For a historical overview of the politics of endangered species prior to the 2002 passage of SARA, see Bocking (2001).

9 COSEWIC, created in 1977, is a non-governmental body consisting of thirty-one independent scientists drawn from each of the thirteen provincial and territorial government wildlife agencies, four federal agencies, three non-government science members, ten co-chairs of the Species Specialist Subcommittees, and one co-chair from the Aboriginal Traditional Knowledge Subcommittee. This body has gained credibility in the assessment of wildlife species in Canada. See Freedman et al. (2001) for a description and history of COSEWIC.

10 Beyond the scholarly literature, these criticisms have also been made by Ecojustice, Nature Canada, the David Suzuki Foundation, the Species at Risk Advisory Committee, Environmental Defence, Conservation West, ForestEthics, and other environmental interest groups inside and outside Canada.

11 There are, however, millions of land managers in Canada who lease Crown lands, usually for ninety-nine years, but such managers would not enter into land trusts.

12 For example, their sample populations are different for the two periods and they measure attitudes as opposed to actual compliance with the policy. Moreover, there is no way they can control for other variables that might have contributed to this attitude change during the 1980s.

13 Not to mention the empirical and legal difficulties of measuring compliance, including possible return trips to the landowner's property as well as monitoring the property to assess if the landowner is complying with the law.

14 As a matter of clarification it is important to note that attitudes are the expressed thoughts and values of an individual while norms are values that are shared in common within a population (Axelrod 1986; Campbell 1998).

15 Bromley is writing about the United States only. I argue that Canadians share the same values and are attracted to the concept for the same reasons.

16 When environment minister David Anderson introduced species-at-risk legislation in Parliament in 1995, he said the federal government would regulate private property in the provinces. This could have been declared unconstitutional under the Canada Act (1982), however, and might have endangered the validity of the entire proposed legislation. Moreover, several provinces, most notably Quebec, were adamantly opposed to federal intrusion into private property and threatened to support any appeal to the Supreme Court of Canada over its constitutionality. See Beazley and Boardman (2001) for a good history of endangered species legislation in Canada prior to SARA.

17 In 1995 the USFWS created a "small landowner exemption" in the case of threatened species, but landowners knew so little about the law that they were not aware of this exemption.

18 Currently about 1,400 animal species are listed as threatened or endangered in the United States, but fewer than half have designated habitat listed.

19 The term "science" is intentionally left vague, since it is used differently by individuals and often varies according to context. For example, Republican congressmen who use the phrase "strengthen the use of science" actually might mean using scientific information about genetic diversity to decrease the number of species listings, whereas environmentalists might mean the exact opposite.

20 Several studies document the use and value, or lack of value, of critical habitat; see, in particular, Hodges and Elder (2008); Salzman (1990); Taylor, Suckling, and Rachlinski (2005). For a specific examination of the Bush administration's response to critical habitat listings, see Senatore, Kostyack, and Wetzler (2003).

21 The Conservative Alliance Party of Canada was on the far right for a Canadian party; it merged with the Progressive Conservative Party of Canada to form the present-day Conservative Party of Canada.

22 It was also during this time that the Roosevelt administration created the National Wildlife Refuge System. Today the system consists of more than thirty-seven million hectares of land and has an established role in conserving species listed under the ESA; see Davison (2011).

23 "Prompted by declining populations caused by disturbance of bats during hibernation and modification of hibernacula," the Indiana bat was listed in 1967 as "in danger of extinction" under the Endangered Species

Preservation Act of 1966. It is listed as "endangered" under the current Endangered Species Act of 1973. Listing under the Endangered Species Act protects the bat from take, and requires federal agencies to work to conserve it (USFWS 2012b).

24 Here I use the same data set (the interviews), but the emphasis is different and in some cases the interviews have been recoded for different themes and areas of interest. To obtain the sample of landowners, I found all the parcel numbers for the land within the Conservation Management Area, which included forty-five privately owned parcels in total. With the parcel numbers I was able to use Indiana's online tax record system to find the names of the parcel owners. I used a county phone book as well as online directories to find the addresses and phone numbers for each parcel owner. From the total of forty-five parcels, four were businesses or churches and excluded from the sample. I attempted to contact all remaining forty-one private landowners through an initial letter stating the purpose of the project and letting them know I would be contacting them by phone to arrange an interview. With institutional review board approval, I offered each landowner $25 to participate in a one-hour interview. Eleven landowners were unreachable for one of three reasons: incorrect/no address, disconnected phone, or no answer in three attempts. Eight landowners refused an interview, usually reporting they did not have time or interest. The remaining twenty-two landowners agreed to an interview, making the response rate 54 per cent. The guided interviews lasted between thirty and sixty minutes. With permission of the landowner, the interviews were digitally recorded and transcribed. The responses were then coded mostly as yes/no/don't know or on a five-point scale ranging from strongly disagree to strongly agree.

25 I spoke with the director of the Partners for Fish and Wildlife program in Nevada, since the program does not exist in Utah. The tortoise is also endangered in Nevada, however, and the director had experience working with landowners and the tortoise in the area. I also interviewed a USFWS field biologist for Utah as well as a USFWS enforcement officer for Utah.

26 The entire Washington County is part of an HCP and there are thousands of landowners within the HCP's designated tortoise areas. The HCP designates ten zones of habitat outside the reserve that are of particular importance because of the type and location of the land. Of these ten zones, four contain private, non-agricultural landowners. I sampled from zone 7, the Hurricane Take Area, with 1,411 acres of private land, because this smaller zone is surrounded on three sides by the reserve and because development has been slow enough that landowner information is the most up

to date. Zone 7 was nothing like the CMA in Indiana – the area I visited was urbanized and under construction.

27 To obtain the sample I travelled to the Auditor's office in St George, Utah, and, using the parcel plat books, I obtained all the parcel numbers in zone 7. From these 457 parcel numbers, I randomly selected 50 parcels for inclusion in my study. Using the online landowner information database, I found the names and parcel addresses for the fifty parcels and, using an online telephone directory, obtained telephone numbers for thirty-eight (twelve had unlisted phone numbers). I sent an introductory letter to the parcel addresses, and a week later began contacting landowners. To the landowners with unlisted numbers I sent a letter urging them to contact me by phone or email; only one did so. On a five-day trip to Hurricane, I interviewed the landowners of fifteen parcels. I later conducted four additional interviews by phone. I also mailed a condensed version of the interview and the survey to all parcels whose landowners had not been interviewed, including those with an unlisted phone number. To improve the response rate, I included a two-dollar bill with the survey and return envelope. From the total of thirty interviews mailed, I received fifteen completed interviews. Therefore, overall I have data for thirty-five land-owners, a response rate of 62 per cent. I also gave each interviewee a short survey regarding demographics, knowledge of the ESA, and attitudes towards government.

28 This ferret was successfully reintroduced into the Grasslands National Park in southern Saskatchewan in 2011. Time will tell if the species will make a comeback in the province more broadly.

29 Of the remaining twelve, five are endangered birds (the burrowing owl, Eskimo curlew, greater sage grouse, piping plover, and whooping crane), one is a mammal (the swift fox), and six are plants (the dwarf woolly herd, hairy prairie clover, slender mouse-ear cress, small white lady's slipper, tiny crypthanthe, and western spider foot).

30 Poisonous and predatory animals are a separate category of species. Much research has examined human-wildlife conflict and the conservation of such species; see, for example, Hegel, Gates, and Eslinger (2009); Jonker et al. (2006); Kaltenborn et al. (2006); and Morgan and Gramann (1989).

31 The demographics of respondents varied greatly. Examining the variation between sample locations (the four cities) as well as the discrepancy between the sample population and the general population in Saskatchewan, it is clear that the sample is very similar to the overall population with few exceptions. Of particular interest is the age of the sample respondents, which is not representative of the population at large. Almost half the

sample is older than sixty-one years old. This is not surprising for survey research, where it is expected that the retired population has more time (and perhaps desire) to participate in studies. The fact that the sample is skewed towards the older population is not necessarily a negative feature, since older people are more likely to vote in elections (Barnes 2010; Burgar and Munkman 2010). Thus, if we are concerned with residents' attitudes because they are ultimately responsible for voting policy into effect, then the sample might be a better indicator of attitudes than a sample skewed towards youth attitudes. Moreover, the fact that the sample population is otherwise generally representative of the overall population in Saskatchewan is important because there is adequate variation on all explanatory variables and because there is little reason to suspect response bias. For example, the sample is not predominately female New Democrats from urban areas. Instead, individuals from different political parties, different religious groups, and various education and income brackets responded.

32 One exception to this was a single landowner in Indiana who owned more than forty acres of forested land that he was prohibited from clear cutting because of the ESA. However, the smaller landowners – those with only a few acres of land and who did not intended to profit economically from resource extraction – had greater freedom because no legal enforcement bothered them.

33 Under the OESA, landowners may apply for a permit that allows them to carry out development activities in an endangered-species-designated habitat area. The minister of natural resources grants these permits on a discretionary basis. To qualify for a permit, a landowner normally would have to agree to mitigation efforts to help the endangered species that he/she is potentially harming with development related activities.

34 To obtain my sample of landowners, I travelled to the auditor's office in Port Clinton, Ohio, and, using the official land parcel plat books, I found the parcel numbers for all the privately owned land on Middle Bass Island bordering Lake Erie. In total there were 317 parcels, from which I randomly selected 50. Using the online landowner information database, I found the names and property addresses for the fifty parcels and, using an online telephone directly as well as the Middle Bass phone directory, I obtained the phone numbers for forty-five parcels (five had unlisted phone numbers). I sent an introductory letter to each parcel address, fifty in total. With institutional review board approval, I offered each landowner $20 to participate in an interview. Over two four-day trips to Middle Bass Island, I spoke with twenty-seven landowners, sometimes married couples and

sometimes just one individual. On one trip through Ohio I spoke with two more landowners at their off-island residence. I also interviewed one landowner over the phone. In total I conducted thirty interviews with forty landowners (thirty individual landowners and, in ten cases, their spouses). I mailed a condensed version of the interview to each remaining parcel owner, fifteen in total. The condensed mail survey included yes/no/don't know questions as well as open-ended questions. Of the fifteen, only three were completed and returned. Therefore, I obtained information about owner attitudes for thirty-four parcels on Middle Bass Island, and attitudes and demographic information (a survey was given at each interview and included in the mail survey) for forty-four landowners on Middle Bass Island, a response rate of 66 per cent, which is fairly high in this type of research.

35 In Ontario I was not able to obtain a publicly available list of property owners or parcel numbers, so random sampling on Pelee Island was not possible. In July 2010 I spent two four-day weekends on the island, where I formally interviewed eighteen landowners, one fieldworker for the OMNR, and two representatives for different land conservation groups on the island. Consistent with the Middle Bass case study, I compensated each landowner $20 for his or her time.

36 The United States did not ratify this treaty and is not bound by Article 8(j), which in part helps explain the relationship (or lack thereof) between Native Americans and the ESA. The United States did not ratify the UNCBD because of supposed pressure from the pharmaceutical industry's concern over intellectual property rights as well as a basic unwillingness to engage in financial arrangements around sharing benefits (Le Prestre and Stoett 2006, 209). Moreover, the United States has a different history of the involvement of indigenous peoples in the conservation of biodiversity, an issue that lies outside the scope of this book.

37 Some communities inside the territory allow private property, but this is very limited.

38 This information was gathered from both personal experience with the funding process and through an informal interview with a Prairie Conservation Action Plan representative in Saskatchewan (17 April 2012).

39 At a 2006 meeting with the minister, NACOSAR presented four key points to guide SARA with regards to Aboriginal peoples: 1) Aboriginal traditional knowledge is equivalent to Western science; 2) NACOSAR can help government avoid infringing on Aboriginal rights and interests; 3) engaging NACOSAR must not be construed as consultation; and 4) engagement of Aboriginal peoples must begin early in the SARA cycle of activities,

such as assessment and listing (NACOSAR 2007). Those recommendations served as an early warning to the federal government that the creation of NACOSAR itself was not enough – that if Canada wants to meaningfully include Aboriginal knowledge in the conservation of biodiversity, it must be prepared to take all the necessary steps.

40 After initially refusing, Canada signed the UN Declaration in November 2010, six months after McNeely spoke before the Committee.

41 Section 3, "Aboriginal and Treaty Rights," states that, "[f]or greater certainty, nothing in this Act shall be construed so as to abrogate or derogate from the protection provided for existing aboriginal or treaty rights of the aboriginal peoples of Canada by the recognition and affirmation of those rights in section 35 of the *Constitution Act, 1982*."

42 The categories included Peace and Security, Economic and Social Development, Environment and Sustainable Development, Human Rights, Education and Health, Human Settlements, Women and Children, Humanitarian Activities, Food, Agricultural, Fisheries and Forests, and Cultural Development.

43 See, for example, Berkes, Colding, and Folke (2000); Gagnon and Berteaux (2009); Schmidt and Dowsley (2010); Tester and Irniq (2008); Usher (2000).

44 For example, in the case of American hunters, the Inuit keep all the pelts because US citizens cannot bring endangered species into the United States.

45 Also included in discussions of the ESA and conservation strategies more broadly should also be other landowners not addressed in this book, including commercial property owners and landowners with charismatic and non-charismatic species as well as threatening and non-threatening species.

46 This instrument was used as the template for the other case studies (Utah, Ohio, and Ontario). The only difference between instruments is around the species in question and the actions that landowners would be willing to take. Those questions are catered to each specific case.

References

Legislation and Legal Cases

Babbitt v. Sweet Home Chapter of Communities for a Great Oregon, 515 U.S. 687 (1995).
Christy v. Hodel, 490 U.S. 1114 (1989).
Endangered Species Act, 2007, S.O. 2007, c. 6 (Ontario).
Endangered Species Act, C.C.S.M. c. E111 (Manitoba).
Endangered Species Act, S.N.B. 1996, c. E-9.101 (New Brunswick).
Endangered Species Act, S.N.L. 2001, c. E-10.1 (Newfoundland and Labrador).
Endangered Species Act, S.N.S. 1998, c. 11 (Nova Scotia).
Endangered Species Act, 1973. Publ. L. No. 93–205, 87 *U.S. Statutes at Large* 884 (23 December 1973) (codified as amended at 16. U.S.C. §1541–43) (United States).
Food, Conservation and Energy Act, 2008. Publ. L. No. 110–234, H.R. 2419, 122 Stat. 923 (22 May 2008) (United States).
Species at Risk Act, S.C. 2002, c. 29 (Canada).
Threatened or vulnerable species, An Act respecting, R.S.Q. c. E-12.01 (Quebec).
TVA v. Hill, 437 U.S. 153 (1978).
Wildlife Act, R.S.A. 2000, c. W-10 (Alberta).
Wildlife Act, R.S.B.C. 1996, c. 488 (British Columbia).
Wildlife Act, S.Nu. 2003, c. 26 (Nunavut).
Wildlife Act, S.S. 1998, c. W-13.12 (Saskatchewan).
Wildlife Conservation Act, R.S.P.E.I 1988, c. W-4.1 (Prince Edward Island).

Other References

Aarluk Consulting Incorporated. 2008. *A Consultation-Based Review of the Harvester Support Programs of the Government of Nunavut and Nunavut*

Tunngavik Inc.: Final Report. Available online at http://www.tunngavik
.com/documents/publications/2008-08-11-Review-of-Harvester-Support-
Programs-Final-Report-ENG.pdf.

Abdollah, Tami. 2008. "Wolves not endangered, U.S. says." *Los Angeles Times,*
22 February, A17.

Adler, Jonathan A. 2011. "The Leaky Ark: The Failure of Endangered Species
Regulation on Private land." In *Rebuilding the Ark: New Perspectives on
Endangered Species Act Reform,* ed. Jonathan H. Adler. Washington, DC:
American Enterprise Institute.

Agyeman, Julian, Peter Cole, Randolph Haluza-Delay, and Pat O'Riley. 2009.
Speaking for Ourselves: Environmental Justice in Canada. Vancouver: UBC
Press.

Ajzen, I., and M. Fishbein. 1980. *Understanding Attitudes and Predicting Social
Behavior.* Englewood Cliffs, NJ: Prentice-Hall, Inc.

Alberta. 2008. Alberta Sustainable Resource Development. Fish and Wildlife
Division. "Alberta's Strategy for the Management of Species at Risk 2009–
2014." Edmonton. Available online at www.assembly.ab.ca/lao/library/
egovdocs/2008/alsrd/171462.pdf.

American Consulting, Inc. 2002. "Habitat Conservation Plan for the
Six Points Road Interchange and Associated Development." Project
DEM-070-3(196)68.

Amos, William, Kathryn Harrison, and George Hoberg. 2001. "In Search of a
Minimum Willing Coalition: The Politics of Species-at-Risk Legislation in
Canada." In *Politics of the Wildlife: Canada and Endangered Species,* ed. Karen
Beazley and Robert Boardman. Oxford: Oxford University Press.

Anderson, David. 2001. In Canada, Parliament, House of Commons, *Debates
and Proceedings,* 37th Parliament, 1st Session, no. 16, 19 February.

Anderson, Terry L., and Lawrence Reed Watson. 2011. "An Economic
Assessment of Environmental Federalism: The Optimal Locus of
Endangered Species Authority." In *The Endangered Species Act and Federalism,*
ed. Kaush Arha and Barton H. Thompson Jr. New York: RFF Press.

Ando, A.W. 1999. "Waiting to Be Protected under the Endangered Species Act:
The Political Economy of Regulatory Delay." *Journal of Law & Economics* 42
(1): 29–60. Available online at http://dx.doi.org/10.1086/467417.

Angell, Angela C., and John R. Parkins. 2011. "Resource Development and
Aboriginal Culture in the Canadian North." *Polar Record* 47 (1): 67–79.
Available online at http://dx.doi.org/10.1017/S0032247410000124.

Annin, Peter. 2006. *The Great Lake Water Wars.* Washington, DC: Island Press.

Arha, Kaush, and Barton H. Thompson Jr. 2011. "Introduction." In *The
Endangered Species Act and Federalism: Effective Conservation through Greater*

State Commitment, ed. Kaush Arha and Barton H. Thompson Jr. New York, NY: RFF Press.

Armstrong, A. 2002. "Critical Habitat Designations under the Endangered Species Act: Giving Meaning to the Requirements for Habitat Protection." *South Carolina Environmental Law Journal* 10 (Summer): 53–86.

Arnold, C.A. 1991. "Conserving Habitats and Building Habitats: The Emerging Impact of the Endangered Species Act on Land Use Development." *Stanford Environmental Law Journal* 10: 1–43.

Atleo, Shawn. 2010. In Canada, Parliament, House of Commons, Standing Committee on Environment and Sustainable Development, *Evidence*, Meeting no. 8, 13 April.

Axelrod, Robert. 1986. "An Evolutionary Approach to Norms." *American Political Science Review* 80 (4): 1095–111. Available online at http://dx.doi.org/10.2307/1960858.

Balis-Larson, Martha, Chuck Dauphine, and Susan Jewell. 1999. "Canada and US Save Shared Species at Risk." *Endangered Species Bulletin* 22 (2): 22–3.

Banks, Tommy. 2002. In Canada, Parliament, Senate, *Debates and Proceedings*, 22 October.

Barnes, Andre. 2010. "Youth Voter Turnout in Canada: Trends and Issues." Library of Parliament Research Publications 2010-19E. Ottawa.

Barrett, Toby. 2007. In Ontario, Legislative Assembly, *Debates and Proceedings*, 28 March.

Barry, D.J. 1991. "Amending the Endangered Species Act, the Ransom of the Red Chief, and Other Related Topics." *Environmental Law* (Northwestern School of Law) 21: 587–604.

Baruch-Mordo, Sharon, Stewart W. Breck, Kenneth R. Wilson, and John Broderick. 2011. "The Carrot or the Stick? Evaluation of Education and Enforcement as Management Tools for Human-Wildlife Conflicts." *PLoS ONE* 6 (1): e15681. Available online at http://dx.doi.org/10.1371/journal.pone.0015681. Medline:21264267.

Bazerman, Max H. 1983. "Negotiator Judgment: A Critical Look at the Rationality Assumption." *American Behavioral Scientist* 27 (2): 211–28. http://dx.doi.org/10.1177/000276483027002007.

Bean, Michael J. 1998. "The Endangered Species Act and Private Land: Four Lessons Learned from the Past Quarter Century." *Environmental Law Reporter* 28 (12): 10701–10.

Bean, Michael J. 2002. "Overcoming Unintended Consequences of Endangered Species Regulation." *Idaho Law Review* 38: 409–20.

Bean, Michael. 2004. "The Agony of Critical Habitat." *Environmental Forum* 21 (6): 18–26.

Bean, Michael J. 2006. "Second-Generation Approaches." In *The Endangered Species Act at Thirty*, vol. 1, *Renewing the Conservation Promise*, ed. Dale D. Goble, J. Michael Scott, and Frank W. Davis. Washington, DC: Island Press.

Bean, M.J., and D.S. Wilcove. 1996. "Ending the Impasse." *Environmental Forum* 13 (4): 22–8.

Beazley, Karen. 2001. "Why Should We Protect Endangered Species? Philosophical and Ecological Rationale." In *Politics of the Wild: Canada and Endangered Species*, ed. Karen Beazley and Robert Boardman. Oxford: Oxford University Press.

Bell, M. 2002. "Nunavut Literacy Development in the Context of Inuit Qaujimajatuqanginnut (IQ) (Inuit Traditional Knowledge)." Yellowknife, NT: Inukshuk Management Consultants. Available online at http://www .nunavutliteracy.ca/english/resource/reports/paper/cover.htm.

Benson, Delwin E., Don W. Steinback, and Ross Shelton. 1999. *Wildlife Stewardship on Private Lands*. College Station: Texas A&M University Press.

Berkes, F. 1990. "The James Bay Hydroelectric Project." *Alternatives* 17 (3): 20.

Berkes, Fikret, Johan Colding, and Carl Folke. 2000. "Rediscovery of Traditional Ecological Knowledge as Adaptive Management." *Ecological Applications* 10 (5): 1251–62. Available online at http://dx.doi.org/10.1890/ 1051-0761(2000)010[1251:ROTEKA]2.0.CO;2.

Binnema, Theodore. 2010. "'Most Fruitful Results': Transborder Approaches to Canadian-American Environmental History." In *A Companion to American Environmental History*, ed. Douglas Cazaux Sackman. Malden, MA: Blackwell.

Blake, J., and K. Davis. 1964. "Norms, Values, and Sanctions." In *Handbook of Modern Sociology*, ed. R.E. Farris. Chicago: Rand McNally.

Bocking, Stephen. 2001. "The Politics of Endangered Species: A Historical Perspective." In *Politics of the Wild: Canada and Endangered Species*, ed. Karen Beazley and Robert Boardman. Oxford: Oxford University Press.

Bonneau, L.A. 2003. "Texas Master Naturalist Program Assessment: Changes in Volunteer Knowledge and Attitudes as a Result of Training." Master's thesis, Department of Forestry, Stephen F. Austin State University.

Bourdages, Jean-Luc. 1996. "Species at Risk in Canada." BP-417E. Ottawa: Library of Parliament. Available online at http://publications.gc.ca/ Collection-R/LoPBdP/BP/bp417-e.htm; accessed 1 October 2012.

Bow, Brian. 2009. *The Politics of Linkage: Power, Interdependence, and Ideas in Canada-US Relations*. Vancouver: UBC Press.

Brandt, J.P. 2009. "The Extent of the North American Boreal Zone." *Environmental Reviews* 17 (1): 101–61. Available online at http://dx.doi .org/10.1139/A09-004.

Briar, Scott, and Ian Piliavin. 1965. "Delinquency, Situational Inducements and Commitment to Conformity." *Social Problems* 13 (1): 35–45. Available online at http://dx.doi.org/10.2307/799304.

British Columbia. 2011a. Ministry of Environment. "Conservation Framework." Available online at http://www.env.gov.bc.ca/conservationframework/; accessed 27 March 2012.

British Columbia. 2011b. Ministry of Forestry, Land and Natural Resources Operations. "Wildlife Program Plan. " Victoria. Available online at http://www.env.gov.bc.ca/fw/docs/WildlifeProgramPlan.pdf; accessed 27 March 2012.

Bromley, Daniel W. 2000. "Private Property and the Public Interest: Land in the American Idea." In *Land in the American West: Private Claims and the Common Good*, ed. William G. Robbins and James C. Foster. Seattle: University of Washington Press.

Brook, Amara, Michaela Zint, and Raymond De Young. 2003. "Landowners' Responses to an Endangered Species Act Listing and Implications for Encouraging Conservation." *Conservation Biology* 17 (6): 1638–49. Available online at http://dx.doi.org/10.1111/j.1523-1739.2003.00258.x.

Brosi, Berry J., Gretchen C. Daily, and Frank W. Davis. 2006. "Agricultural and Urban Landscapes." In *The Endangered Species Act at Thirty*, vol. 2, *Conserving Biodiversity in Human-Dominated Landscapes*, ed. J. Michael Scott, Dale D. Goble, and Frank W. Davis. Washington, DC: Island Press.

Brunson, M.W. 1998. "Social Dimensions of Boundaries: Balancing Cooperation and Self-interest." In *Stewardship Across Boundaries*, ed. R.L. Knight and P.B. Landres. Washington, DC: Island Press.

Bruyneel, Shannon. 2010. "Shared Landscape, Divergent Visions? Transboundary Environment Management in the Northern Great Plains." Diss., Department of Geography and Planning, University of Saskatchewan.

Bryant, Bunyan. 1995. *Environmental Justice: Issues, Policies, and Solutions*. Covelo, CA: Island Press.

Bryden, J., and K. Hart. 2000. "Land Reform, Planning and People: An Issue of Stewardship." Presentation to the RSE/SNH Millennium Conference on the Future for the Environment in Scotland – Resetting the Agenda?, Aberdeen, 3 April.

Bultena, G., D. Field, P. Womble, and Don Albrecht. 1981. "Closing the Gates: A Study of Backcountry Use-Limitations at Mount McKinley National Park." *Leisure Sciences* 4 (3): 249–67. Available online at http://dx.doi.org/10.1080/01490408109512966.

Burgar, Joanna, and Martin Monkman. 2010. "Who Heads to the Polls? Exploring the Demographics of Voters in British Columbia." Victoria: BC

Stats. Available online at http://www.elections.bc.ca/docs/stats/Who-heads-to-the-polls.pdf.

Campbell, John L. 1998. "Institutional Analysis and the Role of Ideas in Political Economy." *Theory and Society* 27 (3): 377–409.

Canada. 2007. Environment Canada. "Natural Areas Conservation Program." Ottawa. Available online at http://www.ec.gc.ca/default.asp?lang=En&n=FEF1141D-1&news=8334AC21-47F1-4734-9182-A5EE2016A388.

Canada. 2009a. *Canada's 4th National Report to the UN Convention on Biological Diversity*. Ottawa: Environment Canada. Available online at http://www.cbd.int/doc/world/ca/ca-nr-04-en.pdf.

Canada. 2009b. "Canada's Northern Strategy: Our North, Our Heritage, Our Future." Ottawa. Available online at http://www.northernstrategy.gc.ca.

Canada. 2010a. Department of Fisheries and Oceans. Canadian Science Advisory Secretariat. "Advice Relevant to the Identification of Critical Habitat for Copper Redhorse (Moxostoma hubbsi)." Science Advisory Report 2010/072. Ottawa.

Canada. 2010b. *Canadian Biodiversity: Ecosystem Status and Trends 2010*. Ottawa: Canadian Council of Resource Ministers.

Canada. 2011. "Energy Relations." Consulate General of Canada in Detroit. Available online at http://www.can-am.gc.ca/relations/energy-energie.aspx?lang=eng); accessed 22 April 2012.

Canada. 2012. Species at Risk Public Registry. "Aboriginal Funds for Species at Risk." Ottawa: Environment Canada. Available online at http://www.sararegistry.gc.ca/involved/funding/faep-asrp_e.cfm; accessed 17 April 2012.

Canada Gazette. 2009. "Order Amending Schedule 1 to the Species at Risk Act." 143 (6), 18 March. Available online at http://www.gazette.gc.ca/rp-pr/p1/2012/2012-04-21/html/reg2-eng.html.

Canadian Boreal Initiative. 2012. "About Us." Available online at http://www.borealcanada.ca; accessed 9 October 2012.

CBC (Canadian Broadcasting Corporation). 2008. "Eastern Arctic bowhead whale not extinct." 16 April. Available online at http://www.cbc.ca/news/canada/north/story/2008/04/16/science-bowhead-arctic.html.

Center for Biological Diversity. 2007. "The Road to Recovery: 100 Success Stories for Endangered Species Day 2007." Tucson, AZ. Available online at http://www.esasuccess.org/reports/.

CESCC (Canadian Endangered Species Conservation Council). 2011. National General Status Working Group. "Wild Species 2010: The General Status of Species in Canada." [Ottawa].

Champagne, D. 2007. *Social Change and Cultural Continuity among Native Nations*. Lanham, MD: AltaMira Press.

Chester, Charles C. 2006. *Conservation Across Borders: Biodiversity in an Interdependent World*. Washington, DC: Island Press.

Church, Thomas, and Milton Heumann. 1989. "The Underexamined Assumptions of the Invisible Hand: Monetary Incentives as Policy Instruments." *Journal of Policy Analysis and Management* 8 (4): 641–57. Available online at http://dx.doi.org/10.2307/3325050.

Clarkson, Stephen, and Matto Mildenberger. 2011. *Dependent America? How Canada and Mexico Construct US Power*. Toronto: University of Toronto Press.

Colburn, Jamison. 2005. "The Indignity of Federal Wildlife Habitat Law." *Alabama Law Review* 57: 417–51.

Colburn, Jamison. 2011. "Permits, Property and Planning in the Twenty-First Century: Habitat as Survival and Beyond." In *Rebuilding the Ark: New Perspectives on Endangered Species Act Reform*, ed. Jonathan H. Adler. Washington, DC: American Enterprise Institute.

Cole, Daniel E. 2002. *Pollution and Property: Comparing Ownership Institutions for Environmental Protection*. New York: Cambridge University Press. Available online at http://dx.doi.org/10.1017/CBO9780511494604.

Comartin, Joe. 2001. In Canada, Parliament, House of Commons, *Debates and Proceedings*, 37th Parliament, 1st Session, no. 016, February.

Coombs, Fred S. 1980. "The Bases of Noncompliance with a Policy." *Policy Studies Journal* 8 (6): 885–900.

Costanza, R., R. d'Arge, R. deGroot, S. Farber, M. Grasso, B. Hannon, K. Limburg, S. Naeem, R.V. Oneill, J. Paruelo, et al. 1997. "The Value of the World's Ecosystem Services and Natural Capital." *Nature* 387 (6630): 253–60. Available online at http://dx.doi.org/10.1038/387253a0.

Czech, Brian, and Paul Krausman. 2001. *The Endangered Species Act: History, Conservation Biology, and Public Policy*. Baltimore: Johns Hopkins University Press.

Daily, G. 2005. "Why Biodiversity Matters." In *Conserving Biodiversity*, ed. Bruce Babbitt, José Sarukhán, and John A. Riggs. Washington, DC: Aspen Institute.

Dana, David A. 2011. "Reforming Section 10 and the Habitat Conservation Program." In *Rebuilding the Ark: New Perspectives on Endangered Species Act Reform*, ed. Jonathan H. Adler. Washington, DC: American Enterprise Institute.

Davis, Frank W., J. Michael Scott, and Dale D. Goble. 2006. "Introduction." In *The Endangered Species Act at Thirty*, vol. 2, *Conserving Biodiversity in Human-Dominated Landscapes*, ed. J. Michael Scott, Dale D. Goble, and Frank W. Davis. Washington, DC: Island Press.

Davison, Robert P. 2011. "The Evolution of Federalism under Section 6 of the Endangered Species Act." In *The Endangered Species Act and Federalism*, ed. Kaush Arha and Barton H. Thompson Jr. New York: RFF Press.

Dearden, Philip. 2001. "Endangered Species and Terrestrial Protected Areas."
    In *Politics of the Wild: Canada and Endangered Species*, ed. Karen Beazley and
    Robert Boardman. Oxford: Oxford University Press.
d'Eca, Michael. 2010. In Canada, Parliament, House of Commons, Standing
    Committee on Environment and Sustainable Development, *Evidence*,
    Meeting no. 15, 6 May.
Desbiens, Carol. 2004. "Nation to Nation: Defining New Structures of
    Development in Northern Quebec." *Economic Geography* 80 (4): 351–66.
    Available online at http://dx.doi.org/10.1111/j.1944-8287.2004.tb00242.x.
De Young, Raymond. 2011. "Localization: Motivating Transition with a
    Conservation Aesthetic." Unpublished. Available online at http://www
    .personal.umich.edu/~rdeyoung/current_paper.html; accessed 4 June 2012.
Diamond, Jared. 2006. *Collapse: How Societies Choose to Fail or Succeed*. New
    York: Penguin Books.
Dietz, Thomas, Amy Fitzgerald, and Rachael Shwom. 2005. "Environmental
    Values." *Annual Review of Environmental Resources* 5 (39): 12.1–12.38.
Dobson, A. 2005. "Monitoring Global Rates of Biodiversity Change:
    Challenges that Arise in Meeting the Convention on Biological Diversity
    (CBD) 2010 Goals." *Philosophical Transactions of the Royal Society of London.
    Series B, Biological Sciences* 360 (1454): 229–41. Available online at http://
    dx.doi.org/10.1098/rstb.2004.1603; Medline:15814342.
Doern, G. Bruce. 2005. *Canadian Energy Policy and the Struggle for Sustainable
    Development*. Toronto: University of Toronto Press.
Doremus, Holly. 2006. "Lessons Learned." In *The Endangered Species Act
    at Thirty*, vol. 1, *Renewing the Conservation Promise*, ed. Dale D. Goble,
    J. Michael Scott, and Frank W. Davis. Washington DC: Island Press.
Dorsey, Kurkpatrick. 1998. *The Dawn of Conservation Diplomacy: US-Canadian
    Wildlife Protection Treaties in the Progressive Era*. Seattle: University of
    Washington Press.
Dowie, Mark. 1996. *Losing Ground*. Cambridge, MA: MIT Press.
Dowsley, Martha. 2009. "Community Clusters in Wildlife and Environmental
    Management: Using TEK and Community Involvement to Improve Co-
    management in an Era of Rapid Environmental Change." *Polar Research* 28 (1):
    43–59. Available online at http://dx.doi.org/10.1111/j.1751-8369.2008.00093.x.
Dowsley, M., and G. Wenzel. 2008. "'The time of the Most Polar Bears':
    A Co-management Conflict in Nunavut." *Arctic* 61 (2): 177–89.
Duffy, Andrew. 2000. "Anderson blasts U.S. critics." *Ottawa Citizen*, 4 March, A6.
Earl, G., A. Curtis, and C. Allan. Apr 2010. "Towards a Duty of Care for
    Biodiversity." *Environmental Management* 45 (4): 682–96. Available online at
    http://dx.doi.org/10.1007/s00267-010-9444-z. Medline:20140433.

Easley, Stephanie, Jason P. Holtman, Janine Scancarelli, and Brian A. Schmidt, eds. 2001. *The Endangered Species Act: A Stanford Environmental Law Society Handbook*. Stanford, CA: Stanford University Press.

Eckersley, Robin. 1992. *Environmentalism and Political Theory*. New York: University of New York Press.

Ecojustice. 2012. *Failure to Protect: Grading Canada's Species at Risk Laws*. Ottawa.

Egan, A., and S. Jones. 1993. "Do Landowner Beliefs Reflect Behavior?" *Journal of Forestry* 91 (10): 39–45.

Ehrlich, P.R., and A.H. Ehrlich. 1996. *Betrayal of Science and Reason: How Anti-Environmental Rhetoric Threatens Our Future*. Washington, DC: Island Press.

Eilperin, Juliet. 2007. "7 species decisions revisited." *Washington Post*, 28 November, A03.

EJRC (Environmental Justice Resource Center). 1991. "Principles of Environmental Justice." Available online at http://www.ejrc.cau.edu/princej.html.

Elgie, Stewart. 1995. *Endangered Species Legislation in Canada: A Bear Necessity*. Toronto: Sierra Legal Defence Fund.

Elgie, Stewart. 2008. "Statutory Structure and Species Survival: How Constraints on Cabinet Discretion Affect Endangered Species Listing Outcomes." *Journal of Environmental Law and Practice* 19: 1–32.

Elgie, Stewart. 2010. "The Politics of Extinction: The Birth of Canada's Species at Risk Act." In *Canadian Environmental Policy and Politics*, ed. Debora L. VanNijnatten and Robert Boardman. Oxford: Oxford University Press.

Elmendorf, Christopher S. 2003. "Ideas, Incentives, and Gifts and Governance: Toward Conservation Stewardship on Private Land, in Cultural and Psychological Perspective." *University of Illinois Law Review* 2: 443–505.

Erickson, D., and R. De Young. 1992–3. "Management of Farm Woodlots and Windbreaks: Some Psychological and Landscape Patterns." *Journal of Environmental Systems* 22: 233–47.

Fairfax, Sally, K. Lauren, Mary Gwin, Anne King, Leigh Raymond, and Laura A. Watt. 2005. *Buying Nature: The Limits of Land Acquisition as a Conservation Strategy, 1780–2004*. Cambridge, MA: MIT Press.

Farrier, David. 1995. "Conserving Biodiversity on Private Land: Incentives for Management or Compensation for Lost Expectations?" *Harvard Environmental Law Review* 19: 303–408.

Federal, Provincial and Territorial Governments of Canada. 2010. "Canadian Biodiversity: Ecosystem Statutes and Trends 2010." Ottawa: Canadian Councils of Resource Ministers.

Ferguson, Ian F. 2008. "United States-Canada Trade and Economic Relationship: Prospects and Challenges." Washington, DC: Congressional Research Service.

Findlay, Scott C., Stewart Elgie, Brian Giles, and Linda Burr. 2009. "Species Listing under Canada's Species at Risk Act." *Conservation Biology* 23 (6): 1609–17. Available online at http://dx.doi.org/10.1111/j.1523-1739.2009 .01255.x. Medline:19500120.

Fischer, Joren, Beery Brosi, Gretchen C. Daily, Paul R. Ehrlich, Rebecca Goldman, Joshua Goldstein, David B. Lindenmayer, Adrian D. Manning, Harold A. Mooney, Liba Pejchar, et al. 2008. "Should Agricultural Polices Encourage Land-Sparing or Wildlife-Friendly Farming?" *Frontiers in Ecology and the Environment* 6 (7): 380–5. Available online at http://dx.doi.org/ 10.1890/070019.

Fischer, J., D.B. Lindenmayer, and A.D. Manning. 2006. "Biodiversity, Ecosystem Function, and Resilience: Ten Guiding Principles for Commodity Production Landscapes." *Frontiers in Ecology and the Environment* 4 (2): 80–6. Available online at http://dx.doi.org/10.1890/1540-9295(2006)004[0080: BEFART]2.0.CO;2.

Fix, Michael E., Jeffrey S. Passel, and Kenneth Sucher. 2003. "Trends in Naturalization." Washington, DC: Urban Institute, Immigration Studies Program. Available online at http://www.urban.org/UploadedPDF/310847_ trends_in_naturalization.pdf.

Fletcher, Thomas. 2003. *From Love Canal to Environmental Justice: The Politics of Hazardous Waste.* Toronto: University of Toronto Press.

Fluker, Shaun. 2010. "Endangered Species under Alberta's Wildlife Act: Effective Legal Protection?" ABlawg. Available online at http://ablawg. ca/2010/03/29/endangered-species-under-alberta%E2%80%99s-wildlife-act-effective-legal-protection/.

Ford, James, Tristan Pearce, Barry Smit, Johanna Wandel, Mishak Allurt Kikshappa, Harry Ittusujurat, and Kevin Qrunnut. 2007. "Reducing Vulnerability to Climate Change in the Arctic: The Case of Nunavut, Canada." *Arctic* 60 (2): 150–66.

Foster, Janet. 1998. *Working for Wildlife: The Beginning of Preservation in Canada.* Toronto: University of Toronto Press.

Fox, Glenn, and Wiktor Adamowicz. 1997. "Should Canadian Legislators Learn Anything from the U.S. Experience with Endangered Species Legislation?" *Canadian Journal of Agricultural Economics* 45 (4): 403–10. Available online at http://dx.doi.org/10.1111/j.1744-7976.1997.tb02163.x.

Francis, Charles A., Twyla E. Hansen, Allison A. Fox, Paula J. Hesje, Hana E. Nelson, Andrea E. Lawseth, and Alexandra English. 2012. "Farmland Conversion to Non-Agricultural Uses in the US and Canada: Current Impacts and Concerns for the Future." *International Journal of Agricultural Sustainability* 10 (1): 8–24. Available online at http://dx.doi.org/10.1080/ 14735903.2012.649588.

Freedman, Bill, Lindsay Rodger, Peter Ewins, and David M. Green. 2001. "Species at Risk in Canada." In *Politics of the Wild: Canada and Endangered Species*, ed. Karen Beazley and Robert Boardman. Oxford: Oxford University Press.

Freyfogle, Eric. 2003. *The Land We Share*. Washington, DC: Island Press.

Freyfogle, Eric T., and Dale D. Goble. 2009. *Wildlife Law: A Primer*. Covelo, CA: Island Press.

Friedman, L.M. 1975. *The Legal System: A Social Science Perspective*. New York: Russell Sage Foundation.

Fry, Earl H. 2005. "Federalism and the Evolving Cross-border Role of Provincial, State and Municipal Governments." *International Journal* 60 (2): 471–82. Available online at http://dx.doi.org/10.2307/40204304.

Gagnon, C.A., and D. Berteaux. 2009. "Integrating Traditional and Scientific Knowledge: Management of Canada's National Parks." In *Climate Change: Integrating Traditional and Scientific Knowledge*, ed. R. Riewe and J. Oaks. Winnipeg: Aboriginal Issues Press.

Gagnon, Liam A. 2011. *Canada: Background and U.S. Relations*. Haupphauge, NY: Nova Science Publishers.

Gelfand, Julie. 2009. In Canada, Parliament, House of Commons, Standing Committee on Environment and Sustainable Development, *Evidence*, Meeting no. 24, 2 June.

George, Susan. 2002. *Conservation in America: State Government Incentives for Habitat Conservation*. Washington, DC: Defenders of Wildlife.

George, Susan, William J. Snoops III, and Michael Senatore. 1998. *State Endangered Species Acts: Past, Present and Future*. Washington, DC: Defenders of Wildlife.

Gerber, Jean-David. 2012. "The Difficulty of Integrating Land Trusts in Land Use Planning." *Landscape and Urban Planning* 104 (2): 289–98. Available online at http://dx.doi.org/10.1016/j.landurbplan.2011.11.002.

Gillis, Peter R., and Thomas R. Roach. 1986. "The American Influence on Conservation in Canada: 1899–1911." *Journal of Forest History* 30 (4): 160–74. Available online at http://dx.doi.org/10.2307/4004729.

Goble, Dale D. 2009. "The Endangered Species Act: What We Talk about When We Talk about Recovery." *Natural Resources Journal* 49: 1–44.

Goble, Dale D., S.M. George, K. Mazaika, J.M. Scott, and J. Karl. 1999. "Local and National Protection of Endangered Species: An Assessment." *Environmental Science & Policy* 2 (1): 43–59. Available online at http://dx.doi.org/10.1016/S1462-9011(98)00041-0.

Goldberg, L.R. 1976. "Man versus Model of Man: Just How Conflicting Is the Evidence?" *Organizational Behavior and Human Perceptions* 16 (1): 13–22. Available online at http://dx.doi.org/10.1016/0030-5073(76)90003-9.

Grabosky, Peter N. 1995. "Regulation by Reward: On the Use of Incentives as Regulatory Instruments." *Law and Policy* 17 (3): 257–82. Available online at http://dx.doi.org/10.1111/j.1467-9930.1995.tb00150.x.

Graf, William L. 1990. *Wilderness Preservation and the Sagebrush Rebellions.* Lanham, MD: Rowman & Littlefield.

Grant, Shelagh D. 2010. *Polar Imperative: A History of Arctic Sovereignty in North America.* Vancouver: Douglas & McIntyre.

Grasmick, Harold G., and Robert J. Bursik Jr. 1990. "Conscience, Significant Others, and Rational Choice: Extending the Deterrence Model." *Law and Society Review* 24 (3): 837–61. http://dx.doi.org/10.2307/3053861.

Grasmick, Harold G., Robert J. Bursik Jr, and Karyl A. Kinsey. 1991. "Shame and Embarrassment as Deterrents to Noncompliance with the Law: The Case of Antilittering Campaign." *Environment and Behavior* 23 (2): 233–51. Available online at http://dx.doi.org/10.1177/0013916591232006.

Green, R.E., S.J. Cornell, J.P.W. Scharlemann, and A. Balmford. 2005. "Farming and the Fate of Wild Nature." *Science* 307 (5709): 550–5. Available online at http://dx.doi.org/10.1126/science.1106049; Medline:15618485.

Greenwald, Noah D., Kieran F. Suckling, and Martin Taylor. 2006. "The Listing Record." In *The Endangered Species Act at Thirty*, vol. 1, *Renewing the Conservation Promise*, ed. Dale D. Goble, J. Michael Scott, and Frank W. Davis. Washington, DC: Island Press.

Hall, David J. 1985. *Clifford Sifton: The Young Napoleon.* Vancouver: UBC Press.

Hardin, Garrett. 13 Dec. 1968. "The Tragedy of the Commons: The Population Problem Has No Technical Solution; It Requires a Fundamental Extension in Morality." *Science* 162 (3859): 1243–8. Medline:5699198.

Harkinson, Josh. 2011. "Obama: Not So Wild about Wildlife." *Mother Jones*, 6 January.

Harrison, Kathryn. 1996. *Passing the Buck: Federalism and Canadian Environmental Policy.* Vancouver: UBC Press.

Hatch, Leila, Maria Uriarte, Daniel Fink, Laura Aldrich-Wolfe, Richard G. Allen, Colleen Webb, Kelly Zamudio, and Alison Power. 2002. "Jurisdiction over Endangered Species' Habitat: The Impacts of People and Property on Recovery Planning." *Ecological Applications* 12 (3): 690–700. Available online at http://dx.doi.org/10.1890/1051-0761(2002)012[0690:JOESHT]2.0.CO;2.

Hayward, Tim. 1994. *Ecological Thought: An Introduction.* Cambridge, UK: Polity Press.

Hegel, Troy M., C. Cormack Gates, and Dale Eslinger. 2009. "The Geography of Conflict between Elk and Agricultural Values in the Cypress Hills, Canada." *Journal of Environmental Management* 90 (1): 222–35. Available online at http://dx.doi.org/10.1016/j.jenvman.2007.09.005; Medline:18082311.

Henderson, A. 2007. *Nunavut: Rethinking Political Culture*. Vancouver: UBC Press.

Herron, Jon. 2001. In Canada, Parliament, House of Commons, *Debates and Proceedings*, 37th Parliament, 1st Session, no. 016., February.

Hicks, Jack. 2007. "The Social Determinates of Elevated Rates of Suicide Among Inuit Youth." *Indigenous Affairs* 4: 30–7.

Hinzman, L.D., N.D. Bettez, W.R. Bolton, F.S. Chapin, M.B. Dyurgerov, C.L. Fastie, B. Griffith, R.D. Hollister, A. Hope, H.P. Huntington, et al. 2005. "Evidence and Implications of Recent Climate Change in Northern Alaska and Other Arctic Regions." *Climatic Change* 72 (3): 251–98. Available online at http://dx.doi.org/10.1007/s10584-005-5352-2.

Hodges, K., and J. Elder. 2008. "Critical Habitat Designation under the US Endangered Species Act: How Are Biological Criteria Used?" *Biological Conservation* 141 (10): 2662–8.

Hoffman, Andrew J., Hannah C. Riley, John G. Troast Jr, and Max H. Bazerman. 2002. "Cognitive and Institutional Barriers to New Forms of Cooperation on Environmental Protection: Insights from Project XL and Habitat Conservation Plans." *American Behavioral Scientist* 45 (5): 820–45. Available online at http://dx.doi.org/10.1177/0002764202045005006.

Hoiberg, E.O., and G.L. Bultena. 1981. "Farm Operator Attitudes toward Governmental Involvement in Agriculture." *Rural Sociology* 46 (3): 381–90.

Houck, Oliver A. 1993. "The Endangered Species Act and Its Implementation by the US Department of Interior and Commerce." *University of Colorado Law Review* 64 (2): 277–370.

Huebert, Robert. 2011. "Canadian Arctic Sovereignty and Security in a Transforming Circumpolar World." In *Canada and the Changing Arctic: Sovereignty and Stewards*, ed. Franklyn Griffiths, Rob Hubert, and P. Whitney Lackenbauer. Waterloo, ON: Wilfrid Laurier University Press.

Hughes, Donald J. 1996. "American Indian Ecology." In *This Sacred Earth*, ed. Rogers S. Gottlieb. New York: Routledge.

Illical, Mary, and Kathryn Harrison. 2007. "Protecting Endangered Species in the US and Canada: The Role of Negative Lesson Drawing." *Canadian Journal of Political Science* 40 (2): 367–94. Available online at http://dx.doi.org/10.1017/S0008423907070175.

Inman, K., and D. Mcleod. 2002. "Property Rights and Public Interests: A Wyoming Agricultural Lands Study." *Growth and Change* 33 (1): 91–114. Available online at http://dx.doi.org/10.1111/0017-4815.00181.

IPCC (Intergovernmental Panel on Climate Change). 2007. *Climate Change 2007: Synthesis Report*. Contribution of Working Groups I, II, and III to the Fourth Assessment. Synthesis Report, ed. R.K. Pachauri and A. Reisinger. Geneva: IPCC Secretariat.

IUCN (International Union for the Conservation of Nature). 2011. "Wildlife in a Changing World." Gland, Switzerland.

Jackson-Smith, Douglas, Urs Kreuter, and Richard S. Krannich. 2005. "Understanding the Multidimensionality of Property Rights Orientations: Evidence from Utah and Texas Ranchers." *Society & Natural Resources* 18 (7): 587–610. Available online at http://dx.doi.org/10.1080/08941920590959578.

Jacobs, Harvey M. 1998. "The Wisdom, but Uncertain Future, of the Wise-Use Movement." In *Who Owns America? Social Conflict over Property Rights*, ed. Harvey M. Jacobs. Madison: University of Wisconsin Press.

James, Frances C. 1999. "Lessons Learned from a Study of Habitat Conservation Planning." *Bioscience* 49 (11): 871–4. Available online at http://dx.doi.org/10.2307/1313646.

Jia, G.J., H.E. Epstein, and D.A. Walker. 2009. "Vegetation Greening in the Canadian Arctic Related to Decadal Warming." *Journal of Environmental Monitoring* 11 (12): 2231–8. Available online at http://dx.doi.org/10.1039/b911677j; Medline:20024021.

Johnson, Kennon. 2010. In Canada, Parliament, House of Commons, Standing Committee on Environment and Sustainable Development, *Evidence*, Meeting no. 15, 6 May.

Johnston, Josee, Michael Gismondi, and James Goodman. 2006. "Politicizing Exhaustion: Eco-social Crisis and the Geographic Challenge for Cosmopolitans." In *Nature's Revenge*, ed. Josee Johnston, Michael Gismondi, and Hames Goodman. Peterborough, ON: Broadview Press.

Jonker, Sandra, Robert Muth, John Organ, Rodney Zwick, and William Siemer. 2006. "Experiences with Beaver Damage and Attitudes of Massachusetts Residents toward Beaver." *Wildlife Society Bulletin* 34 (4): 1009–21. Available online at http://dx.doi.org/10.2193/0091-7648(2006)34[1009:EWBDAA]2.0.CO;2.

Kagan, Robert A., and John Scholz. 1980. "The Criminology of the Corporation and Regulatory Enforcement Strategies." In *Enforcing Regulation*, ed. Keith Hawkins and John Thomas. Hingham, MA: Kluwer-Nijhoff. Available online at http://dx.doi.org/10.1007/978-3-322-83669-4_21.

Kaltenborn, Bjorn P, Tore Bjerke, Julius W. Nyahongo, and Daniel R. Williams. 2006. "Animal Preferences and Acceptibility of Wildlife Management Actions around Serengeti National Park, Tanzania." *Biodiversity and Conservation* 15 (14): 4633–49. Available online at http://dx.doi.org/10.1007/s10531-005-6196-9.

Kareiva, Peter, Timothy H. Tear, Stacey Solie, Michelle L. Brown, Leonardo Sotomayor, and Christopher Yuan-Farrell. 2006. "Nongovernmental Organizations." In *The Endangered Species Act at Thirty*, vol. 1, *Renewing the Conservation Promise*, ed. Dale D. Goble, J. Michael Scott, and Frank W. Davis. Washington, DC: Island Press.

Kenny, Alex, Stewart Elgie, and Dave Sawyer. 2011. "Advancing the Economics of Ecosystems and Biodiversity in Canada: A Survey of Economic Instruments for the Conservation & Protection of Biodiversity." Background paper. Ottawa: Sustainable Diversity.

King, Gary, Robert O. Keohane, and Sidney Verba. 1994. *Designing Social Inquiry: Scientific Inference in Qualitative Research*. Princeton, NJ: Princeton University Press.

King, Richard B. 1986. "Population Ecology of the Lake Erie Watersnake, Nerodia sipedon insularum." *Copeia* 1986 (3): 757–72. Available online at http://dx.doi.org/10.2307/1444959.

Kirmayer, Laurence J., Gregory Brass, Tara Holton, Ken Paul, Cori Simpson, and Caroline Tait. 2007. *Suicide among Aboriginal People in Canada*. Ottawa: Aboriginal Healing Foundation.

Knickerbocker, Brad. 2007. "Controversy erupts over Endangered Species Act." *Christian Science Monitor*, 25 July, A2.

Knudtson, Peter, and David Suzuki. 1992. *Wisdom of Elders*. Toronto: Stoddart.

Kohler, Nicholas. 2012. "We're Shooting Polar Bears?" *Maclean's*, 16 February. Available online at http://www2.macleans.ca/2012/02/16/were-shooting-polar-bears/; accessed 4 June 2012.

Kraus, Stephen J. 1995. "Attitudes and the Prediction of Behavior: A Meta-Analysis of the Empirical Literature." *Personality and Social Psychology Bulletin* 21 (1): 58–75. Available online at http://dx.doi.org/10.1177/0146167295211007.

Kreuter, Urs, Malini V. Nair, Douglas Jackson-Smith, J. Richard Conner, and Janis E. Johnston. 2006. "Property Rights Orientations and Rangeland Management Objectives: Texas, Utah, and Colorado." *Rangeland Ecology and Management* 59 (6): 632–9. Available online at http://dx.doi.org/10.2111/05-173R1.1.

Kulchyski, Peter, and Frank James Tester. 2007. *Kiumajut (Talking Back): Game Management and Inuit Rights 1900–70*. Vancouver: UBC Press.

Lackenbauer, Whitney P. 2011. "From Polar Race to Polar Saga: An Integration Strategy for Canada and the Circumpolar World." In *Canada and the Changing Arctic: Sovereignty and Stewards*, ed. Franklyn Griffiths, Rob Huebert, and P. Whitney Lackenbauer. Waterloo, ON: Wilfrid Laurier University Press.

Langpap, Christian, and Joe R. Kerkvliet. 2010. "Allocating Conservation Resources under the Endangered Species Act." *American Journal of Agricultural Economics* 92 (1): 110–24. Available online at http://dx.doi.org/10.1093/ajae/aap001.

Langpap, Christian, and JunJie Wu. 2004. "Voluntary Conservation of Endangered Species: When Does No Regulatory Assurance Mean No Conservation?" *Journal of Environmental Economics and Management* 47 (3): 435–57. Available online at http://dx.doi.org/10.1016/j.jeem.2003.06.001.

Laugrand, Frederic B., and Jarich G. Oosten. 2010. *Inuit Shamanism and Christianity: Transitions and Transformations in the Twentieth Century.* Montreal; Kingston, ON: McGill-Queen's University Press.

Le Prestre, Philippe G., and Peter Stoett. 2001. "International Initiatives, Commitments, and Disappointments: Canada, CITES and the CBD." In *Politics of the Wild: Canada and Endangered Species*, ed. Karen Beazley and Robert Boardman. Oxford: Oxford University Press.

Le Prestre, Philippe G. and Peter J. Stoett, eds. 2006. *Bilateral Ecopolitics: Continuity and Change in Canadian-American Environmental Relations.* Farnham, UK: Ashgate Publishing.

Leaky, Richard E., and Roger Lewin. 1995. *The Sixth Extinction: Patterns of Life and the Future of Humankind.* New York: Anchor.

Leonard, D.L. 2009. "Social and Political Obstacles to Saving Hawaiian Birds: Realities and Remedies." In *Conservation Biology of Hawaiian Forest Birds: Implications for Island Avifauna*, ed. T.K. Pratt, C.T. Atkinson, P.C. Banko, J.D. Jacobi, and B.L. Woodworth. New Haven, CT: Yale University Press.

Leopold, Aldo. 1949. *A Sand County Almanac.* New York: Oxford University Press.

Leslie, Keith. 2012. "Ontario Liberals ignoring rules, defying will of legislature: environmental watchdog." *National Post*, 19 September.

Levi, Margaret. 1997. *Consent, Dissent and Patriotism.* New York: Cambridge University Press. Available online at http://dx.doi.org/10.1017/CBO9780511609336.

Lueck, Dean, and Jeffrey A. Michael. 2003. "Preemptive Habitat Destruction under the Endangered Species Act." *Journal of Law and Economics* 46 (1): 27–60. Available online at http://dx.doi.org/10.1086/344670.

MacDougall, John. 2006. *Drifting Together: The Political Economy of Canada-US Integration.* Toronto: University of Toronto Press.

MacEachern, Alan. 2003. "The Conservation Movement." In *Canada: Confederation to Present*, CD-ROM, ed. Chris Hacket and Bob Hesketh. Edmonton: Chinook Media.

Main, M.B. 2004. "Mobilizing Grass-roots Conservation Education: The Florida Master Naturalist Program." *Conservation Biology* 18 (1): 11–16. Available online at http://dx.doi.org/10.1111/j.1523-1739.2004.01801.x.

Manitoba. 2012. Conservation and Water Stewardship. Wildlife Branch. "Legislation and Permits." Winnipeg. Available online at http://www.gov.mb.ca/conservation/wildlife/legislation/endang_act.html; accessed 4 June 2012.

Marcel, Pat. 2010. In Canada, Parliament, House of Commons, Standing Committee on Environment and Sustainable Development, *Evidence*, Meeting no. 8, 13 April.

Mathews, Jud. 2004. "Turning the Endangered Species Act Inside Out?" *Yale Law Review* 113 (4): 947–54. Available online at http://dx.doi.org/10.2307/4135687.

May, Peter J. 2002. "Social Regulation." In *Tools of Government: A Guide to the New Governance*, ed. Lester M. Salamon. Oxford: Oxford University Press.

May, Peter J. 2004. "Compliance Motivations: Affirmative and Negative Bases." *Law and Society Review* 38 (1): 41–68. Available online at http://dx.doi.org/10.1111/j.0023-9216.2004.03801002.x.

May, Peter J. 2005. "Regulation and Compliance Motivations: Examining Different Approaches." *Public Administration Review* 65 (1): 31–44. Available online at http://dx.doi.org/10.1111/j.1540-6210.2005.00428.x.

May, Peter J., and Soren Winter. 1999. "Regulatory Enforcement and Compliance: Examining Danish Agro-environmental Policy." *Journal of Policy Analysis and Management* 18 (4): 625–51. Available online at http://dx.doi.org/10.1002/(SICI)1520-6688(199923)18:4<625::AID-PAM5>3.0.CO;2-U.

May, Peter J., and Robert S. Woods. 2003. "At the Regulatory Front Lines: Inspectors' Enforcement Styles and Regulatory Compliance." *Journal of Public Administration: Research and Theory* 13 (2): 117–39. Available online at http://dx.doi.org/10.1093/jopart/mug014.

McCarthy, Shawn. 2012. "Budget bill gives Harper cabinet free hand on environmental assessment." *Canadian Press*, 9 May.

McDermott, P.W. 1947. "Snake Stories from the Lake Erie Islands." *Inland Seas* 3: 83–8.

McKenzie, Judith. 2002. *Environmental Politics in Canada: Managing the Commons into the Twenty-First Century*. Oxford: Oxford University Press.

McNeely, Joshua. 2010. In Canada, Parliament, House of Commons, Standing Committee on Environment and Sustainable Development, *Evidence*, Meeting no. 8, 13 April.

McPhee, Alastair. 2010. In Canada, Parliament, House of Commons, Standing Committee on Environment and Sustainable Development, *Evidence*, Meeting no. 8, 13 April.

Meek, Chanda L., Amy Lauren Lovecraft, Riku Varjopuro, Martha Dowsley, and Aaron T. Dale. 2011. "Adaptive Governance and the Human Dimension of Marine Mammal Management: Implications for Policy in a Changing North." *Marine Policy* 35 (4): 466–76. Available online at http://dx.doi.org/10.1016/j.marpol.2010.10.021.

Merrill, Karen M. 2002. *Public Lands and Political Meaning: Ranchers, the Government and the Property Between Them*. Los Angeles: University of

California Press. Available online at http://dx.doi.org/10.1525/california/
9780520228627.001.0001.

MHHC (Manitoba Habitat Heritage Corporation). *Annual Report 2010–2011*.
Winnipeg. Available online at http://www.mhhc.mb.ca/pdf/ar-10-11.pdf.

Millennium Ecosystem Assessment. 2005. *Ecosystems and Human Well-being:
Biodiversity Synthesis*. Washington, DC: World Resources Institute.

Miller, Alan S. 1991. *Gaia Connections*. Boston: Beacon Press.

Miller, J.K., J.M. Scott, C.R. Miller, and L.P. Waits. 2002. "The Endangered
Species Act: Dollars and Sense?" *Bioscience* 52 (2): 163–8. Available online at
http://dx.doi.org/10.1641/0006-3568(2002)052[0163:TESADA]2.0.CO;2.

Mills, Robert. 2001. In Canada, Parliament, House of Commons, *Debates and
Proceedings*, 37th Parliament, 1st Session, no. 016, February.

Minteer, Ben A. 2006. *The Landscape of Reform: Civic Pragmatism and
Environmental Thought in America*. Cambridge, MA: MIT Press.

Monroe, Kristen. 1996. *The Heart of Altruism*. Princeton, NJ: Princeton
University Press.

Mooers, A.Ø., D.F. Doak, S.C. Findlay, D.M. Green, C. Grouios, L.L. Manne,
A. Rashvand, M.A. Rudd, and J. Whitton. 2010. "Science, Policy, and
Species at Risk in Canada." *BioScience* 60 (10): 843–9.

Morales, Daniel S., and Luis A. Medina. 2011. *U.S. Economic and Trade Relations
with Canada and Mexico*. Haupphauge, NY: Nova Science Publishers.

Morgan, Mark J., and James H. Gramann. 1989. "Predicting Effectiveness
of Wildlife Education Programs: A Study of Students' Attitudes and
Knowledge Toward Snakes." *Wildlife Society Bulletin* 17 (4): 501–9.

Murphy, Kristina. 2003. "Procedural Justice and Tax Compliance." *Australian
Journal of Social Issues* 38 (33): 379–408.

Mussell, Al, Claudia Schmidt, and Bob Seguin. 2010. "The Ontario ESA:
Understanding the Incentives, Implications and Alternatives." Guelph, ON:
George Morris Centre.

NACOSAR (National Aboriginal Council on Species at Risk). 2007. *Annual
Report 2006–2007*. Ottawa.

Napier, Ted L., and Silvana M. Camboni. 1988. "Attitudes toward a Proposed
Soil Conservation Program." *Journal of Soil and Water Conservation* 43 (2):
186–91.

Nash, Jonathan Remy. 2011. "Mark to Ecosystem Service Market: Protecting
Ecosystems through Revaluing Conservation Easements." In *Rebuilding
the Ark: New Perspectives on Endangered Species Act Reform*, ed. Jonathan H.
Adler. Washington, DC: American Enterprise Institute.

Nature Conservancy. 2012. "About Us: Private Lands Conservation."
Available online at www.nature.org/about-us/private-lands-conservation.

Nature Saskatchewan. 2009. "Operation Burrowing Owl." Regina.

Nature Saskatchewan. 2010. "Saskatchewan Important Bird Areas Program." Regina.

Nature Saskatchewan. 2011. "Plovers on Shore." Regina.

NatureServe Explorer. 2012. "NatureServe Explorer: An Online Encyclopedia of Life." Available online at http://www.natureserve.org/explorer.

Naugle, David E., ed. 2011. *Energy Development and Wildlife Conservation in Western North America*. Washington, DC: Island Press. Available online at http://dx.doi.org/10.5822/978-1-61091-022-4.

Newfoundland and Labrador. 2011. Department of Environment and Conservation. "Newfoundland and Labrador Species at Risk." St John's. Available online at http://www.env.gov.nl.ca/env/wildlife/endangered-species/Species-at-Risk_Policy.pdf; accessed 22 April 2012.

Nikiforuk, Andrew. 2010. *Tar Sands: Dirty Oil and the Future of a Continent*. Vancouver: Greystone.

Niles, L., and K. Korth. 2006. "State Wildlife Diversity Programs." In *The Endangered Species Act at Thirty*, vol. 1, *Renewing the Conservation Promise*, ed. Dale D. Goble, J. Michael Scott, and Frank W. Davis. Washington, DC: Island Press.

NLCA (Nunavut Land Claims Agreement). 1993. "Agreement between the Inuit of the Nunavut Settlement Area and Her Majesty the Queen in Right of Canada." Ottawa: Tunngavik and the Minister of Indian Affairs and Northern Development.

Noss, R.F., T.E. LaRoe III, and J.M. Scott. 1995. "Endangered Ecosystems of the United States: A Preliminary Assessment of Loss and Degradation." National Biological Service Biological Report 28. Washington, DC.

Noss, Reed F., Michael A. O'Connell, and Denis D. Murphy. 1997. *The Science of Conservation Planning: Habitat Conservation under the Endangered Species Act*. Washington, DC: Island Press.

Nova Scotia. 2011. Department Natural Resources. "Legislation: NS Endangered Species Act." Halifax. Available online at http://www.gov.ns.ca/natr/wildlife/biodiversity/legislation_nsesa.asp; accessed 27 March 2012.

NTI (Nunavut Tunngavik Incorporated). 2012. "Science Shows Polar Bears in Nunavut Are Abundant and Healthy." Available online at http://www.tunngavik.com/blog/2012/04/03/science-shows-polar-bears-in-nunavut-are-abundant-and-healthy/; accessed 4 June 2012.

Nunavut. 2010. "Minister of Environment: Polar Bear Not an At-Risk Species." News Release, 28 May. Available online at http://pbsg.npolar.no/export/sites/pbsg/en/docs/Nunavut-norisk.pdf.

Nussbaum, Martha. 2000. *Women and Human Development: The Capabilities Approach*. Oxford: Oxford University Press. Available online at http://dx.doi.org/10.1017/CBO9780511841286.

Nussbaum, Martha. 2006a. *Frontier of Justice: Disability, Nationality, Species Membership*. Cambridge, MA: Harvard University Press.

Nussbaum, Martha. 2006b. "The Moral Status of Animals." *Chronicle of Higher Education* 52 (22): B6–8. Available online at Medline:16789292.

Nussbaum, Martha, and Amartya Sen. 1992. *The Quality of Life*. Oxford: Claredon Press.

Northwest Territories. 2009. Environment and Natural Resources. "Wildlife Management in the Northwest Territories: Media Guide 2009." Yellowknife. Available online at http://www.enr.gov.nt.ca/_live/documents/content/Wildife_Management_in_the_NWT.pdf.

NWMB (Nunavut Wildlife Management Board). 2000. *Final Report of the Inuit Bowhead Knowledge Study*. Iqaluit.

Olive, Andrea. 2011. "Can Stewardship Work for Species at Risk? A Pelee Island Case Study." *Journal of Environmental Law and Practice* 22 (3): 223–38.

Olive, Andrea. 2012a. "Endangered Species Policy in Canada and the US: A Tale of Two Islands." *American Review of Canadian Studies* 42 (1): 84–101. Available online at http://dx.doi.org/10.1080/02722011.2012.649925.

Olive, Andrea. 2012b. "A Research Note on Gendered Perceptions of Wildlife: Ethic of Care Meets a Snake and a Tortoise." *Journal of Women, Politics & Policy* 33 (2): 176–87. Available online at http://dx.doi.org/10.1080/1554477X.2012.667750.

Olive, Andrea. 2012c. "Does Canada's Species at Risk Act Live Up to Article 8?" *Canadian Journal of Native Studies* 32 (1): 173–89.

Olive, Andrea, and L. Raymond. 2010. "Reconciling Norm Conflict in Endangered Species Conservation on Private Land." *Natural Resources Journal* 50 (2): 431–54.

Olson, Mancur. 1965. *The Logic of Collective Action*. Cambridge, MA: Harvard University Press.

Ontario. 2012. Ministry of Natural Resources. "Final Recovery Strategies." Toronto. Available online at http://www.mnr.gov.on.ca/en/Business/Species/2ColumnSubPage/287123.htmla; accessed 1 October 2012.

Opotow, Susan, and Amara Brook. 2003. "Identity and Exclusion in Rangeland Conflict." In *Identity and the Natural Environment: The Psychological Significance of Nature*, ed. S. Clayton and Susan Opotow. Cambridge, MA: MIT Press.

Owen, Ted. 2000. "Washington County's HCP: Four Years Later." *Endangered Species Bulletin* 25 (4): 16–17.

Parkhurst, Gregory M., and Jason F. Shogren. 2003. "Evaluating Incentive Mechanisms for Conserving Habitat." *Natural Resources Journal* 43 (Fall): 1093–149.

Peters, E.J. 2003. "Views of Traditional Ecological Knowledge in Co-Management Bodies in Nunavik, Quebec." *Polar Record* 39 (1): 49–60. Available online at http://dx.doi.org/10.1017/S0032247402002759.

Peterson, Tarla Rai. 1991. "Telling the Farmers' Story: Competing Responses to Soil Conservation Rhetoric." *Quarterly Journal of Speech* 77 (3): 289–308. Available online at http://dx.doi.org/10.1080/00335639109383961.

Peterson, Tarla Rai, and Cristi Choat Horton. 1995. "Rooted in the Soil: How Understanding the Perspectives of Landowners Can Enhance the Management of Environmental Disputes." *Quarterly Journal of Speech* 81 (2): 139–66. Available online at http://dx.doi.org/10.1080/00335639509384106.

Pew Oceans Commission. 2003. *America's Living Oceans: Charting a Course for Sea Change*. Arlington, VA.

Pinkus, Susan. 2010. In Canada, Parliament, House of Commons, Standing Committee on Environment and Sustainable Development, *Evidence*, Meeting no. 12, 27 April.

Plotkin, Rachel. 2010. In Canada, Parliament, House of Commons, Standing Committee on Environment and Sustainable Development, *Evidence*, Meeting no. 12, 27 April.

Polasky, Stephen, and Holly Doremus. 1998. "When the Truth Hurts: Endangered Species Policy on Private Land with Imperfect Information." *Journal of Environmental Economics and Management* 35 (1): 22–47. Available online at http://dx.doi.org/10.1006/jeem.1998.1021.

Powledge, Fred. 2009. "Environmental Science after Bush." *Bioscience* 59 (3): 200–4. Available online at http://dx.doi.org/10.1525/bio.2009.59.3.3.

Preece, Rod. 1999. *Animals and Nature: Cultural Myths, Cultural Realities*. Vancouver: UBC Press.

Prince Edward Island. 2011. Department of Agriculture and Forestry. "Species at Risk." Charlottetown.

Ramsay, David. 2007. In Ontario, Legislative Assembly, *Debates and Proceedings*, 28 March.

Rankin, R., M. Austin, and J. Rice. 2010. "Ecological Classification System for the Ecosystem Status and Trends Report." Canadian Biodiversity: Ecosystem Status and Trends 2010, Technical Thematic Report Series 1. Ottawa: Canadian Councils of Resource Ministers.

Raymond, Leigh. 2003. *Private Rights in Public Resources: Equity and Property Allocation in Market-Based Environmental Policy*. Washington, DC: Resources for the Future.

Raymond, Leigh, and Andrea Olive. 2008. "Landowner Beliefs Regarding Biodiversity Protection on Private Property: A Indiana Case Study." *Society & Natural Resources* 21 (6): 483–97. Available online at http://dx.doi.org/10.1080/08941920801905203.

Reading, R.P., T.W. Clark, and S.R. Kellert. 1994. "Attitudes and Knowledge of People Living in the Greater Yellowstone Ecosystem." *Society & Natural Resources* 7 (4): 349–65. Available online at http://dx.doi.org/10.1080/08941929409380871.

Reckless, Walter C., and Simon Dinitz. 1967. "Pioneering with Self-Concept as a Vulnerability Factor in Delinquency." *Journal of Criminal Law Criminology and Police Studies* 58 (4): 515–23. Available online at http://dx.doi.org/10.2307/1141910.

Reed, Nathaniel, and Dennis Drabelle. 1984. *The United States Fish and Wildlife Service*. Boulder, CO: Westview Press.

Restani, M., and J.M. Marzluff. 2002. "Funding Extinction? Biological Needs and Political Realities in the Allocation of Resources to Endangered Species Recovery." *Bioscience* 52 (2): 169–77. Available online at http://dx.doi.org/10.1641/0006-3568(2002)052[0169:FEBNAP]2.0.CO;2.

Rockefeller, Stephen C. 1992. "Faith and Community in an Ecological Age." In *Spirit and Nature: Why the Environment Is a Religious Issue*, ed. Steven C. Rockefeller and John C. Elder. Boston: Beacon Press.

Rockström, J., W. Steffen, K. Noone, A. Persson, F.S. Chapin III, E.F. Lambin, T.M. Lenton, M. Scheffer, C. Folke, H.J. Schellnhuber, et al. 2009. "A Safe Operating Space for Humanity." *Nature* 461 (7263): 472–5. Available online at http://dx.doi.org/10.1038/461472a; Medline:19779433.

Roosevelt, Theodore. 1913. *Theodore Roosevelt: An Autobiography*. New York: Macmillan.

Rosenzweig, Michael R. 2003. *Win-Win Ecology: How Earth's Species Can Survive in the Midst of Human Enterprise*. New York: Oxford University Press.

Rosenzweig, Michael R. 2006. "Beyond Set-Asides." In *The Endangered Species Act at Thirty*, vol. 1, *Renewing the Conservation Promise*, ed. Dale D. Goble, J. Michael Scott, and Frank W. Davis. Washington, DC: Island Press.

Roush, W. 1995. "When Rigor Meets Reality." *Science* 269 (5222): 313–5. Available online at http://dx.doi.org/10.1126/science.269.5222.313; Medline:17841242.

Russell, D., and A. Gunn. 2011. "Caribou and Reindeer (Rangifer)." *Arctic Report Card: Update 2011*. Washington, DC: National Oceanic and Atmospheric Administration. Available online at http://www.arctic.noaa.gov/reportcard/caribou_reindeer.html.

Sagoff, Mark. 1988. *The Economy of the Earth: Philosophy, Law, and the Environment*. New York: Cambridge University Press.

Salzman, J. 1990. "Evolution and Application of Critical Habitat under the Endangered Species Act." *Harvard Environmental Law Review* 14: 311–42.

Sanders, Marren. 2007. "Implementing the Federal Endangered Species Act in Indian Country." Joint Occasional Papers on Native Affairs 2007–01. Tucson, AZ; Cambridge, MA: Native Nations Institute for Leadership, Management, and Policy and the Harvard Project on American Indian Economic Development.

Saskatchewan. 2012. Bureau of Statistics. "Population & Statistics." Available online at http://www.stats.gov.sk.ca/pop.

Save Ontario's Species. 2009. "Ontario's Endangered Species Report Card June 2009." Toronto. Available online at http://www.ecojustice.ca/publications/reports/ontarios-endangered-species-act-report-card/attachment.

Sax, Joseph. 1983. "Some Thoughts on the Decline of Private Property." *Washington Law Review* 58: 481–96.

SCBD (Secretariat of the Convention on Biological Diversity). 2010. "Global Biodiversity Outlook 3." Montreal: Convention on Biological Diversity.

Schlosberg, David. 2007. *Defining Environmental Justice: Theories, Movements, and Nature.* New York: Oxford University Press. Available online at http://dx.doi.org/10.1093/acprof:oso/9780199286294.001.0001.

Schlosberg, David, and David Carruthers. 2010. "Indigenous Struggles, Environmental Justice, and Community Capabilities." *Global Environmental Politics* 10 (4): 12–35. Available online at http://dx.doi.org/10.1162/GLEP_a_00029.

Schmidt, Jeremy J., and Martha Dowsley. 2010. "Hunting with Polar Bears: Problems with the Passive Properties of the Commons." *Human Ecology* 38 (3): 377–87. Available online at http://dx.doi.org/10.1007/s10745-010-9328-0.

Schwartz, Mark W. 2008. "The Performance of the Endangered Species Act." *Annual Review of Ecology Evolution and Systematics* 39 (1): 279–99. Available online at http://dx.doi.org/10.1146/annurev.ecolsys.39.110707.173538.

Schwartz, Mark W., Nicole L. Jurjavcic, and James O'Brien. 2002. "Conservation's Disenfranchised Urban Poor." *Bioscience* 52 (7): 601–6. Available online at http://dx.doi.org/10.1641/0006-3568(2002)052[0601:CSDUP]2.0.CO;2.

Scoffield, Heather. 2012. "As Tories rewrite rules, watchdog details cost of law environmental legislation." *Canadian Press*, 8 May.

Scott, J.M., D.D. Goble, A.M. Haines, J.A. Wiens, and M.C. Neel. 2010. "Conservation-reliant Species and the Future of Conservation." *Conservation Letters* 3 (2): 91–7. Available online at http://dx.doi.org/10.1111/j.1755-263X.2010.00096.x.

Scott, J. Michael, Dale D. Goble, Leona Svancara, and Anna Pidgorna. 2006.
"By the Numbers." In *The Endangered Species Act at Thirty*, vol. 1, *Renewing the Conservation Promise*, ed. Dale D. Goble, J. Michael Scott, and Frank W. Davis. Washington, DC: Island Press.

Scott, J.M., Dale D. Goble, John A. Wiens, David S. Wilcove, Michael Bean, and Timothy Male. 2005. "Recovery of Imperiled Species under the Endangered Species Act: The Need for a New Approach." *Frontiers in Ecology and the Environment* 3 (7): 383–9. http://dx.doi.org/10.1890/1540-9295(2005)003 [0383:ROISUT]2.0.CO;2.

Senatore, M., J. Kostyack, and A. Wetzler. 2003. "Critical Habitat at the Crossroads: Responding to the G.W. Bush Administration's Attacks on Critical Habitat under the ESA." *Golden Gate University Law Review* 33: 447–71.

Shaffer, Mark L., J. Michael Scott, and Frances Casey. 2002. "Noah's Options: Initial Cost Estimates of a National System of Habitat Conservation Areas in the United States." *BioScience* 52 (5): 439–43. Available online at http:// dx.doi.org/10.1641/0006-3568(2002)052[0439:NSOICE]2.0.CO;2.

Shogren, Jason F., and John Tschirhart, eds. 2001. *Protecting Endangered Species in the United States: Biological Needs, Political Realities and Economic Choices.* Cambridge, UK: Cambridge University Press. Available online at http:// dx.doi.org/10.1017/CBO9780511625916.

Sinclair, Peter. 2010. *Energy in Canada.* Oxford: Oxford University Press.

Smallwood, Kate. 2003. *A Guide to Canada's Species at Risk Act.* Vancouver: Sierra Legal Defence Fund.

Soule, Michael E., and B.A. Wilcox. *Conservation Biology: An Evolutionary-Ecological Perspective.* Sunderland, MA: Sinauer Associates.

Sparrow, Malcolm. 2000. *The Regulatory Craft: Controlling Risks, Solving Problems, and Managing Compliance.* Washington, DC: Brookings Institution Press.

Spivak, Mira. 2002. In Canada, Parliament, Senate, *Debates and Proceedings*, 22 October.

Spohr, David, and Lara B. Fowler. 2009. "Application of the Endangered Species Act to Tribal Actions: Can Ambiguity Be a Good Thing?" *Seattle Journal of Environmental Law* (Spring): 64–121.

Stanford, K.M. 2012. "Spatial and Temporal Variation in Demographic Parameters of the Lake Erie Watersnake (Nerodia sipedon insularum)." Diss., Northern Illinois University.

Sterling, Norman. 2007. In Ontario, Legislative Assembly, *Debates and Proceedings*, 28 March.

Stern, Stephanie. 2006. "Encouraging Conservation on Private Lands: A Behavioral Analysis of Financial Incentives." *Arizona Law Review* 48: 541–92.

Stone, Deborah. 1990. *Policy Paradox: The Art of Political Decision Making*. New York: Norton and Company.

Strankman, Peggy. 2009. In Canada, Parliament, House of Commons, Standing Committee on Environment and Sustainable Development, *Evidence*, Meeting no. 25, 4 June.

Sullivan, B.K., R.W. Bowker, K.B. Malmos, and E.W.A. Gergus. 1996. "Arizona Distribution of Three Sonoran Desert Anurans: *Bufo retiformis*, *Gastrophryne olivacea*, and *Pternohyla fodiens*." *Great Basin Naturalist* 56 (1): 38–47.

Suluk, Thomas K., and Sherrie L. Blakney. 2008. "Land Claims and Resistance to the Management of Harvester Activities in Nunavut." *Arctic* 61 (1): 62–70.

Suzuki, David. 2007. *Sacred Balance: Rediscovering our Place in Nature*. Vancouver: Greystone Books.

Suzuki, David. 2011. "Beyond the Species at Risk Act: Recognizing the Sacred." *Journal of Environmental Policy and Practice* 22 (3): 239–54.

Svancara, L.K., J.M. Scott, D.D. Goble, F.W. Davis, and D. Brewer. 2006. "Endangered Species Timeline." In *The Endangered Species Act at Thirty*, vol. 2, *Conserving Biodiversity in Human-Dominated Landscapes*, ed. J. Michael Scott, Dale D. Goble, and Frank W. Davis. Washington, DC: Island Press.

Taylor, M., K. Suckling, and J. Rachlinski. 2005. "The Effectiveness of the Endangered Species Act: A Quantitative Analysis." *Bioscience* 55 (4): 360–7. Available online at http://dx.doi.org/10.1641/0006-3568(2005)055[0360: TEOTES]2.0.CO;2.

Teal, G.A., and J.B. Loomis. 2000. "Effects of Gender and Parental Status on the Economic Valuation of Increasing Wetlands, Reducing Wildlife Contamination and Increasing Salmon Populations." *Society & Natural Resources* 13 (1): 1–14. Available online at http://dx.doi.org/10.1080/089419200279207.

TEEB (The Economics of Ecosystems and Biodiversity). 2010. "Report for Business: Executive Summary." Geneva: United Nations Environmental Program. Available online at http://www.teebweb.org/wp-content/uploads/ Study%20and%20Reports/Reports/Business%20and%20Enterprise/ Executive%20Summary/Business%20Executive%20Summary_English.pdf.

Tester, Frank James, and Peter Irniq. 2008. "Inuit Qaujimajatuqangit: Social History, Politics and the Practice of Resistance." *Arctic* 61 (1): 48–61.

Thompson Jr, Benjamin H., 2006. "Managing the Working Landscape." In *The Endangered Species Act at Thirty*, vol. 1, *Renewing the Conservation Promise*, ed. Dale D. Goble, J. Michael Scott, and Frank W. Davis. Washington, DC: Island Press.

Torbit, Steve, and Jody McNaught. 2001. "Restoring the Prairie, Mending the Sacred Hoop: Prairie Conservation and Restoration on the Cheyenne River Reservation." Boulder, CO: National Wildlife Federation.

Toronto. 2011. "City of Toronto: Backgrounder." Toronto: City of Toronto.
   Available online at http://www.toronto.ca/demographics/pdf/2011-
   census-backgrounder.pdf.
Trainor Fleiser, Sarah, Anna Godduhn, Lawrence K. Duffy, F. Stuart Chapin
   III, David C. Natcher, Gary Kofinas, and Henry P. Huntington. 2009.
   "Environmental Injustice in the Canadian Far North." In *Speaking for
   Ourselves: Environmental Justice in Canada,* ed. Julian Agyeman, Peter Cole,
   Randolph Haluza-Delay, and Pat O'Riley. Vancouver: UBC Press.
Tyler, Tom. 1990. *Why People Obey the Law.* New Haven, CT: Yale University
   Press.
Tyler, Tom, and J. Darley. 2000. "Building a Law-Abiding Society: Taking
   Public Views about Morality and the Legitimacy of Legal Authorities into
   Account when Formulating Substantive Law." *Hofstra Law Review* 28: 707–39.
Tyler, Tom, and Y.J. Huo. 2002. *Trust in the Law: Encouraging Public Cooperation
   with the Police and Courts.* New York: Russell Sage Foundation.
United Nations. 2000. Convention on Biological Diversity. Subsidiary Body on
   Scientific, Technical and Technological Advice. "Sustaining Life on Earth."
   Available online at http://www.cbd.int/doc/publications/cbd-sustain-en.pdf.
UNEP (United Nations Environmental Programme). 2010. "Convention on
   Biological Diversity: Framework for Measuring Progress." Available online
   at http://www.unep.org/geo/pdfs/geo5/Measuring_progress.pdf;
   accessed 1 May 2012.
United States. 1992. Environmental Protection Agency. "Environmental Justice."
   Washington, DC. Available online at http://www.epa.gov/
   environmentaljustice/.
United States. 2011. Department of State. "Background Note – Canada."
   Available online at http://www.state.gov/r/pa/ei/bgn/2089.htm; accessed
   22 April 2012.
United States. 2012. Environmental Protection Agency. "Ecoregions of North
   America." Washington, DC. Available online at http://www.epa.gov/wed/
   pages/ecoregions/na_eco.htm.
USFWS (United States Fish and Wildlife Service). 1994. *Report to Congress on
   the Recovery Program for Threatened and Endangered Species.* Washington, DC.
USFWS. 2003. *Lake Erie Water Snake Recovery Plan.* Fort Snelling, MN:
   Department of the Interior, Fish and Wildlife Service, Region 3.
USFWS. 2011a. "FY2011 Cooperative Endangered Species Conservation Fund."
   Washington, DC. Available online at http://www.fws.gov/endangered/
   grants/Sect%206%20FY2011%20Combined%20Award %20Summaries%
   20Final%208–22.pdf.; accessed 13 January 2012.

USFWS. 2011b. "Partners for Fish and Wildlife Program." Washington, DC. Available online at http://www.fws.gov/partners/aboutus.html.

USFWS. 2012a. "Endangered Species Permits: Habitat Conservation Plans." Washington, DC. Available online at www.fws.gov/midwest/endangered/permits/hcp/hcp_wofactsheet.html; accessed 22 April 2012.

USFWS. 2012b. "Indiana Bat Recovery Sheet." Washington, DC. Available online at http://www.fws.gov/midwest/endangered/mammals/inba/inbafctsht.html; accessed 1 October 2012.

USFWS. 2013. "Endangered Species." Washington, DC. Available online at http://www.fws.gov/endangered/.

US Geological Survey. 2008. "90 billion barrels of oil and 1,670 trillion cubic feet of natural gas assessed in the Arctic." News release, 23 July. Available online at http://www.usgs.gov/newsroom/article.asp?ID=1980; accessed 4 June 2012.

Usher, P. 2000. "Traditional Ecology Knowledge in Environmental Assessment and Management." *Arctic* 53 (2): 183–93.

Usher, P., Gérard Duhaime, and Edmund Searles. 2003. "The Household as an Economic Unit in Arctic Aboriginal Communities, and Its Measurement by Means of a Comprehensive Survey." *Social Indicators Research* 61 (2): 175–202. Available online at http://dx.doi.org/10.1023/A:1021344707027.

Van Den Berg, Heather A., Shawn J. Riley, and Shari L. Dann. 2011. "Conservation Education for Advancing Natural Resource Knowledge and Building Capacity for Volunteerism." *Society & Natural Resources* 24 (3): 205–20. Available online at http://dx.doi.org/10.1080/08941920902960404.

VanderZwagg, David L., Maria Cecilia Engler-Palma, and Jeffery A. Hutchings. 2011. "Canada's Species at Risk Act and Atlantic Salmon: Cascade of Promises, Trickles of Protection, Sea of Challenges." *Journal of Environmental Law and Practice* 22 (3): 267–307.

Vaske, Jerry J., Maureen P. Donnelly, Daniel R. Williams, and Sandra Jonker. 2001. "Demographic Influences on Environmental Value Orientations and Normative Beliefs about National Forest Management." *Society & Natural Resources* 14 (9): 761–76. Available online at http://dx.doi.org/10.1080/089419201753210585.

Vaughn, Jacqueline. 2011. *Environmental Politics: Domestic and Global Dimensions*. Boston: Wadsworth.

Venter, Oscar, Nathalie N. Brodeur, Leah Nemiroff, Brenna Belland, Ivan J. Dolinsek, and James W.A. Grant. 2006. "Threats to Endangered Species in Canada." *Bioscience* 56 (11): 903–10. Available online at http://dx.doi.org/10.1641/0006-3568(2006)56[903:TTESIC]2.0.CO;2.

Vogel, Stephan. 1996. "Farmer's Environmental Attitudes and Behavior: A
    Case Study for Austria." *Environment and Behavior* 28 (5): 591–613. Available
    online at http://dx.doi.org/10.1177/001391659602800502.
Waggoner, P.E. 1996. "How Much Land Can Ten Billion People Spare for
    Nature?" *Daedalus* 125 (3): 73–93.
Watkins, M., and S. Hilts. 2001. "Land Trusts Emerge as an Important
    Conservation Force in Canada: A Summary of the Land Protected by Land
    Trusts and the Current Issues and Challenges Facing the Growing Land
    Trust Movement in Canada." Guelph, ON: University of Guelph, Centre
    for Land and Water Stewardship. Available online at www.uoguelph.ca/
    claws/conference/landtrustsincanada.doc.
Wenzel, G. 2001. "Nunamiut or Kabloonamiut: Which Identity Best Fits Inuit
    (and Does It Matter)?" *Inuit Studies* 25 (1/2): 37–52.
White, Graham. 2006. "Cultures in Collision: Traditional Knowledge and
    Euro-Canadian Governance Processes in Northern Land Claim Boards."
    Arctic 59 (4): 401–14.
Wilcove, David S., Michael J. Bean, Bob Long, William J. Snape III, Bruce
    M. Beehler, and Jeff Eisenberg. 2004. "The Private Side of Conservation."
    Frontiers in Ecology and the Environment 2 (6): 326–31. Available online at
    http://dx.doi.org/10.2307/3868410.
Wilcove, David S., Michael J. Bean, Robert Bonnie, and Margaret McMillan.
    1996. *Rebuilding the Ark: Toward a More Effective Endangered Species Act for
    Private Land*. Washington, DC: Environmental Defense Fund.
Wilcove, David S., and L.L. Master. 2005. "How Many Endangered Species
    Are There in the United States?" *Frontiers in Ecology and the Environment* 3
    (8): 414–20. Available online at http://dx.doi.org/10.1890/1540-9295(2005)
    003[0414:HMESAT]2.0.CO;2.
Wilcove, D.S., D. Rothstein, J. Dubow, A. Phillips, and E. Losos. 1998.
    "Quantifying Threats to Imperiled Species in the United States." *Bioscience*
    48 (8): 607–15. Available online at http://dx.doi.org/10.2307/1313420.
Wilkins, Neal R. 2011. "Improving the ESA's Performance on Private Land."
    In *Rebuilding the Ark: New Perspectives on Endangered Species Act Reform*,
    ed. Jonathan H. Adler. Washington, DC: American Enterprise Institute.
Wilshire, Howard G., Jane E. Nielson, and Richard W. Hazlett. 2008. *The
    American West at Risk: Science, Myths, and Politics of Land Abuse*. New York:
    Oxford University Press.
Wilson, E.O. 1992. *The Diversity of Life*. Cambridge, MA: Harvard University Press.
Winter, Soren C., and Peter J. May. 2001. "Motivation for Compliance with
    Environmental Regulations." *Journal of Policy Analysis and Management*
    20 (4): 675–98. Available online at http://dx.doi.org/10.1002/pam.1023.

Wojciechowski, Stephane, Sue McKee, Christopher Brassard, C. Scott Findlay, and Stewart Elgie. 2011. "SARA's Safety Net Provisions and the Effectiveness of Species at Risk Protection on Non-Federal Lands." *Journal of Environmental Law and Practice* 22 (3): 203–22.

Wren, Sarah. 2009. In Canada, Parliament, House of Commons, Standing Committee on Environment and Sustainable Development, *Evidence*, Meeting no. 24, 2 June.

Wright, J.B. 1992. "Land Trusts in the USA." *Land Use Policy* 9 (2): 83–6. http://dx.doi.org/10.1016/0264-8377(92)90015-O.

Yaffee, Steven L. 2006. "Collaborative Decision Making." In *The Endangered Species Act at Thirty*, vol. 1, *Renewing the Conservation Promise*, ed. Dale D. Goble, J. Michael Scott, and Frank W. Davis. Washington, DC: Island Press.

Zuckerman, Laura. 2011. "Montana governor threat: shoot wolves now, ask questions later." *Reuters*, 16 February.

Index

Studies in Comparative Political Economy and Public Policy